The Therapeutic Relationship:
Foundations for an
Eclectic Psychotherapy

C.H. PATTERSON

The Therapeutic Relationship: Foundations for an Eclectic Psychotherapy

The Therapeutic Relationship:
Foundations for an
Eclectic Psychotherapy

C. H. PATTERSON

UNIVERSITY OF ILLINOIS
URBANA-CHAMPAIGN
and
UNIVERSITY OF NORTH CAROLINA
GREENSBORO

BROOKS/COLE PUBLISHING COMPANY
MONTEREY, CALIFORNIA

Brooks/Cole Publishing Company
A Division of Wadsworth, Inc.

Printed in the United States of America

10 9 8 7 6 5 4 3 2 1

Library of Congress Cataloging in Publication Data

Patterson, C. H. (Cecil Holden), 1912–
  The therapeutic relationship.

  Includes bibliographies and index.
  1. Psychotherapist and patient. I. Title.
  [DNLM: 1. Professional-Patient Relations. 2. Psycho-
therapy. WM 420 P317t]
  RC 480.8.P37   1985   616.89'14   84-29326
  ISBN 0-534-04944-3

The discussion of the Carkhuff scales in Chapters 4, 5, and 7 is based on R. R. Carkhuff,
Helping and Human Relations: Vol. 2. Practice and Research. New York: Holt, Rinehart
and Winston, 1960. Used by permission of R. R. Carkhuff.

Sponsoring Editor: *Claire Verduin*
Production Editor: *Fiorella Ljunggren*
Manuscript Editor: *Lorraine Anderson*
Interior and Cover Design: *Victoria Van Deventer*
Typesetting: *Linda Andrews, Ashland, Oregon*
Printing and Binding: *Malloy Lithographing, Inc., Ann Arbor, Michigan*

Preface

The precursor to this book, titled *Relationship Counseling and Psychotherapy*, was written during my tenure as a Fulbright-Hays Senior Lecturer at the University of Aston, Birmingham, England.

The preface to that book began with the statement: "The days of 'schools' in counseling and psychotherapy are drawing to a close." That statement was apparently premature. Since then we have seen a proliferation of new methods, techniques, and strategies of intervention, although few if any of them would warrant the designation of a school. And few have any systematic theoretical foundation or research support.

Yet, in a sense, the days of schools or theories have passed. The emphasis has been on techniques and has spawned a return of so called eclecticism. In a 1982 survey of 422 members and fellows of Divisions 12 (Clinical Psychology) and 17 (Counseling Psychology) of the American Psychological Association, 41 percent reported their orientation as eclectic; several other surveys have also found that the largest single group of respondents consists of those who identify themselves as eclectics. In the 1982 survey, the most favored theoretical systems were psychoanalytic (11 percent), cognitive behavioral (10 percent), and person centered (9 percent).[1]

I refer to this eclecticism as "so-called" because the atheoretical, even antitheoretical, stance of most of those who call themselves eclectic is inconsistent with the definition of *eclecticism* by English and English: "In theoretical system building, the selection and orderly combination of compatible features from diverse sources . . . the effort to find valid elements in all doctrines or theories and to combine them into a harmonious whole. . . . Eclecticism is to be distinguished from unsystematic and uncritical combination for which the name is syncretism."[2] Most of those who call themselves eclectics are actually syncretists.

Those who presently call themselves eclectics have little in common. They do not subscribe to any common system; thus there are as many eclectic approaches as there are eclectic counselors or therapists. Each operates out of his or her own unique bag of techniques, on the basis of his or her particular training, experience, and biases, on a case-by-case basis, with no general theory or set of principles for guidance. The claim that practice is based on what works is supported only by the subjective evaluation of the practitioner. Essentially, it amounts to flying by the seat of one's pants. Garfield notes that "eclecticism is perceived as the adherence to a nonsystematic and rather haphazard clinical approach."[3] Prochaska and Norcross, noting that the need for theoretical integration has been recognized, write that "few, if any, adequate models of systematic eclecticism have been created to aid the clinical practitioner and researcher. Beyond its conceptual relativity and personal appeal, eclecticism in its current state may not possess adequate clinical utility or validity for increasing numbers of therapists."[4]

Recent publications purporting to present eclectic approaches to psychotherapy in fact represent syncretic approaches.[5] They are lacking in any theoretical base and in any integration of the various methods and techniques that are gathered together. Garfield has stated that "one important step in the desired direction [toward integration in psychotherapy] is to delineate and to operationalize clearly some of the common variables which seem to play a role in most psychotherapies, and, perhaps to regard them as the basis for a clearer delineation of psychotherapeutic principles and procedures."[6] This book takes that step.

There does exist, however, a theoretical base for a truly eclectic system. Such a system must include the conditions proposed by Rogers in 1957 as the necessary and sufficient conditions for therapeutic personality change.[7] Truax and Carkhuff presented evidence that these conditions are included, either implicitly or explicitly, in the major theoretical orientations.[8] There has been increasing recognition of these common elements in theory and practice, and of their importance, indeed their necessity, for effective psychotherapy.

These conditions, then, must be part of any eclectic system of psychotherapy, since they are the very foundation on which any such system must be built. They cannot be ignored, dismissed, or relegated to a background position, as some writers have done. The evidence for their effectiveness, evaluated in Chapter 13 of this book, is too strong, and there is little or no evidence for the effectiveness of any other methods or techniques.

The focus of this book differs from that of most current texts in counseling and psychotherapy. These texts emphasize so-called skills, strategies, and techniques and pay scant attention to theory and philosophical concepts. This book, instead, pays a great deal of attention to theory, philosophy, and attitudes, because it is my conviction, based on over 25 years of experience in teaching counseling or psychotherapy, that theory, philosophy, and the concurrent attitudes are central to the preparation of counselors and psychotherapists. When students have a thorough grasp and understanding of, and some commitment to, a philosophy and a theory, they quickly master the necessary skills as a logical implementation of such philosophy and theory. Lengthy skill training before a student begins working with actual clients is unnecessary. Too many graduates of counselor education programs are technicians, without an understanding of why they do what they were trained to do.

This book, then, presents a theory-based eclectic system that focuses on the elements that constitute the therapy relationship. Integrated into this position are the methods and techniques common to all approaches to psychotherapy—catharsis, conditioning, confrontation, desensitization, empathy, extinction, genuineness, immediacy, insight, interpretation, listening, placebos, probing, reinforcement, reflection, resistance, respect, shaping, silence, and transference. Since this approach derives from client-centered or relationship therapy, I have used these two terms rather than coin a new one. The terms *counseling* and *psychotherapy*, as well as *client* and *patient*, are used interchangeably.

Much of the material in this book comes from my experience as a teacher and supervisor of students in counseling or psychotherapy over a 25-year period. It includes many apparently simple yet basic ideas and suggestions often overlooked in textbooks and teaching, ideas and suggestions I have found particularly useful in helping beginning counselors in practicum. I am indebted to the many students who, over the years, have stimulated me to formulate them and to express them in writing, particularly the students at the University of Aston during my year there, who responded to my writing with comments and suggestions. I am also grateful to the following reviewers of the manuscript: Michael Dougherty of Western Carolina University, Abraham Gelfond of Montclair State College, Lenore Harmon of the University of Illinois, Kenneth R. Newton of the University of Tennessee, and Bernard Nisenholz of California State University, Northridge.

C. H. Patterson

NOTES

1. D. Smith. Trends in counseling and psychotherapy. *American Psychologist*, 1982, *37*, 802–809.
2. H. B. English and A. C. English. *A comprehensive dictionary of psychological and psychoanalytic terms*. New York: McKay, 1958.
3. S. L. Garfield. Eclecticism and integration in psychotherapy. *Behavior Therapy*, 1982, *13*, p. 612.
4. J. O. Prochaska and J. C. Norcross. Contemporary psychotherapists: A national survey of characteristics, practices, orientations, and attitudes. *Psychotherapy: Theory, Research, and Practice*, 1983, *20*, p. 171.
5. S. L. Garfield. *Psychotherapy: An eclectic approach*. New York: Wiley-Interscience, 1980; L. E. Beutler. *Eclectic psychotherapy: A systematic approach*. New York: Pergamon Press, 1983; J. Hart. *Modern eclectic therapy: A functional orientation to counseling and psychotherapy*. New York: Plenum, 1983; S. Palmer. *A primer of eclectic psychotherapy*. Monterey, CA: Brooks/Cole, 1979.
6. Garfield, Eclecticism and integration, p. 620.
7. C. R. Rogers. The necessary and sufficient conditions for therapeutic personality change. *Journal of Consulting Psychology*, 1957, *21*, 95–103.
8. C. B. Truax and R. R. Carkhuff. *Toward effective counseling and psychotherapy*. Chicago: Aldine, 1967.

Contents

PART ONE

Core Concepts 1

PART THREE
Implications   197

CHAPTER 11
The Therapeutic Relationship: Essence or Placebo?   199

CHAPTER 12
Other Issues and Questions   213

PART FOUR
Research Evidence   229

CHAPTER 13
Evaluation of the Research   231

Self-realization can be encouraged if the therapist has a profound knowledge not of therapeutic theories and formulations but of people and their personal experiences.

JURGEN RUESCH (*Therapeutic Communication.*
New York: Norton, 1961, p. 290)

As man's control of his environment has proceeded . . . he has progressively uncovered more and more complication, but, at the same time, he has succeeded in discovering more and more unifying principles which accept the ever increasing variety, but recognize an underlying unity. He has, in short, discovered the many and the one. . . . The diversity . . . is a surface phenomenon: When one looks underneath and within, the universal unity again becomes apparent.

WARREN WEAVER (Confessions of a Scientist-Humanist,
Saturday Review, May 28, 1966)

PART ONE

Core Concepts

CHAPTER 1

A Model for Facilitative Interpersonal Relationships

Counseling or psychotherapy is an interpersonal relationship. Note that I don't say that counseling or psychotherapy *involves* an interpersonal relationship—it *is* an interpersonal relationship. That is the thesis of this book. As an interpersonal relationship, counseling or psychotherapy obviously must bear some resemblance to other facilitative interpersonal relationships. Conversely, facilitative interpersonal relationships must share the characteristics of counseling or psychotherapy.

Actually, the model to be presented was not constructed from any theory of interpersonal relationships. Rather it derives from theory, experience, and research on the nature of counseling or psychotherapy. It is therefore couched in the vocabulary of this field. Nevertheless, the terms and concepts can be generalized to other interpersonal relationships—friendships, parent-child relationships, husband-wife relationships, teacher-student relationships (see, for example, Patterson[1]), supervisor-supervisee relationships (see, for example, Patterson[2]), and employer-employee relationships. The model specifies the characteristics all such relationships must have if they are to be positive, or facilitative of the personal growth, development, and well-being (or self-actualization) of the participants.

The model as presented here is not a formal or mathematical model. It is rather a conceptual model, representing an attempt to organize or integrate what we know into a comprehensive general

3

view of the nature and process of facilitative or helping relationships. Table 1-1 presents a summary of the model as an aid in following the discussion.

TABLE 1-1. A Model for Facilitative Interpersonal Relationships

	Goals		
Conditions	*Immediate (Process)*	*Mediate (Subgoals)*	*Ultimate*
1. Empathic understanding	Self-Exploration: Self-disclosure Self-awareness	Common: Empathy Respect for others Genuineness	Self-Actualization: Empathy Acceptance of self and others Respect for others Autonomy Creativity Spontaneity Genuineness
2. Respect, concern, compassion, liking, warmth	Self-understanding Self-acceptance Self-esteem Respect for self and others	Individual: Actualization of potentials—in education, work, family, and personal relationships	
3. Therapeutic genuineness, honesty	Honesty, genuineness in relationships		
4. Concreteness, specificity	Acceptance and understanding of others		

Any comprehensive model of facilitating behavior change—and helping relationships, including counseling or psychotherapy, are an important means of facilitating voluntary change—has three broad aspects: (1) goals or objectives, both general and more specific, (2) the process, which is actually the immediate goal in the relationship, and (3) the conditions required for initiating and continuing the process. In this chapter I shall present a summary of these aspects, each of which will be considered in more detail in succeeding chapters as it relates to counseling or psychotherapy.

GOALS

Philosophers and others such as religious leaders have long debated the purpose, or goal, of life. Discussions have been confused, in part because of a lack of discrimination among various levels of goals. I have divided goals into three levels—ultimate, mediate, and immediate—and will discuss each in turn here.

The Ultimate Goal

In the search for an ultimate goal we are looking for something that is applicable to all interpersonal relationships, not simply to counseling or psychotherapy. Thus, such goals as curing or remedying pathological conditions are not acceptable. We are concerned with a positive goal. Moreover, we need a goal that not only applies to all persons, but one that is not time-bound or culture-bound. In essence, we are searching for the goal of life itself.

For my model, I have selected the goal of self-actualization. While this choice might be—indeed, has been—disputed, it seems to incorporate all other goals that have been or might be proposed. Other terms that have been used for the same concept are *self-enhancement, self-realization,* and *full functioning.* In Chapters 2 and 3 I shall justify this choice and consider the nature of self-actualization. Here I note that among the many characteristics of a self-actualizing person are empathy, respect and concern for others, and genuineness or honesty.

The Mediate Goals

Self-actualization is a goal common to all persons. It is a general goal. Many of the goals discussed by counselors or therapists are more specific, and vary with individuals. Mediate goals include these more specific, individual goals, though some mediate goals may be general in the sense that they apply to all or most individuals, since they may be elements of the general goal of self-actualization. Mediate goals can also be considered as subgoals, or as steps toward reaching the ultimate goal. Self-actualization as an ultimate goal may never be completely achieved—if it were easily achieved it would no longer constitute a goal, and life would from then on be goalless, except for maintaining one's achievement. Thus most of life is focused upon achieving mediate goals, or subgoals. An ultimate goal provides a guide or criterion for accepting or rejecting mediate goals, or subgoals. Such goals are acceptable or not depending on whether they contribute to the *process* of self-actualization.

From another point of view, mediate or subgoals may be conceived of as by-products of self-actualization. They follow, in a sense, from being a self-actualizing person. The self-actualizing person utilizes his or her potentials, finds ways to actualize them, seeks out the information, instruction, education, or training required.

The Immediate Goal

The immediate goal of facilitative interpersonal relationships is to initiate and continue the activity or process of helping one become a self-actualizing person. In counseling or psychotherapy this has been identified as the process of self-exploration. This begins with self-disclosure, leading through self-exploration to self-discovery, self-awareness, and self-understanding, followed by self-acceptance and the development of a realistic self-concept and a sense of self-esteem. In general, the process might be described as that of being oneself. One is able to see oneself for what one really is and what one can be or become, in a relationship free from threat or fear, in which one does not have to be defensive and engage in deception, or distortion of oneself. In a good interpersonal relationship people are able to look at and explore themselves and reach an awareness and understanding of self, can see themselves for what they really are and as they want to be. One is or becomes one's best self in the presence of persons who offer a facilitative interpersonal relationship. One becomes more self-actualizing, including becoming more understanding and respectful of others and more open, more honest, more genuine.

CONDITIONS

There are a number of conditions for good interpersonal relationships that appear to be specified in all theories of or approaches to counseling or psychotherapy. Three common elements in particular have been identified and defined or described by Rogers[3] : empathy, respect, and genuineness. These elements are complex and may eventually be analyzed into their components; there may indeed be other elements of a facilitative interpersonal relationship. But these three are generally recognized and accepted as necessary conditions. Truax and Carkhuff[4] point to the evidence for these common elements in the writings of numerous therapists. In addition to the three elements proposed by Rogers, a fourth condition has been identified as important: concreteness or specificity.

Empathy or Empathic Understanding

Empathy is the ability to put oneself in the place of another and to see things—the other as well as his or her world—as he or she sees them. This is not easy to do in a world in which everyone is so concerned about and focused upon oneself. We seldom if ever realize that things as we see them are not what they really are—indeed, if there is a reality beyond ourselves we cannot know it. Each of us lives in his or her own world, and it is that world that is *real* for us.

Being listened to and understood by another has a powerful influence on how one feels, thinks, and behaves. It is basic to all good human relationships. Unless we have to some extent the ability to share the world of another, we cannot establish any relationship with that other.

Respect

The second condition for good interpersonal relationships is a real respect for the other person. Respect is perhaps a mild term, though a deep respect for another encompasses a number of aspects—

a genuine concern and liking for, a real interest in, the other, a non-judgmental attitude, compassion. It accepts a person as he or she is, yet can have high expectations of that person. It does not require that one approve of another's behavior or agree with all his or her thoughts and ideas. A parent can reject particular behaviors of a child, yet see and treat the child as a person worthy of respect.

Genuineness

Genuineness is a difficult concept to define. Genuineness in the sense of being oneself is not always helpful to another person—one may not be a helpful or therapeutic person. It is perhaps necessary to talk about a facilitative or therapeutic genuineness. Thus one is not necessarily brutally frank in one's relations with others. Being therapeutically genuine may involve not expressing hurtful or threatening thoughts and feelings. The essential condition is that whatever one does say or express is real and genuine, that one is not presenting a facade or role, trying to appear to be what one is not. Openness and honesty, and lack of deceit and deception, are necessary for any good interpersonal relationship.

Specificity or Concreteness

A fourth condition has been identified as important in counseling or psychotherapy. It also appears to be important in all interpersonal relationships. It involves focusing upon the concrete and specific concerns of the other person. This means avoiding glossing over the other person's concerns with generalizations, abstractions, or reassurances. It involves dealing with the down-to-earth, nitty-gritty, everyday things of concern to the other person.

When these conditions are present in a relationship, they provide an environment that is nonthreatening, thus allowing one to look at and explore oneself and one's situation and concerns in a constructive manner conducive to learning and behavior change. Respect, acceptance, and interest are reinforcing for self-disclosure and self-exploration. Cassius, in Shakespeare's *Julius Caesar*, expressed it well:

> And since you cannot see yourself,
> So well as by reflection,
> I, your glass,
> Will modestly discover to yourself that of
> Yourself which you
> Yet know not of.

A glance at the model as summarized in Table 1-1 will show an interesting repetition in the conditions, the process, and the goals or outcomes of facilitative interpersonal relationships. Empathy, respect, and genuineness are present in all. The conditions lead to the process and to the outcomes. That is, the conditions are also the goal. The principle of reciprocity operates here. A self-actualizing person facilitates self-actualization in others; a relationship with a self-actualizing person is the condition for becoming a self-actualizing person.

The Central Importance of Love

The essence of these conditions is love, in the sense of the Greek *agape*. Thus they are not new discoveries. Research and experience in counseling or psychotherapy have simply confirmed what human experience shows us. St. Paul's little essay on love (I Cor. 13, 4–8) states it. All religions have reiterated the central importance of love in human relationships. Folk culture and pop songs pour it out: *Love Is the Answer; What the World Needs Now Is Love, Sweet Love; You're Nobody Until Somebody Loves You;* and the couplet from *Nature Boy*:

> The greatest thing you'll ever learn
> Is just to love and be loved in return.*

Love is the most effective agent for change that we know. Science is demonstrating that love is not only necessary for normal psychological development, but also for life itself. Barry Stevens tells about an incident when her husband was in charge of the pediatric ward at a hospital in New York in the twenties. "There was an infant whom none of the doctors could find anything wrong with, but all of them agreed the baby was dying. My husband spoke privately to a young nurse who loved babies. He swore her to secrecy before telling her what he wanted her to do. The secret was, 'Take care of this baby as if it were your own. Just *love* it.' At that time 'love' was nonsense even to psychologists. . . . The baby took hold. All the doctors agreed on that."[5] Since then the work of Rene Spitz[6] has documented the deleterious physical as well as psychological effects of lack of love in infancy. Burton, while discouraging a search for the single overriding trauma causing emotional disturbance, nevertheless states that "the basic pathogen is, for me, a disordered maternal or care-taking environment rather than any specific trauma as such."[7] Baumrind, a researcher in child development, states it simply and starkly: "Someone must, when no one else will, provide the attention, stimulation, and continuous personal relationship without which a child is consigned to psychosis, psychopathy, or marasmus."[8]

The importance—indeed, necessity—of love for the survival of the race has long been recognized. William James many years ago

*By Eden Ahbez. © 1948 by Crestview Music Corp.

wrote: "I saw . . . that the foundation principle of the worlds, of all the worlds, is what we call love."[9] A decade and a half later Maria Montessori noted that "scientists have at last perceived, after much research, this most evident fact: that it is love which preserves the animal species, and not the struggle for existence."[10] The poet W. H. Auden put it simply: "We must love each other or we must die." More recently Eric Hoffer phrased it as follows: "It may well be that the survival of the species will depend upon the capacity to foster a boundless capacity for compassion."[11] Man does not live by bread alone: bread is *necessary*, but not sufficient. Love is also necessary *and* sufficient, for when there is love there will be bread for those who need it.

A CONTINUUM OF HELPING RELATIONSHIPS

The model for facilitative interpersonal relationships suggests a continuum of helping activities or helping relationships. Table 1-2 shows this continuum.

TABLE 1-2. A Continuum of Psychological Helping Relationships

Information Giving	Instruction in Subject Matter: Education	Instruction in Habits and Skills: Behavior Modification	Reeducation: Behavior Therapy	Counseling: Psychotherapy
Cognitive				Affective
Impersonal				Personal
Specific				General
Learning (response not in repertoire)				Performance (response in repertoire)
Relationship as the medium				Relationship as the essence
Structured				Unstructured
Problem oriented				Person oriented

There are a number of variables underlying this continuum. The degree to which they are present varies in the different helping relationships. The kinds of relationships listed on the continuum do not exhaust all the possible kinds of helping relationships. Their exact placement on the continuum is arbitrary. The relationships at one extreme are not characterized by a complete lack of the variables at the other extreme—it is a matter of degree. For example, even the simplest or most casual helping relationship probably has an affective element, and the most intensive psychotherapy relationship has cognitive elements.

At one end of the continuum are helping relationships that are essentially cognitive rather than affective, impersonal rather than highly personal, specific and limited rather than broad and general in their concerns. In learning theory terms, relationships toward this end of the continuum involve the acquisition of new information, knowledge, or behaviors, while at the other end of the continuum the concern is with freeing for use or unblocking what is already known or with the performance of behaviors already learned.

A basic variable is the place or importance of the personal relationship in the helping process. A personal relationship—or a psychological relationship—is involved in every helping relationship, even if information is conveyed in an apparently impersonal manner, as through the printed word; a writer does establish a kind of psychological relationship with the reader, or perhaps more accurately, the reader creates or constructs some kind of relationship. Thus, a positive personal relationship of some kind or degree is a necessary part of the helping process. In many kinds of helping processes the relationship is not sufficient, however. The helper also must provide information, direction, guidance, resources, instruction. Thus, in teaching or reeducation, or remedial education, a good relationship with the student is necessary for effective teaching and learning, but it is not sufficient. The relationship is the medium through which teaching/learning is achieved. In some teaching, however—perhaps the best teaching—it appears that creating a suitable relationship may be sufficient for some kinds of learning by some kinds of learners. Such teaching approaches counseling or psychotherapy. The psychotherapy relationship—a highly affective, personal, open, or general relationship—is the necessary and sufficient condition for personality or behavior change of a particular kind or for resolving problems or fulfilling needs of a particular kind. It is the thesis of this book that the therapy relationship, or relationship therapy, is the specific treatment for persons whose problems inhere in or relate to the lack of or inadequacy of good interpersonal relationships in their past and/or current life experience.

This is perhaps not as narrow or restrictive a definition of psychotherapy as it may at first appear to be. The exact extent of psychological or emotional disturbances stemming from inadequate human relationships is not known. Certainly it is great, and experience suggests that it is the most frequent basic reason for seeking counseling or psychotherapy.

SUMMARY

In this chapter a conceptual model for facilitative interpersonal relationships was summarized. It involved a consideration of the goal or goals of counseling or psychotherapy. These goals were divided into three levels—the ultimate goal, the mediate goals or subgoals, and the immediate goal, which relates directly to the therapy process. Then the conditions for this process were considered, and four were specified: (1) empathic understanding, (2) respect, (3) therapeutic genuineness, and (4) specificity or concreteness.

A continuum of helping relationships was presented, ranging from a relatively superficial kind of helping involving simple information-giving to the intensive relationship known as psychotherapy. While some kind of interpersonal relationship is involved in, and is necessary for, all helping relationships, in psychotherapy a facilitative interpersonal relationship is both the necessary and the sufficient condition for positive personality and behavior change or for facilitating self-actualization.

NOTES

1. C. H. Patterson. *Humanistic education.* Englewood Cliffs, NJ: Prentice-Hall, 1973.
2. C. H. Patterson. Client-centered supervision. *The Counseling Psychologist,* 1983, *11*, 21-25.
3. C. R. Rogers. The necessary and sufficient conditions of therapeutic personality change. *Journal of Consulting Psychology,* 1957, *21*, 95-103.
4. C. B. Truax and R. R. Carkhuff. *Toward effective counseling and psychotherapy.* Chicago: Aldine, 1967, pp. 23-43.
5. In C. R. Rogers and B. Stevens. *Person to person: The problem of being human.* Lafayette, CA: Real People Press, 1967, p. 31.
6. R. Spitz. Hospitalism: An inquiry into the genesis of psychiatric conditions in early childhood. In R. S. Eissler et al. (Eds.), *The psychoanalytic study of the child* (Vol. I). New York: International Universities Press, 1945, pp. 53-74. See also J. J. Lynch. *The broken heart: The medical consequences of loneliness.* New York: Basic Books, 1977; and S. H. Frazier and A. C. Carr. *Introduction to psychopathology.* New York: Macmillan, 1964, p. 13.
7. A. Burton. *Interpersonal psychotherapy.* Englewood Cliffs, NJ: Prentice-Hall, 1972, p. 14.
8. D. Baumrind. New directions in socialization research. *American Psychologist,* 1980, *35*, 639-652.
9. W. James. *Varieties of religious experience.* New York: Modern Library, 1902, p. 391.
10. M. Montessori. *Spontaneous activity in education.* New York: Stokes, 1917, p. 326.
11. E. Hoffer, in *Saturday Review,* November 11, 1979.

CHAPTER 2

Goals and Values in Psychotherapy

Until relatively recently, the literature on counseling or psychotherapy has contained very little regarding its goals. One would think that the goals, objectives, or purpose of such an important process would be of great concern. In contrast, the goals and objectives of the educational process have been of continuing concern. It is difficult to understand how so much could be written about the process of counseling or psychotherapy, with so little consideration of its goals, since ends influence, or should influence, means.

In recent years, however, more attention has been given to this area. Two influences have perhaps contributed to this greater concern. One has been the greatly increased research on the effectiveness of counseling or psychotherapy, with the focus on outcomes of the process. The second has been the influence of the behaviorists, with their focus upon specifying objectives, even though their concern has been with relatively immediate, concrete, easily measured outcomes. The emphasis of the behaviorists upon stating and defining the objectives of treatment is an example for those who advocate other methods or approaches, even though there might be disagreement with the highly specific and limited objectives of behavior therapy.

The volume *The Goals of Psychotherapy*, edited by Mahrer[1], provides a comprehensive discussion of the goals of various theories and approaches to counseling or psychotherapy. In Mahrer's book, there appear to be as many goals of psychotherapy as there are authors of chapters. The number and variety of goals are almost endless. Included are such specific goals as the removal or elimination of symptoms, and reduction or elimination of test anxiety, phobias, fear of speaking in public, frigidity, impotence, enuresis, alcoholism, and so on. The chapter authors speak of unlearning nonadaptive habits and learning adaptive habits,[2] reduction of anxiety, relief from suffering, curing of a mental disease or illness, personality reorganization, effective biological and social functioning, and adjustment to the environment, society, or culture. Still other authors express even broader and more general goals: insight, self-understanding, optimal functioning, maturity, the facilitation of growth, the development of a philosophy of life, and the achievement of meaning in life.[3] Burton, after a survey of the literature, listed forty different aims of psychotherapy, most of them general rather than specific.[4]

It would appear to be almost impossible to combine, or integrate, these and other goals into a generally acceptable goal. The concept of mental health might seem to be an organizing focus. But concepts of mental health vary, being defined in almost as many ways as the goals of psychotherapy. Jahoda, recognizing that "there exists no psychologically meaningful description of what is commonly understood to constitute mental health," examined five criteria: (1) absence of mental disorder or symptoms; (2) normality of behavior; (3) adjustment to the environment; (4) unity of the personality; and (5) correct perception of the environment.[5] The first two were discarded, since symptoms are normal or abnormal depending on the cultural context, so that it is difficult to define what is normal in any absolute sense. Adjustment may be "passive acceptance of social conditions to the detriment . . . of mental health," and thus represent conformity (psychotherapy has been accused of being an instrument of social control and for maintaining the status quo[6]). Jahoda proposed a criterion of active adjustment, or "mastery of the environment, involving a choice of what one adjusts to, and a deliberate modification of environmental conditions."[7] Integration, or unity of the personality, or self-consistency, she felt, is useful as a criterion, though it is not acceptable alone, since it doesn't imply freedom from conflicts with the environment. Correct perception of reality, both of the world and of oneself, while difficult to establish (since the majority judgment is not necessarily correct), is still useful as a criterion.[8] (One is reminded of the remark of Nathaniel Lee, the English dramatist, on being confined to the Bedlam insane asylum: "The world and I differed as to my being mad, and I was outvoted."[9]) Jahoda thus proposed a triple criterion, in which Smith concurred.[10]

This proposal, or solution, to the problem of the nature of mental health, or of the goal of counseling or psychotherapy, does not seem to have been adopted or to have influenced the field, though a considerable period of time has elapsed during which it has received attention. Thus, we are still in need of an integrating concept that can encompass the suggested goals, which are of varied degrees of specificity as well as varying widely in nature. A resolution of this problem is offered here.

A LEVELS CONCEPT OF GOALS

One of the difficulties of specifying or agreeing upon the goals of psychotherapy is the fact that the goals stated by different writers vary in specificity, or, to use another term, in level. If goals could be organized in terms of levels, perhaps we would find, or gain, greater agreement. Parloff proposed two levels of goals—mediating and ultimate. Mediating goals, according to his classification, are those that are aspects of the psychotherapy process, for example, recovery of repressed memories. He notes that while there may be great differences in mediating goals, "differences in the stated ultimate goals will in all likelihood be small."[11] Halleck, discussing the need for study of the optimum human condition, writes that "probably no two psychiatrists would agree on what was best for a given patient on any specific issue, but they might eventually discover that there are a few general principles that could provide guidelines for intervention."[12] It is to this problem that the search for, and agreement upon, ultimate goals is directed. We briefly touched upon levels of goals in Chapter 1; here we will consider them in greater detail.

The Ultimate Goal

Ultimate goals are broad and general in nature. They are concerned with long-term outcomes. They relate to the questions: What do we want to be? What should people strive to be? What should people be like? What kind of persons do we want and need? These questions have been the concern of philosophers since before Aristotle.

We have noted that Jahoda's concept of positive mental health doesn't appear to be adequate. Two other suggested concepts are White's concept of competence[13] and psychological effectiveness. Both Bonner and Maslow have pointed out that competence conceptualizes behavior in the adjustment framework.[14] One must ask: Competence for what? Effectiveness for what? These questions indicate the need for a criterion of competence and effectiveness, so that these cannot themselves be the criterion. An ultimate goal must itself be the criterion.

There are a number of terms or concepts that appear to transcend these limitations and to constitute an ultimate goal. These terms include *self-realization, self-enhancement, full functioning* and *self-actualization.* Perhaps the most commonly used term is the last. We propose, as mentioned in Chapter 1, that self-actualization is the ultimate goal of counseling or psychotherapy.

Self-actualization as the goal of counseling or psychotherapy has a number of significant characteristics.

1. It constitutes a criterion in the sense that it is not vulnerable to the question: For what? Self-actualization is a given, inherent in the biology of living organisms.

2. Self-actualization as a goal avoids the problems of the medical model and its illness-health dilemma. The goal is more than the elimination of pathology and the achievement of some undefined (and undefinable) level of "normality." It is not a negative concept, such as the absence of disturbance, disorder, or "mental illness." It is a positive goal.

3. It avoids the problems of an adjustment model, with its question of adjustment to what, and the accompanying questions of conformity and (political) control.[15]

4. Self-actualization as a goal eliminates the conflict or dichotomy between intrapersonal and interpersonal goals. It encompasses both aspects of the person.

5. Self-actualization as a goal encompasses all persons—self-actualizing persons share characteristics and behaviors in common. Yet it allows for individual differences—each person has somewhat different potentialities that can be actualized. "Self-actualization is actualization of a self, and no two selves are altogether alike."[16]

6. The goal is a process, not a static condition to be achieved once and for all. It is the development of self-actualizing persons. This brings the concept of self-actualization within the existential framework. It is not an end, which once achieved is no longer a goal, but a continuing process of becoming. A goal should be an ideal that is continuously strived for though never completely reached.

7. Self-actualization is not the isolated goal of counseling or psychotherapy, limited to the treatment of disturbed or abnormal individuals. As noted above, it goes beyond the absence of disturbance or abnormality. It is the goal for all persons, the "normal" as well as the abnormal—for the person who, though not suffering from psychopathology, is dissatisfied, unhappy, unfulfilled, and not fully utilizing his or her potentialities, not being the person he or she is capable of being. Self-actualization is the goal of life and, as such, it should be the goal of society and of all its institutions—religion, education, marriage and the family, political and economic-occupational systems—all of which should exist for the benefit of individuals. Thus, counseling or psychotherapy is of a piece with the

rest of life, not something apart from it. Its purpose is to contribute, with other social institutions, to the personal development and fulfillment of individuals. In fact, counseling or psychotherapy has come into existence as a means by which society provides special assistance to those whose progress toward self-actualization has been blocked, interrupted, or impeded in a particular way, specifically by the lack of good human relationships.

8. There is another aspect of self-actualization that is particularly significant. Goals are related to drives or motives—in fact, they are the obverse of motivation. Thus, when we talk about the goal of life, we become involved in purpose, needs, drives, or motives, since goals are influenced by, indeed determined by, needs. The ultimate goal of counseling or psychotherapy, and of life itself, should be directly related to the basic needs of human beings.

Self-actualization is not only the goal of life—it is the basic motive of human beings, and indeed of all living organisms. It is the nature of every living organism to strive to actualize its potentials. The drive toward self-actualization as the single basic motive has been recognized by a number of writers. Goldstein was perhaps the first to use this term to indicate such motivation when he stated that "an organism is governed by a tendency to actualize, as much as possible, its individual capacities, its nature in the world."[17]

9. Finally, the concept of self-actualization as representing the basic motivation of all human beings provides a solution to the problem of organizing the myriad of specific and temporary needs or drives (see Chapter 3).

Combs and Snygg, in their perceptual theory of human behavior, refer to the maintenance and enhancement of the self, which they equate with self-actualization, as the "all inclusive human need which motivates all behavior in all times and in all places."[18] Rogers has said that "the organism has one basic tendency and striving—to actualize, maintain and enhance the experiencing organism."[19] This single basic drive appears to be inherent in the human organism and, though based upon a value orientation, to have a biological basis. Ashley Montagu, the distinguished anthropologist, emphasizes a biological basis for human values:

> We can here demonstrate that there are certain values for human life which are not matters of opinion, but which are biologically determined. If we do violence to these inbuilt values, we disorder our lives, as persons, as groups, as nations, and as a world of human beings.[20]

Self-actualization is the basic inbuilt value in human beings.

Thus, the concept of self-actualization provides a single universal goal, or common need, not only for counseling or psychotherapy and all helping relationships, but for life. Counseling or psychotherapy is thus consistent with life and living, and its goal is not something apart from life and everyday living but inherent in it. This goal is implicit, if not explicit, in the writings of many counselors and psychotherapists. Mahrer recognized it in his attempt to summarize the apparently diverse goals of the authors represented in his book when he included "achieving optimal functioning" as a common characteristic of many of their statements.[21] Rollo May stated that "the goal of therapy is to help the patient actualize his potentialities."[22]

The concept of self-actualization provides an integrating term for incorporating many, if not most, of the broad, general goals of psychotherapy expressed by writers in the field, as well as for the goals and objectives of life developed by many philosophers. It can encompass Freud's genital man, Jung's individuation, Adler's perfection, Binswanger's authentic one, even Frankl's will to meaning. For although Frankl suggested that self-actualization is a by-product of the attainment of meaning, it would seem that it is actually self-actualization that gives life itself meaning. Even the behaviorists recognize that these are desirable outcomes beyond their specific objectives. Wolpe, in describing the results of his treatment, includes general changes such as "increased productiveness, . . . improved interpersonal relationships—and ability to handle psychological conflict and reasonable stresses."[23]

Many philosophers in their search for the ultimate good have arrived at concepts closely resembling self-actualization. Aristotle's highest or supreme good was in effect self-actualization: the basic function (or motivation) of human beings is to exercise their highest capacities.[24] This concept of the development of one's potentials as the goal of life has persisted in the writings of other philosophers (for example, Locke and Rousseau) as well as in those of many psychologists.

The Immediate Goal and Mediate Goals

The immediate goal in counseling or psychotherapy, as noted in Chapter 1, is to set in motion and to continue the process that will lead to the client's achievement of the ultimate goal. The mediating goals of Parloff are aspects of the process and thus would be considered immediate goals. The counseling or therapy process as the immediate goal will be considered in detail in Chapters 6 and 7.

As the model presented in Chapter 1 was being developed, a third level of goals, designated mediate goals, was included. A category of mediate goals was considered desirable for two reasons. First, the ultimate goal is a common goal, universal for all clients, in all situations and cultures. It was felt that there should be a level of goals that would allow for the presence of individual differences, or the various ways in which individuals might actualize themselves. Second, such a level would meet the demand of the behaviorists and others for more specific, concrete goals, which again would vary among individuals. In an earlier model, mediate goals were considered to be subgoals, or steps toward the ultimate goal. In turn, the ultimate goal of self-actualization would serve as a criterion for the acceptance or rejection of mediate goals as justifiable or desirable goals.

Examples of mediate goals would be such things as achieving educational levels necessary for the full utilization of one's potentials (thus, not dropping out of school); obtaining employment (since holding a job is usually considered necessary for self-actualization in our society); saving or, if desirable, terminating a marriage; and other more specific goals such as eliminating phobias, examination anxiety, and fear of public speaking.

Two things became apparent, however, as the model developed. First, many of the more specific goals were the objectives of other helping processes, in terms of the continuum presented in Chapter 1; that is, they involved education or reeducation or skill training. Second, it became apparent that, in many cases at least, these specific goals or subgoals can be considered not only as steps toward self-actualization but as by-products of self-actualization. That is, as people become more self-actualized—more open, free, independent or autonomous, more aware of themselves, others, and their environment, and more capable in interpersonal relationships—they are able to achieve these goals themselves, on their own, or to seek and obtain the specific assistance—such as tutoring, skill instruction, information, education, or reeducation—necessary to achieve them.

The by-products of self-actualization are different for individual clients. As by-products, they are not necessarily goals to be directly achieved or specifically sought. Indeed, they need not be considered or planned for in advance as outcomes, thus avoiding the problem of determining in advance specific outcomes, which may only be developed by the client during or even following therapy.

It thus appears to be sufficient, at least in some cases, to provide the conditions leading to the development of self-actualizing persons. As individuals become more self-actualizing, they develop, seek, and achieve their own more specific goals. That this actually does occur is indicated by research showing that a good therapeutic relationship leads to a wide variety of changes, including the achievement of specific goals, in a wide variety of clients with a wide variety of problems.

VALUES AND PSYCHOTHERAPY

A generation ago the prevalent view regarding values and psycho-therapy was simple: values and psychotherapy, like alcohol and gasoline, should not be mixed. The model was the orthodox psycho-analyst, who claimed to be neutral, a blank screen upon which the client projected his or her beliefs, attitudes, and values without the therapist's values being involved. According to Weisskopf-Joelson "many psychotherapists still believe that the therapist's values should not influence the client. They may feel that imposing one's values on the patient is a miniature way of playing God."[25] Wilder, comment-ing upon a paper by Ginsburg, states that "it has been taken for granted that the analyst must not try to impose his value systems on the patient, and I still think this to be true."

But Wilder noted that there were "rising voices to the effect that the analyst not only does but should transmit his own value system to the patient" and notes that "a patient often says, 'Doctor, after all, you seem to have found a measure of peace and stability, why don't you shorten the therapy by simply telling me your philosophy.'"[26] Weisskopf-Joelson proposes that the inculcation of a philosophy of life be considered as one of the objectives of psychotherapy.[27] Thorne includes reeducation in a philosophy of life as a method of counseling.[28] Ellis's rational-emotive psychotherapy is essentially instruction in a philosophy of life.[29] Viktor Frankl also instructs clients in values and an approach to life.[30]

There are a number of reasons why it might be undesirable for a therapist to indoctrinate clients or attempt to inculcate a philosophy of life in them. We will consider each in turn.

1. First of all, while there are no doubt some generally, or even universally, accepted principles or ethical standards or rules, these do not constitute a philosophy of life. Each individual's philosophy, while sharing much in common with others, particularly in the same culture, is unique. No individual's philosophy is adequate for another individual.

2. It is too much to expect all counselors or psychotherapists to have a fully developed, adequate, generally accepted philosophy of life ready to be impressed on clients. Murphy, while admitting that "no one knows enough to construct an adequate philosophy of life," says that "it is not true that the wise man's sharing of a philosophy of life is an arrogant imposition upon a defenseless client."[31] Un-fortunately, all counselors are not wise men or women.

3. It may be questioned whether the counseling relationship is the appropriate place for direct instruction in ethics and a philoso-

phy of life. The home, the church, and the school are more appropriate places for such instruction. Particularly appropriate for the consideration of alternative philosophies and ethical systems is the school.

4. An individual usually does not adopt a system or code of ethics or a philosophy of life from one source and at a particular time. These are products of many influences over a long period of time.

5. It would appear to be best for each individual to develop one's own unique philosophy from many sources and not to be deprived of the experience of doing so. Such a philosophy will probably be more meaningful and useful than one adopted readymade from someone else, no matter how wise a person it may be. It cannot be imposed from without but must be developed from within.

6. We must still accept the right of the client to refuse to accept or develop any system of ethics or any philosophy of life and to accept or suffer the consequences.

This does not mean that counselors should refuse to discuss ethics, values, or a philosophy of life. In the process of doing so, they may, sometimes at the request of the client, disclose and discuss their own values, always clearly identifying them as their own preferences and avoiding the implication that the client ought to accept them. There may also be times when counselors, whether by request of the client or not, feel it necessary not only to state their own attitudes and values but to inform the client of the attitudes, ethics, or values of society—or some part of society.

But the problem is not simply whether therapists should openly impose their own values on clients, but whether therapists can avoid influencing clients. The therapist's values, whether or not the therapist is clearly aware of them, and whether or not the therapist intends it or is aware of it, influence the values of clients. If therapists value dreams, their clients dream and report their dreams; if therapists value sexual material, or any other particular kind of content, their clients produce it, thus "validating" the theories of their therapists. Moreover, therapists respond to the client's productions from a value orientation, whether they are aware of it or not. It might even be contended that if therapists were amoral (and especially if defensively so), they would be unable to empathize with a client in a moral conflict and thus be unable to help the client. Further, value orientation is communicated, at least to some extent, in words, tone of voice, or nonverbal ways, whether the therapist intends to or not. Thus therapists are not neutral in their values, and it is not possible for them to conceal their values from the client.

Ingham and Love were among the earliest to recognize the intrusion of the therapist's values into the therapy:

> The existence of the therapeutic relationship puts the therapist in a position in which he does, without choice, influence values in the mind of the patient. It is almost impossible for a therapist to avoid giving some impression of whether he favors such things as general law and order, personal self-development, and emotional maturity. The development of the relationship partly depends on the expression of such standards, because if the therapist were able to withdraw to such an extent that no evaluative attitudes would be apparent, he would not be able to participate sufficiently. But in an area in which the therapist does avoid revealing his ideas, the patient will project some onto him. So even if he could keep complete silence, he would still represent judgmental attitudes in the mind of the patient. If they have discussed an issue that involves moral values for a period of time, it is evident that the patient will have a concept of what the therapist thinks. His attitudes about right and wrong, or good and bad, are likely to be particularly influential for the patient.[32]

Wolberg, in a comment on the paper by Ginsburg, writes that

> no matter how passive the therapist may believe himself to be, and no matter how objective he remains in an attempt to permit the patient to develop his own sense of values, there is an inevitable incorporation within the patient of a new super-ego patterned after the character of the therapist as he is perceived by the patient. There is almost inevitably an acceptance by the patient of many of the values of the therapist as they are communicated in the interpretation or through direct suggestion, or as they are deduced by the patient from his association with the therapist.[33]

Parloff notes that "the disclosure of many of the therapist's values is inevitable . . . such disclosure and communication may occur without the therapist being aware of it."[34] It might be expected that the therapist, by reason of position and prestige, would be an example or model for the client, who would tend to pattern himself or herself after the therapist, intentionally or unintentionally.

An early study by Rosenthal provides evidence for the therapist's influence. Rosenthal studied 12 patients with a wide variety of diagnoses, ages 18 to 46, with from three weeks to one year of psychotherapy. The patients and their therapists were given a series of tests early in therapy and at the conclusion of treatment. Patients' scores on a test of moral values changed over therapy; those patients rated as improved became more like their therapists, while those rated as unimproved tended to become less like their therapists.[35] Parloff and his associates also found similar results. Observers listed topics discussed by two schizophrenic patients. The patients and therapists ranked them from most to least important after each therapy hour. After nine months, therapists and patients predicted each others' rankings. At the beginning of therapy the values (as indicated by the ranking of topics) of both patients differed from those of the therapist. As therapy progressed, the patients' values came closer to those of the therapist, though for one patient no further convergence occurred after the first six weeks.[36]

The recognition that the values of the therapist cannot be kept out of psychotherapy makes it incumbent on therapists to be clearly aware of their values. By recognizing that their values do enter into counseling or psychotherapy, therapists are freed of the belief or pressure that it is necessary or desirable to be neutral, and can better recognize and accept their values and become more aware of them in the therapy relationship. When therapists feel that the relationship would be improved by acknowledging and expressing their attitudes, beliefs, and values, they can do so. That is, therapists can freely be themselves, without guilt about not being neutral and without feeling they should not have any strong beliefs or values. This contributes to the openness and honesty of the relationship. When the counselor's attitudes, beliefs, and values are unexpressed (and deliberately withheld), they may (and apparently do) exert a pressuring influence on the client, who senses or deduces what they are. Where they are expressed by counselors and labeled as their own (or identified as those of others or of society in general), there is less coerciveness about them.

In addition to being aware of their values, beliefs, and attitudes, counselors should know how their values influence the client in the counseling process. There are two major ways in which values enter into the counseling relationship: in the assumptions and attitudes of the counselor about clients, and in the perceived goal or goals of the counseling process. The following discussion considers these from the client-centered or relationship therapy viewpoint.

Assumptions about and Attitudes toward Clients

The client-centered or relationship therapist holds certain assumptions about clients. These assumptions are reflected in the therapist's attitudes toward clients; they are as follows.

1. All clients are motivated by the drive toward growth or toward self-actualization. This is what brings them to therapy and keeps them in therapy.

2. All clients are capable of assuming responsibility for themselves, their thoughts, feelings, and actions, including choices and decisions.

3. All clients are capable of resolving their own problems and difficulties in a facilitative human relationship leading to self-understanding.

4. Clients are the experts on themselves—they know themselves better than anyone else does. They may be unaware of what they know or how much they know, and unable to verbalize this knowledge at the beginning of therapy.

5. The basic attitude of the therapist is a deep respect for the client as a person of worth. The client is viewed positively, as able rather than unable, capable rather than incapable, responsible rather than irresponsible, independent rather than dependent, helpful rather than helpless. The client is valued, not devalued or evaluated.

These are, as stated, assumptions, but they represent values held by the therapist. They are not always borne out, of course. But they should not be easily or quickly abandoned with any client. The implications of abandoning the assumptions are serious—consigning the client to a state of dependence, irresponsibility, or helplessness, in which someone else, often the state or an institution, assumes responsibility for him or her.

On the other hand, holding to the assumptions invokes the power of expectations; the client responds by supporting the assumptions. Indeed, it may be that the most important factor in therapy is how much faith and confidence the therapist has in the client, a faith and confidence expressed by the therapist in the relationship and communicated to the client.

There are some implications of or corollaries to these assumptions that should be noted.

1. If clients are the experts on themselves, then the therapist does not have to be an all-knowing expert, being expected to know clients better than clients know themselves.

2. If clients can take responsibility for themselves, beginning in the therapy situation, then the therapist does not have to assume responsibility for the direction of therapy, or give advice, answer all questions, solve clients' problems, make choices or decisions for them, or lead or push them toward counselor-selected choices or decisions.

3. The therapist does not have to possess a detailed textbook knowledge of theories of psychopathology or theories of personality. These are only theories, and there are different theories.

4. The therapist is not an initiator in the therapy process, but a responder—responsive to the material provided by the client at the client's own rate or pace. The therapist's responsiveness facilitates client self-exploration and self-understanding. An axiom I use in my

teaching is that anything therapeutic that can be achieved by therapist initiation—by questioning, probing, leading, guiding—can be
achieved in a more meaningful and useful way by the responsive
mode, thereby not robbing the client of the initiative in the process.

Too many therapists fail because they do not adequately test the
assumptions. They have too little faith in their clients.

Goals as Values

Goals are values, and, conversely, values are goals. Counselors or
therapists who value educational achievement, economic or occupational success, or social success will see these as desirable goals for
their clients, while counselors or therapists who value independence
and responsibility will see these as goals for their clients. Whether the
client or the counselor should determine goals has been a trouble-
some question, with the behaviorists insisting that clients should
determine their own goals. Yet, therapists have their own goals.
Many feel, however, that therapists should not impose their own
goals on the client. Should therapists abandon their own goals and
accept those of the client?

The model presented here provides a solution to this dilemma.
The problem of the therapist imposing goals on the client arises when
therapists have a variety of relatively specific goals, which may not
be relevant to all clients. The acceptance of a single, broad, ultimate
goal applicable to all clients would change this situation. The reluctance of therapists to adopt such a goal is based upon the difficulties
of defining a goal that appears to be applicable or best for all clients.
Halleck points out that "philosophers, theologians, political scientists,
and psychologists have struggled with this problem for centuries,
searching for value systems founded upon religious beliefs, social
utility, ethical relativism, or human biology."[37] Self-actualization is
a goal that more and more psychologists and psychotherapists appear
to be adopting.

If self-actualization is seen not only as a goal but as the basic,
dominant motive of life, then its acceptance as a goal does not mean
that the therapist is imposing an external, arbitrary goal upon clients,
but is recognizing and accepting a goal that is inherent in all clients.
The ultimate goal is not determined by either the therapist or the
client but by life itself.

Within the context of the ultimate goal, the client has the freedom to determine subgoals. Therapists who disclaim any ultimate
goal or who are unaware of their implicit (and more specific) goals,
may impose their own goals on the client without being aware of it.
This may be encouraged by the fact that many clients, when they

enter therapy, have no clear or explicit goals. Halleck notes that "if the therapist takes time to investigate a patient's social situation, he will usually find that when the patient enters therapy he doesn't have a clear idea of what he wants. The patient comes to the therapist in the role of a supplicant."[38] Therapists sometimes disagree with or refuse to accept the stated goals of the client. The behaviorists often appear to direct or force the client into having a problem or goal that their technique can deal with, ignoring or rejecting other problems or goals as being too vague, general, or not susceptible of operational definition.

The specific goals of therapy are selected by the client, in terms of their contribution toward his or her becoming a more self-actualizing person, or, from another point of view, they are by-products of increasing self-actualization. As a more fully self-actualizing person, the client is then more capable of achieving these specific goals. If clients require assistance from others—information, education, training, or reeducation—they seek and obtain it, or they may be referred by the therapist to sources of such specific help.

Self-actualization is the goal not only of psychotherapy, but since it is the basic motivation of the human being, it is, or should be, the goal of society and all its institutions—the family, the school, the church. It is the goal of all helping relationships. The various kinds of helping relationships referred to in Chapter 1 are concerned, each in its own way, with facilitating self-actualization. Counseling or psychotherapy is only one way of facilitating self-actualization. It is appropriate for those individuals whose self-actualization is prevented or inhibited by the lack of, or the inadequacy of, good human relationships.

VALUES CLARIFICATION AND COUNSELING

For the past decade and a half an approach to values in education known as values clarification[39] has attracted considerable attention, from both professionals and the public. This is essentially a method of discussing values with students by the use of clarifying questions. More recently it has been suggested that this approach to values be used in counseling settings.[40] This would involve the introduction into counseling of the value problems and conflicts of the client.

The process of values clarification is essentially a rational, cognitive process guided by the questioning of the counselor. This questioning puts the counselor in the position of leading and directing the discussion. It seems clear that this is a teaching or, in the case of a single client, a tutoring process; simply because it involves a single or a small number of clients doesn't make it counseling.

Clients in a counseling situation do of course have the value problems and conflicts dealt with in values clarification. Counseling, however, recognizes the affect-laden aspects. In my view, where there are value conflicts and problems within the client, or between the client and others, or between the client and society or an element in society, these will arise spontaneously in counseling—the client will bring them up without their being introduced by the counselor. In a counseling process in which the counselor responds sensitively and understandingly, clients will explore these problems and conflicts as they would any other problems or concerns. They will do so in their own way, at their own pace, including the affective and emotional aspects as well as the cognitive elements, and including the kinds of questions posed by values clarification. The advantages of this approach, with the client in control, are that clients will explore the more personal aspects and nuances, and reach conclusions that are more meaningful, useful, and to which they will feel a greater commitment since they are achieved on the client's own— with, of course, the counselor's participation, not as a Socratic guide, but as an understanding facilitator. This approach to dealing with values in counseling with its goal of the self-actualizing person (which includes responsibility, independence, self-acceptance, and self-esteem) leads to clients' perception of the locus of control as within themselves rather than outside,[41] to the perception of themselves as competent,[42] as capable rather than helpless,[43] and as efficacious.[44] Bandura[45] provides evidence that perceived self-efficacy is related to a wide variety of desirable behaviors—increased coping behavior, less physiological stress reactions, self-regulation of refractory behavior, and positive reactions to resignation, dependency, and failure experiences, among others.

SUMMARY

This chapter was concerned with the goals of counseling or psychotherapy. Since goals are values, the place of values in psychotherapy was also considered.

Three levels of goals were proposed: an ultimate goal, mediate goals, and an immediate goal. The ultimate goal is the development of self-actualizing persons. This is a goal that is inherent in the human organism and is common to all clients. An intermediate level of goals, which might be called subgoals, vary with different clients, and include the more specific behavior changes that are often considered to be goals or outcomes of therapy. These may also be considered by-products of self-actualization. Persons who, as a result of the therapy relationship, become more self-actualizing, move toward the achievement of these goals or changes on their own, seeking and obtaining where necessary or desirable the specific kinds of help they want.

The immediate goal of counseling or psychotherapy is the initiating and continuing of the therapeutic process or relationship, which leads the client to become a more self-actualizing person.

The problem of values in counseling or psychotherapy was considered, including the overt teaching of values and the method known as values clarification. An approach to values in client-centered or relationship therapy that allows values questions to be introduced spontaneously by the client was discussed.

NOTES

1. A. R. Mahrer (Ed.). *The goals of psychotherapy.* New York: Appleton-Century-Crofts, 1967.
2. J. Wolpe. Behavior therapy and psychotherapeutic goals. In Mahrer, *Goals of psychotherapy,* pp. 129–144.
3. V. E. Frankl. *The doctor and the soul* (2nd ed.). New York: Knopf, 1965.
4. A. Burton. *Interpersonal psychotherapy.* Englewood Cliffs, NJ: Prentice-Hall, 1972, pp. 10–11.
5. M. Jahoda. Toward a sociology of mental health. In M. J. E. Senn (Ed.), *Symposium on the healthy personality.* Supplement II. *Problems of infancy and childhood.* New York: Josiah Macy Foundation, 1950.
6. S. L. Halleck. *The politics of therapy.* New York: Science House, 1971.
7. Jahoda, Toward a sociology of mental health.
8. M. Jahoda. *Current concepts of positive mental health* New York: Basic Books, 1958.
9. Cited in S. De Grazia. *Errors in psychotherapy.* Garden City, NY: Doubleday, 1952, p. 146.
10. M. B. Smith. Optima of mental health: A general frame of reference. *Psychiatry,* 1950, *13,* 503–510.
11. M. B. Parloff. Goals in psychotherapy: Mediating and ultimate. In Mahrer, *Goals of psychotherapy,* pp. 5–19.
12. Halleck, *Politics of therapy,* pp. 197–198.
13. R. W. White. Motivation reconsidered: The concept of competence. *Psychological Review,* 1959, *66,* 297–333.
14. H. Bonner. *On being mindful of man.* Boston: Houghton Mifflin, 1965, p. 190. A. H. Maslow. *Toward a psychology of being.* Princeton, NJ: Van Nostrand Reinhold, 1962, pp. 168–169.
15. Halleck, *Politics of therapy.*
16. A. H. Maslow. Self-actualizing people: A study of psychological health. In C. E. Moustakas (Ed.), *The self: Explorations in personal growth.* New York: Harper & Row, 1956, pp. 160–194.
17. K. Goldstein. *The organism.* New York: Harcourt Brace Jovanovich, 1939, p. 196.
18. A. W. Combs and D. Snygg. *Individual behavior.* New York: Harper & Row, 1959, p. 38.

19. C. R. Rogers. *Client-centered therapy.* Boston: Houghton Mifflin, 1951, p. 195.
20. A. Montagu. *On being human.* New York: Hawthorn Books, 1950, p. 52.
21. Mahrer, *Goals of psychotherapy.*
22. R. May. *Psychology and the human dilemma.* Princeton, NJ: Van Nostrand Reinhold, 1967, p. 109.
23. J. Wolpe. *Psychotherapy by reciprocal inhibition.* Stanford, CA: Stanford University Press, 1958, p. 200.
24. Aristotle, *Ethics, I,* 7, 1098a.
25. E. Weisskopf-Joelson. Values: The *enfant terrible* of psychotherapy. *Psychotherapy: Theory, Research, and Practice,* 1980, *17,* 459–466.
26. J. Wilder. Comment. In S. W. Ginsburg and J. L. Herma, Values and their relationship to psychiatric principles and practice. *American Journal of Psychotherapy,* 1953, 7, 546–573.
27. E. Weisskopf-Joelson. Some suggestions concerning Weltanschauung and psychotherapy. *Journal of Abnormal and Social Psychology,* 1953, *48,* 601–604.
28. F. C. Thorne. *Psychological case handling.* Brandon, VT: Clinical Psychology, 1968.
29. A. Ellis. *Reason and emotion in psychotherapy.* New York: Lyle Stuart, 1953.
30. Frankl, *Doctor and the soul.*
31. G. Murphy. The cultural context of guidance. *Personnel and Guidance Journal,* 1955, *34,* 4–9.
32. H. V. Ingham and L. R. Love. *The process of psychotherapy.* New York: McGraw-Hill, 1954, pp. 75–76.
33. L. R. Wolberg. Comment. In Ginsburg and Herma, *Values.*
34. M. B. Parloff. Communication of values and therapeutic change. Paper presented at the annual convention of the American Psychological Association, New York, August 31, 1957. M. B. Parloff. Therapist-patient relationship and outcome of psychotherapy. *Journal of Consulting Psychology,* 1961, *25,* 29–38.
35. D. Rosenthal. Changes in some moral values following psychotherapy. *Journal of Consulting Psychology,* 1955, *19,* 431–436.
36. M. B. Parloff, B. Iflund, and N. Goldstein. Communication of "therapy values" between therapist and schizophrenic patients. *Journal of Nervous and Mental Disease,* 1960, *130,* 193–199.
37. Halleck, *Politics of therapy,* p. 196.
38. *Ibid.,* p. 80.
39. L. E. Raths, M. Harmin, and S. B. Simon. *Values and teaching* (2nd ed.). Columbus, OH: Charles E. Merrill, 1978. S. B. Simon, L. Howe, and H. Kirschenbaum. *Values clarification: A handbook of practical strategies for teachers and students.* New York: Hart, 1972.
40. B. Glaser and H. Kirschenbaum. Using values clarification in counseling settings. *Personnel and Guidance Journal,* 1980, *58,* 569–574.
41. J. B. Rotter, J. E. Chance, and E. J. Phares. *Applications of a social learning theory of personality.* New York: Holt, Rinehart and Winston, 1972.
42. R. W. White. Motivation reconsidered: The concept of competence. *Psychological Review,* 1959, *66,* 297–333.
43. M. E. Seligman. *Helplessness.* San Francisco: Freeman, 1975.
44. A. Bandura. Self-efficacy mechanism in human agency. *American Psychologist,* 1982, *37,* 122–147.
45. *Ibid.*

CHAPTER 3

The Nature of
Self-Actualization

To be what we are, and to become what we are capable of becoming, is the only end of life.

R. L. STEVENSON

A major criticism of goals such as self-actualization is that they are too general, broad, and amorphous to be useful. The behaviorists, particularly, ask for operational definitions in terms of specific behaviors. This is a legitimate question. If a concept is significant and pertinent, it can, at least in principle or eventually, be reduced to specific, objective, or measurable variables. However, the process of doing so may require considerable time and effort. It is indefensible to reject out of hand, as the behaviorists sometimes do, any concept or objective that cannot be immediately, easily, and objectively measured. Simplicity, or ease of measurement, is not an appropriate criterion. To refuse to be concerned with anything that cannot now be objectively measured is to rule out of consideration many potentially significant and important concepts and to delay progress in attempts to define, objectify, and measure them.

Some progress has already been made in defining and objectifying the concept of self-actualization. This chapter is concerned with the results of efforts in this direction. First, however, it is desirable that we consider the theoretical background from which the concept of self-actualization has developed.

THE NATURE OF HUMANS

What is the nature of the human being? A number of different theories have been offered on this topic, some supporting more than others the concept of self-actualization as our ultimate goal. Here I will focus on four assumptions that support this concept: (1) Humans are active as well as reactive beings; (2) humans are inherently good; (3) humans have a single basic motivation; and (4) humans are social beings.

Humans Are Active as Well as Reactive Beings

Allport has described three concepts or images of human beings.[1] The first concept is that of humans as reactive beings. We are objects, biological organisms, responding to stimuli in the environment. Our behavior is determined by the stimuli to which we are exposed. Past stimuli have made us what we are. Our present and future are determined by past stimuli and the potential stimuli that we will encounter. Thus, we are not free to determine our own behavior. Our behavior is reflective, reactive, or responsive to external stimuli, rewards, or reinforcements. Though it may exist, consciousness—thinking and feeling—is irrelevant in the study of our behavior. This is the traditional or "scientific" approach to humans, the view of stimulus-response psychology and of the behaviorists, exemplified by J. B. Watson and B. F. Skinner.

The second concept is that of humans as reactive beings in depth. We are a result of our past experiences, and our past as well as present and future are determined by our internal drives or instincts. Chief among these drives or instincts are sex or libido and death or aggression. This is the view of depth psychologies, chief among which is psychoanalysis.

Allport contrasts a third concept of humans with these two, which he calls beings in the process of becoming. This model sees people as proactive, as personal, conscious, and future-oriented. We are in control of our behavior and of our destiny (within limits, of course). This is the model of existentialism and humanistic psychology.

These three concepts or images of humans can be reduced to two apparently opposing models. The first two concepts are similar, presenting humans as reactive beings, whether in response to the environment or to instincts and drives. We react to stimuli from without and from within. Thus, in the first model, humans are controlled by stimuli, victims of the environment and innate drives. The second model, of beings in the process of becoming, reverses this view. We are determiners, not determined; we are not controlled but control, both the environment and ourselves. We have something to say about what we shall do or become.

Human behavior is less controlled by instinct than is any other animal's. Rather than being manipulated by the environment, we manipulate the environment for our own purposes. We are not creatures of instinct or of environmental stimuli alone—of the past and of the present alone. Unlike the animals, we have a future and are forward-looking, influenced by anticipation, expectation, and foresight. In fact, we create, to some extent at least, our own environment, our own world. We are free, within limits, of course, and since we are free, we can and must make choices. And since we are free to choose, we are responsible for our choices and behavior.

These two models are in conflict. They appear to be antithetical, so that one is compelled to choose one or the other. The prevailing view, the one that is fostered by our current scientific approach, is that of humans as reactive beings, as determined. The concept of freedom appears to be inconsistent with the assumption of determinism. Moreover, there is overwhelming support in psychology for the view that humans are reactive beings. We cannot reject or deny this view. But must we then, as the behaviorists insist, reject the existentialist or humanistic view?

The difficulty is in stating the problem as an either/or choice. It is not necessary to accept one view and reject the other. The solution is to recognize that neither model alone is a complete or accurate model. Each, by itself, gives us only a partial view. The reactive model is a limited one, a "nothing but" model. But people are this and something more. This "something more" is significant, even crucial, in understanding people and their behavior and in developing an adequate theory of human behavior. The danger of the reactive model is not that it is true, but that it is regarded as the *whole* truth. If people are treated as nothing but reactive objects, they will in fact become objects.

A major difficulty in accepting the humanistic view is the freedom-determinism dilemma. Philosophy has never resolved—and may never resolve—this dilemma, and it is not possible here, nor necessary, to go into its philosophical aspects. Science has accepted determinism—at least at this point it appears to be a necessary assumption. But science, especially psychology, must recognize and deal with human experience. A major aspect of human experience is the influence of beliefs—or assumptions—on human behavior. There are two factors related to the freedom-determinism dilemma that must be recognized. The first is the fact of the psychological existence of the feeling or experience of freedom and choice in the individual. This feeling or experience must be recognized and included in any theory of human behavior. Second, and of perhaps more importance, is the fact that beliefs exert an influence upon behavior. It makes a tremendous difference in our conception of human beings and in the way we act and in the way we deal with each other whether the assumption of determinism or of freedom is accepted. To view people as free means that we treat them differently than if we view them as completely determined, and our different treatment leads to different behavior on their part.

To accept the existence of freedom does not necessitate rejection of the existence of causation, or control, or order. Freedom would be meaningless without the existence of control. Freedom is not an absolute, but a matter of degree. Freedom in the psychological sense is the introduction of the individual as a causal or controlling factor in his or her behavior.

The behaviorists emphasize that the environment, through its rewards, selects and molds the individual's behavior. Yet, from another point of view, it is the individual who selects the responses that produce what to him or her is rewarding or desirable. And this is often done in a conscious manner, with the experience of choice. The term *instrumental response* carries this connotation of choice and purpose. This view is represented by the cartoon of the rat in a Skinner box pressing a bar to receive pellets. The caption read (if my memory is correct) something like this: "Look how I've got him conditioned. Every time I press this bar he gives me a pellet." The way the behaviorists insist that everything is externally determined while at the same time talking about the control and creation of environments also illustrates the paradox, or the importance of the point of view one takes. Behavior is determined, but not entirely by the environment. Human beings are also determiners of their own behavior.

People are living, active beings, not inactive objects waiting to be stimulated. We search for stimuli and seek experiences. We organize stimuli and the environment, the world, in terms of our needs, or actually in terms of the single basic need, the preservation and enhancement of the self—self-actualization.

Humans Are Inherently Good

Many, if not most, religions view human beings as innately depraved. Freud was pessimistic regarding human nature. He believed that the individual's instincts were antisocial and must be controlled by culture or society:

> It does not appear certain that without coercion the majority of human individuals would be ready to submit to the labour necessary for acquiring new means of supporting life. One has, I think, to reckon with the fact that there are present in all men destructive, and therefore anti-social and anti-cultural, tendencies, and that with a great number of people these are strong enough to determine their behavior in society.[2]

People are not only antisocial but actually hostile to other people, according to Freud:

> Civilized society is perpetually menaced with disintegration through this primary hostility of men toward one another. . . . Culture has to call up every possible reinforcement in order to erect barriers against the aggressive instinct of man.[3]

Aggression has long been considered an instinct. Adler originally proposed that aggression was the single basic human motive or instinct.[4] The strength and practical universality of aggression argue for its innateness. However, many have questioned its innateness or instinctiveness. Anthropologists have found societies with little trace or evidence of aggression.[5] Ashley Montagu writes:

> My own interpretation of the evidence, strictly within the domain of science, leads me to the conclusion that man is born good and is organized in such a manner from birth as to need to grow and develop his potentialities for goodness. . . . [The view that aggressiveness is inherited] is not scientifically corroborated. In fact, *all* the available evidence gathered by competent investigators indicates that man is born without a trace of aggressiveness.[6]

He refers to Lauretta Bender's finding that hostility in the child is a symptom complex resulting from deprivation in development. Charlotte Buhler in her studies of infants also found that there is "evidence of a primary orientation toward 'reality' into which the baby moves with a positive anticipation of good things to be found. Only when this reality appears to be hurtful or overwhelming does the reaction become one of withdrawal or defense."[7] Maslow also declares that impulses of hate, jealousy, hostility, and so on are acquired. "More and more," he writes, "aggression is coming to be regarded as a technique or mode of compelling attention to the satisfaction of one's need."[8] There is no instinct of aggression that seeks expression or discharge without provocation or without regard to circumstances.

In other words, aggression is not primary but is a reaction to deprivation, threat, or frustration. This is the frustration-aggression hypothesis put forward in 1939 by the Yale anthropologist Dollard and his psychologist associates.[9] A more general term for the stimuli that provoke aggression is *threat*. Aggression is universal because threat, in some form or other, is universal. The psychoanalyst Bibring, in criticizing Freud's theories, questions "whether there are any phenomena of aggression at all outside the field of the ego-preservative functions" and notes "the empirical fact that aggressiveness appears only or almost only when the life instincts or the ego instincts are exposed to harm."[10] A popular novel purporting to demonstrate the innateness of aggressiveness in man inadvertently supports the view that aggression is the result of threat, since the development of aggression in the group of castaway boys occurs under conditions of fear and feelings of being threatened.[11]

There is evidence that people are inherently good in the continual striving toward an ideal society, with the repeated and independent development of essentially similar religious and ethical systems whose ideals have withstood the test of time. In spite of deprivation, threat, and frustration, these ideals have been held and practiced by many individuals. Humans have developed systems of government and law that, though imperfectly, especially in their applications, represent these ideals.

It might actually be argued that goodness or cooperation has a survival value[12] and that innate aggression would be selectively eliminated by evolution. If there were not an inherent drive toward good, or if aggression were innate, it is difficult to understand how the human race could have continued to survive. The potential for good has survived in the face of continued threat and frustration. When we can reduce deprivation and threat, the manifestations of good will increase and aggression will decrease. It is important to add that aggression does not include assertive behavior, initiative behavior, nor even much of competitive behavior. The confusion of these kinds of behavior with aggression has perhaps contributed to the belief that aggression is innate.

Emotional disturbance, an important manifestation of which, in many people, is aggression, is the result of the frustration of the drive toward self-actualization by a threatening, depriving, or misunderstanding social environment.

Humans Have a Single Basic Motivation

In Chapter 2 I stated that the single basic motivation of all human beings is the actualization of one's potentials. A number of psychologists have reached this conclusion, apparently independently, including Goldstein, Angyal, Rogers, and Combs and Snygg. Angyal defines life as a "process of self-expansion" and adds that "the tendency of the organism is toward increased autonomy," or toward self-determination. He also refers to self-realization as being the intrinsic purpose of life.[13] Lecky, impressed by the integration and organization of the self, felt that a need for self-consistency and its preservation is the single basic need of the organism.[14]

Self-actualization is a part of Rogers's general organismic actualizing tendency: "The organism has one basic tendency and striving— to actualize, maintain, and enhance the experiencing organism."[15]

Rogers also uses terms such as *independence, self-determination, integration,* and *self-actualization.* Thus, although writers use different terms—*self-enhancement, self-fulfillment, self-realization, self-actualization*—to designate the single basic motivation of all human beings, they all seem to be referring to the same concept or phenomenon. People are by nature engaged in the process of actualizing their potentials.

Combs and Snygg have perhaps developed the unitary theory of motivation most extensively:

> From birth to death the maintenance of the phenomenal self is the most pressing, the most crucial, if not the only task of existence. . . . Man seeks not only the maintenance of *a* self. . . . Man seeks both to maintain and enhance his perceived self.[16]

The use of the terms *preservation* and *maintenance* along with *enhancement* and *actualization* poses the question of whether there aren't actually two motives. Maslow perhaps was influenced by some such consideration in his concepts of efficiency motivation and growth motivation.[17]

But preservation or maintenance, and enhancement or actualization, may be seen as two aspects of the same motive operating under different conditions. Adler recognized the different expression of the same motive in neurotics and normals. The neurotic, threatened and compensating for deep feelings of inferiority, reacts to preserve or restore self-esteem, or to overcome inferiority with superiority through a striving for power. The normal individual, on the other hand, free of threat and without feelings of inferiority, can strive for completeness or perfection.[18] For the unhealthy, disturbed, or abnormal individual under stress and threatened, enhancement or positive striving is impossible. He or she must defend against attack or threat, and strive to safeguard, defend, or secure what he or she is or has. Energies are absorbed in preservation. Goldstein has made the same point. He considers the drive for self-preservation a pathological phenomenon. The drive for self-actualization, he suggests, undergoes a change in the sick (or threatened) individual, in whom the scope of life is reduced so that he or she is driven to maintain (or defend) a limited state of existence. Preservation or maintenance of the self is thus the pathological form of self-actualization, the only form of self-actualization left to the disturbed or threatened individual (or, in Goldstein's work, the brain-damaged individual[19]).

A more serious question about the concept of a single basic motive is raised by those who contend that man has many motives and propose various hierarchical orderings of them. Maslow's hierarchy is the most widely known proposal of this kind. It starts with the basic physical needs, which are prepotent and take precedence, when they are unmet, over all other needs. When these basic needs are met, the safety needs emerge. Then come the belongingness need, the love need, the esteem need, and then the need for self-actualization.[20] The problem is that the order is not invariant, as Maslow himself recognized. It is not always true that the lower, more basic physiological needs take precedence over the higher, less prepotent needs. A person may sacrifice life for honor. We need, therefore, some organizing principle to explain this apparent inconsistency.

The concept of self-actualization as the single basic need provides this organizing principle. It clarifies, or eliminates, the confusion we face when we attempt to understand and order, or integrate, the multiplicity of often contradictory or opposing specific drives or motives that are attributed to human beings. There is no need to attempt to order drives or needs in a hierarchy. There *is* no hierarchy in the sense that certain needs always take precedence over other needs. All the specific needs are subservient to the basic tendency for the preservation and enhancement of the self. The individual's specific needs are organized and assume temporary priority in terms of their relationship to the basic need for self-actualization. At any one time, the most relevant specific need assumes priority or prepotence or, to use Gestalt terminology, becomes the figure against the ground of other needs.[21] When it is satisfied, the next most relevant need in terms of self-actualization assumes prepotence or becomes the figure, while the others recede into the background. All are organized by the basic need for self-actualization, and their significance or relevance is determined by this basic need.

Humans Are Social Beings

Human beings need others to actualize themselves. Humans are, as Aristotle noted, social animals. Because of our prolonged infancy, humans learn to become dependent on others and remain dependent on others for affection. Humans become persons and develop a self only in a society or a group.

> In most societies most people typically want to receive a maximum degree of warmth and tenderness from another person and to express such feelings toward another person. When man is unable to develop intimate relationships with others, he is miserable and his physical well-being is threatened. Children can be permanently damaged if they have no intimacy. Even if they receive adequate nourishment and shelter, infants who have no contact with loving adults become ill.[22]

Occasionally, reports are published about the discovery of a child, or even an adult, who has been extremely neglected, isolated from human contact, and treated worse than an animal. Such persons, if they have been treated this way for a long time, are barely human. There are stories, some of them documented, of children who though lost for a long time have managed to survive. But when they have been found, they are no longer human. The "wild boy" of Aveyron discovered in a forest in France in the early 1800s never became human, though the French physician Itard spent much time and effort with him. While it is suspected that he was mentally retarded, his dehumanization went beyond his supposed mental deficiencics. Patients in mental institutions often deteriorate when they are not treated as real persons or human beings. Persons confined in prison become "stir crazy" from lack of human relationships.

It would seem to be clear that one cannot be a self-actualizing person except in a group or society. The condition for self-actualizing persons is a facilitative relationship with other persons. People contribute to each other's self-actualization in a group or society characterized by such relationships. These relationships are reciprocal. Rogers notes that the enhancement of the self "inevitably involves the enhancement of other selves as well. . . . The self-actualization of the organism appears to be in the direction of socialization, broadly defined."[23]

THE SELF-ACTUALIZING PERSON

A number of writers have contributed to the description and definition of the self-actualizing person, sometimes using other designations for such a person. Combs and Snygg discuss the characteristics of the *adequate* person, the person who has developed an adequate self. Adequate persons perceive themselves in positive ways: they have positive self-concepts, they accept themselves. The adequate person also accepts others:

> We are so entirely dependent upon the goodwill and cooperation of others in our society that it would be impossible to achieve feelings of adequacy without some effective relationship with them. The adequate personality must be capable of living effectively and efficiently with his fellows.[24]

In addition, adequate persons are aware of and able to accept all their perceptions without distortion. From a behavioral point of view, adequate persons are characterized by efficient behavior, since they are not handicapped by defensiveness and are more open to experience. They are spontaneous and creative because, being secure, they can take chances, experiment, and explore. Being secure and accepting themselves, they are capable of functioning independently; they find their own feelings, beliefs, and attitudes adequate guides to behavior. Finally, adequate persons are compassionate. They can relate to others with concern rather than with the hostility and fear of defensiveness.

In discussing the actualizing tendency, Rogers notes that it leads to or is manifested by growth and motivation, differentiation, independence and autonomy, and self-responsibility. Rogers's concept of the fully functioning person is similar to the adequate-person concept of Combs and Snygg. Rogers describes three major characteristics of fully functioning persons: (1) They are open to experience, to all external and internal stimuli. They have no need to be defensive. They are keenly aware of themselves and the environment. They experience both positive and negative feelings without repressing the latter. (2) Fully functioning persons live existentially. Each moment is new. Life is fluid, not fixed. They are changing, in process, flexible, and adaptive. (3) Fully functioning persons find their organism "a trustworthy means of arriving at the most satisfying behavior in each existential situation."[25] Their behavior is determined from within; the locus of control is internal. Since they are open to all experience, they have available the relevant data on which to base behavior. Behavior is not always perfect, since some relevant data may be missing. But the resulting unsatisfying behavior is corrected on the basis of feedback. Such a person is a creative and self-actualizing person.

Earl Kelley describes the fully functioning person in similar terms. Such persons think well of themselves and feel able or competent while being aware of limitations. They also think well of others, recognizing their importance as opportunities for self-development. Fully functioning persons develop and live by human values rather than by external demands. They are creative. A characteristic not mentioned by Rogers or Combs and Snygg is the ability of the fully functioning person to recognize the value of mistakes as a source of learning and to profit from them.[26]

These descriptions of the self-actualizing person were developed through observation, experience, and, in Rogers's case, research in education and psychotherapy. Maslow, in a study devoted to self-actualization, lists these same characteristics as well as some others and so provides a comprehensive picture of the self-actualizing person.[27] Maslow used an accepted and sound method in his study of self-actualization. He selected a criterion group of persons (living and dead) who, on the basis of professional judgment, were deemed outstanding self-actualizing persons. Included among the historical persons studied were Lincoln, Einstein, Franklin and Eleanor Roosevelt, William James, Whitman, Thoreau, Beethoven, and Freud (living persons were not identified). As a general definition, Maslow used the following:

[Self-actualizing people are characterized by] the full use and exploitation of talents, capacities, potentialities, etc. Such people seem to be fulfilling themselves and to be doing the best that they are capable of doing. They are people who have developed or are developing the full stature of which they are capable.[28]

The subjects were studied intensively to ascertain the characteristics they had in common that differentiated them from ordinary or average people. Fourteen characteristics emerged.

1. *More efficient perception of reality and more comfortable relations with it.* This characteristic includes the detection of the phony and dishonest person and the accurate perception of what exists rather than a distortion of perception by one's needs. *Self-actualizing people are more aware of their environment,* both human and nonhuman. They are not afraid of the unknown and can tolerate the doubt, uncertainty, and tentativeness accompanying the perception of the new and unfamiliar. This is clearly the characteristic described by Combs and Snygg and Rogers as awareness of perceptions or openness to experience.

2. *Acceptance of self, others, and nature.* Self-actualizing persons are not ashamed or guilty about their human nature, with its shortcomings, imperfections, frailties, and weaknesses. Nor are they critical of these aspects of other people. *They respect and esteem themselves and others.* Moreover, they are honest, *open, genuine, without pose or facade.* They are not, however, self-satisfied, but are concerned about discrepancies between what is and what might be or should be in themselves, others, and society. Again, these characteristics are those that Kelley, Rogers, and Combs and Snygg include in their descriptions.

3. *Spontaneity.* Self-actualizing persons are not hampered by convention, but they do not flout it. *They are not conformists,* but neither are they anticonformist for the sake of being so. They are not externally motivated or even goal-directed—rather, their motivation is the internal one of growth and development, the actualization of themselves and their potentialities. Rogers and Kelley both speak of growth, development and maturation, change and fluidity.

4. *Problem-centeredness.* Self-actualizing persons are not ego-centered but focus on problems outside themselves. They are *mission-oriented,* often on the basis of a sense of *responsibility, duty, or obligation* rather than personal choice. This characteristic would appear to be related to the security and lack of defensiveness leading to compassionateness emphasized by Combs and Snygg.

5. *Detachment; need for privacy. Self-actualizing persons enjoy solitude and privacy.* It is possible for them to remain unruffled and undisturbed by what upsets others. They may even appear to be asocial. This is a characteristic that does not appear in other

descriptions. It is perhaps related to a sense of security and self-sufficiency.

6. *Autonomy, independence of culture and environment.* Self-actualizing persons, though dependent on others for the satisfaction of the basic needs of love, safety, respect, and belongingness, "are not dependent for their main satisfactions on the real world, or other people or culture or means-to-ends, or, in general, on extrinsic satisfactions. *Rather they are dependent for their own development and continued growth upon their own potentialities* and latent resources."[29] Combs and Snygg and Rogers include independence in their descriptions, and Rogers also speaks of an internal locus of control.

7. *Continued freshness of appreciation.* Self-actualizing persons repeatedly, though not continuously, experience awe, pleasure, and wonder in their everyday world.

8. *Mystic experiences, oceanic feelings.* In varying degrees and with varying frequencies, *self-actualizing persons have experiences of ecstasy, awe, and wonder* with feelings of limitless horizons opening up, followed by the conviction that the experience was important and had a carry-over into everyday life. This and the preceding characteristic appear to be related and to add something not in other descriptions, except perhaps as it may be included in the existential living of Rogers.

9. *Gemeinschaftsgefühl. Self-actualizing persons have a deep feeling of empathy, sympathy, or compassion for human beings in general.* This feeling is, in a sense, unconditional in that it exists along with the recognition of the existence in others of negative qualities that provoke occasional anger, impatience, and disgust. Although empathy is not specifically listed by others (Combs and Snygg include compassion), it would seem to be implicit in other descriptions, including acceptance and respect.

10. *Deep interpersonal relations. Self-actualizing people have deep relations with others.* They are selective, however, and their circle of friends may be small, usually consisting of other self-actualizing persons, but the capacity is there. They attract others to them as admirers or disciples. This characteristic, again, is at least implicit in the formulations of others.

11. *Democratic character structure. Self-actualizing persons do not discriminate* on the basis of class, education, race, or color. They are humble in the recognition of what they know in comparison with what could be known, and are ready and willing to learn from anyone. They *respect everyone* as potential contributors to their knowledge, but also just because they are human beings.

12. *Discernment of means and ends.* Self-actualizing persons are highly ethical. *They clearly distinguish between means and ends* and subordinate means to ends.

13. *Philosophical, unhostile sense of humor.* Although the self-actualizing persons studied by Maslow had a sense of humor, it was not of the ordinary type. Their sense of humor was the spontaneous, thoughtful type, intrinsic to the situation. Their humor did not involve hostility, superiority, or sarcasm. Many have noted that a sense of humor characterizes people who could be described as self-actualizing, though it is not mentioned by those cited here.

14. *Creativeness.* All of Maslow's subjects were judged to be creative, each in his or her own way. The creativity involved here is not the special-talent creativeness. It is a creativeness potentially inherent in everyone but usually suffocated by acculturation. *It is a fresh, naive, direct way of looking at things.* Creativeness is a characteristic that most would agree characterizes self-actualizing persons.

The description of the self-actualizing person is a description of the kind of individual who functions at a high level, using his or her potentials and experiencing personal satisfaction. He or she is also a desirable member of society. In fact, it can be said that, unless there are enough individuals possessing to a minimal degree the characteristics of the self-actualizing person, society cannot survive. These characteristics, in Skinner's terminology, are the conditions that lead to the "ultimate strength of men."

> If a science of behavior can discover those conditions of life which make for the ultimate strength of men, it may provide a set of 'moral values' which, because they are independent of the history and culture of any one group, may be generally accepted.[30]

Historically, self-actualizing men and women have been the major contributors to the development of civilization, and where societies have disintegrated or disappeared, it was probably because of the lack of enough such people.

The characteristics of self-actualizing people can be defined and stated in ways that permit their being evaluated and measured; they are observable. In fact, we observe and evaluate them continuously in our everyday interpersonal relationships. At the very least, they can be rated by judges on the basis of observation of a person's behavior. In fact, some of these characteristics can be measured by instruments now available. We shall consider these measurements in our discussion of the nature of the therapy relationship.

It is interesting to compare the description of the self-actualizing person with that of the young child. Young children are naturally self-actualizing, providing evidence for the innateness or naturalness of this state. The infant and young child are curious and exploratory of their environment. They don't have to be stimulated to be active. As Skinner says, "No one asks how to motivate a baby. A baby naturally explores everything he can get at, unless restraining forces have been at work. . . ."[31] Young children are naturally open, gener-ous, spontaneous, honest, trusting, accepting, creative. Their behav-ior is positive, cooperative, and loving, rather than negative, competi-tive, or aggressive—until they are taught the latter.

CRITICISMS OF THE CONCEPT OF SELF-ACTUALIZATION

Self-actualization is an integrating concept in terms of both the goals of psychotherapy and human motivation. Yet objections have been raised against the concept. These objections appear to be based upon some misconceptions or misunderstandings concerning the nature of self-actualization.

One objection appears to be the belief that self-actualization is inimical to individuality. In this view, the self-actualizing person appears to be a collection of traits that are the same for all persons and that manifest themselves in standard, identical behaviors. It is true that, as the model indicates, self-actualizing persons have many common characteristics or behaviors. But since what is actualized is the individual self, there is allowance for different interests and different potentials. Maslow makes the point, quoted earlier, that "self-actualization is actualization of a self, and no two selves are altogether alike."[32]

A second, and opposite, widespread misconception is that a self-actualizing person is antisocial, or at least asocial. Salvatore Maddi, criticizing self-actualization as the good life, writes that this view holds that

> actualization will tend to take place without the aid of socialization. Indeed, society is usually regarded, in this view, as an obstruction, because it forces individuals into molds, roles, conventions that have little to do with their own unique potentialities. The best thing society can do is impinge upon the individual as little as possible.[33]

In another place Maddi writes:

> According to Rogers, . . . what blocks individuals is society, in the form of persons and institutions reacting with conditional positive regard and therefore being too judgmental to be facilitative of self-actualization. . . . The definition of the good life involved emphasizes spontaneity rather than planfulness, openness rather than critical judgment, continual change rather than stability, and an unreflective sense of well-being. Enacting this, one would more likely live in the woods than enter public life."[34]

This involves a subtle misrepresentation by quoting out of context, using clever comparisons, and making unjustified inferences and extrapolations from statements by Rogers.

The idea that the self-actualizing person is—or can be—antisocial has been expressed by Williamson. Pointing out that human nature is potentially both good and evil, and that "man seems to be capable both of becoming his 'best' bestial and debasing self, as well as those forms of 'the best' that are of high excellence," he contends that it cannot be accepted that "the nature or form of one's full potential and self-actualization will thus be the 'best possible' or the 'good' form of human nature."[35] While one could contend that psychotherapy would provide the conditions for the actualizing of one's "best" potential, Williamson questions the "implicit assumption that the 'best' potentiality will be actualized under optimum counseling relationships."[36] He appears to believe that counseling or psychotherapy, by accepting self-actualization as its goal, is in danger of encouraging "growth through demolishing all barriers restricting free development in any and all directions, irresponsibly and without regard for the development of others."[37] He questions the assumption that "any and all forms of growth contain within themselves their own, and sufficient, justification," and asks, "Do we believe that the fullest growth of the individual inevitably enhances the fullest growth of all other individuals?"[38] Again, note the use of extreme statements and the straw-man approach.

M. Brewster Smith also appears to accept this view of self-actualization as including undesirable, or antisocial, behaviors: "The problem of evil remains: people may realize their potentialities in ways that are humanly destructive, of others if not themselves."[39] Indeed, some people *may exercise* their potentialities in antisocial ways, but (by definition) they are not self-actualizing people.

Even the eminent Harvard psychologist Robert White sees self-actualization as self-centered or selfish. Recognizing that Maslow included "focusing on problems outside oneself and being concerned with the common welfare" in his concept of self-actualization, he questions its inclusion: "To call working for the common welfare 'self-actualization' instantly falsifies it into something done for one's own satisfaction."[40] Thus, it is apparent that he views self-actualization as self, or selfish, satisfaction. "I ask readers," he continues, "to observe carefully whether or not self-actualization, in its current use by psychological counselors and others, is being made to imply anything more than adolescent preoccupation with oneself and one's impulses." These remarks seem to reflect the equating of self-actualization with the ego-centered "culture of narcissism" of the "me decade" of the 1970s so widely popularized by writer Tom Wolfe and historian Christopher Lasch.

These are serious misconceptions or misunderstandings, if not misrepresentations, of the concept of self-actualization as it is used by Maslow, Rogers, myself, and others. The implicit assumption in these criticisms is that there is an inevitable conflict between the individual and society, and that the full development or self-actualization of individuals is inimical to the self-actualization of other individuals.

The formulation by Rogers of the self-actualizing person deals with this issue. Individuals live, and must live, in a society composed of other individuals. The person can actualize only in interaction with others. Selfish and self-centered behavior does not lead to experiences that are self-actualizing or satisfying in nature. The self-actualizing person "will live with others in the maximum possible harmony, because of the rewarding character of reciprocal *positive regard.*"[41] "We do not need to ask who will socialize him, for one of his own deepest needs is for affiliation and communication with others. As he becomes more fully himself, he will become more realistically socialized."[42] The self-actualizing person is more mature, more socialized in terms of the goal of social evolution, though he may not be conventionally or socially adjusted in a conforming sense.

> We do not need to ask who will control his aggressive impulses, for when he is open to all his impulses, his need to be liked by others and his tendency to give affection are as strong as his impulses to strike out or to seize for himself. He will be aggressive in situations in which aggression is realistically appropriate, but there will be no runaway need for aggression.[43]

The self-actualizing person needs to live in harmony with others to meet his or her own needs to love and to be loved—in short, in order to be a self-actualizing person. Thus the self-actualizing person provides the conditions for the self-actualization of others, rather than being a negative social influence. A corollary of this is that the therapist must be a self-actualizing person if he or she is to facilitate the self-actualization of his or her clients.

THE NATURE OF EMOTIONAL DISTURBANCE

If the goal of psychotherapy is the development of self-actualizing persons, then it follows that the problem, or the "pathology," for which psychotherapy is the remedy is the inability of the client to become a self-actualizing person. As indicated in Chapter 1, clients fail at this task because they have not had and/or do not now have the personal environment that allows and encourages them to be self-actualizing. Specific problems are aspects of, indications of, or symptoms of this failure to be self-actualizing. Anxiety, guilt, and aggression are results of the frustration of the drive toward self-actualization. The discrepancy between what persons are and what they are capable of being is the source of anxiety and guilt. Persons who are not self-actualizing are lacking in some or all of the characteristics of self-actualizing persons. They do not accept themselves; they have low self-esteem. They are not open to their environment and the experience of their organism and their senses; their relationships with reality are disturbed. They do not accept or respect others, and are disturbed in their interpersonal relationships. They are self-centered rather than problem-centered (in the sense of devoting themselves to a problem or cause outside themselves). They are dependent, inhibited rather than spontaneous, and wear a mask or facade rather than being real and genuine. Their creativity is suppressed, so that they are unable to utilize and develop their potentials.

This concept of self-actualization as the goal of psychotherapy, and of life, and of its frustration as the source and nature of emotional disturbance, avoids the problems connected with the term *mental hygiene* and the nature of "good" or "positive" mental hygiene. We start with the positive, with a goal inherent in the nature of human beings, so that its lack, its frustration, or its blocking is the problem or the "pathology."

Perhaps it should be reiterated here that many things can impede the development of self-actualizing persons. Impediments can include physical deprivation, physical illness, and lack of education, training, experience, and opportunities for the development of one's potentials. Psychotherapy is concerned with a particular class of impediments to self-actualization—the lack of or inadequacy of the appropriate personal environment or personal or psychological conditions for self-actualization, what might be called emotional deprivation. Other kinds of treatment or help are appropriate for dealing with other kinds of impediments to self-actualization. Counseling or psychotherapy is the specific treatment for the lack of self-actualization resulting from emotional deprivation.

SUMMARY

This chapter began with a consideration of the nature of human beings as background for developing a description of the self-actualizing person. People are active as well as reactive beings. They are inherently good rather than bad. Aggression is a reaction to threat rather than an instinct expressed regardless of conditions in the environment. People have a single basic motivation, the preservation and enhancement of the self, or the drive toward self-actualization.

People are by nature social beings; they become human only in a group or society of other persons. They are able to actualize themselves most adequately in a society of other self-actualizing persons as a result of reciprocal influence.

The characteristics of the self-actualizing person were explored, drawing heavily from the research of Maslow. Among other characteristics of the self-actualizing person is the ability to develop good interpersonal relationships. This involves acceptance of and respect for others, understanding or empathy with others, and openness, genuineness, or honesty in interpersonal relationships. Self-actualizing persons accept themselves and their human nature with its fallibilities. They are secure and thus do not have to be defensive; they are not easily threatened. They are in close touch with their environment, being sensitive and aware of stimuli. Their locus of control is internal rather than external, so that they are autonomous, independent, and develop their own value systems.

These characteristics are observable and thus in principle can be defined operationally so that they can be measured. In fact, it is now possible to measure some of them.

It is the inability to become a self-actualizing person because of a deprived social and emotional environment that constitutes emotional disturbance or psychological pathology. It is this disturbance, or this source of the frustration of the drive toward self-actualization, to which counseling or psychotherapy is directed and for which it is the specific treatment.

NOTES

1. G. W. Allport. Psychological models for guidance. *Harvard Educational Review*, 1962, *32*, 373–381.
2. S. Freud. *The future of an illusion*. London: Hogarth Press, 1949, pp. 10–11.
3. S. Freud. Civilization and its discontents. New York: Harrison Smith, n.d. Quoted in D. E. Walker, Carl Rogers and the nature of man. *Journal of Counseling Psychology*, 1956, *3*, 89–92.
4. H. L. Ansbacher and R. R. Ansbacher (Eds.). *The individual psychology of Alfred Adler*. New York: Basic Books, 1956, p. 34.
5. For an excellent survey by an anthropologist of the problem of aggression, see A. Alland, Jr. *The human imperative*. New York: Columbia University Press, 1972.
6. A. Montagu. *The humanization of man*. Cleveland, OH: World Publishing, 1962.
7. C. Buhler. *Values in psychotherapy*. New York: Free Press, 1961, p. 71.
8. A. Maslow. Our maligned human nature. *Journal of Psychology*, 1949, *28*, 273–278.
9. J. Dollard, L. W. Doob, N. E. Miller, O. H. Mowrer, and R. R. Sears. *Frustration and aggression*. New Haven: Yale University Press, 1939.

10. E. Bibring. The development and problems of the theory of instincts. In C. L. Stacy and M. F. Martino (Eds.), *Understanding human motivation*. Cleveland, OH: Howard Allen, 1958, pp. 474–498.
11. W. Golding. *Lord of the flies*. New York: Coward McCann, 1955.
12. A. Montagu. *On being human*. New York: Henry Schuman, 1950.
13. A. Angyal. *Foundations for a science of personality*. New York: Commonwealth Fund, 1941, pp. 29, 47, 354.
14. P. Lecky. *Self-consistency: A theory of personality*. New York: Island Press, 1945.
15. C. R. Rogers. *Client-centered therapy*. Boston: Houghton Mifflin, 1951, p. 487.
16. A. W. Combs and D. Snygg. *Individual behavior* (rev. ed.). New York: Harper & Row, 1959.
17. A. H. Maslow. Deficiency motivation and growth motivation. In M. R. Jones (Ed.), *Nebraska symposium on motivation, 1955*. Lincoln, NE: University of Nebraska Press, 1955, pp. 1–30.
18. Ansbacher and Ansbacher, *Adler*, p. 114.
19. K. Goldstein. *The organism*. New York: Harcourt Brace Jovanovich, 1939.
20. A. H. Maslow. *Motivation and personality* (2nd ed.). New York: Harper & Row, 1970, pp. 35–47.
21. F. S. Perls. *Ego, hunger and aggression*. New York: Random House, 1969.
22. S. L. Halleck. *The politics of therapy*. New York: Science House, 1971, p. 204. Halleck refers to a summary of research by L. J. Yarrow. Separation from parents during early childhood. In M. Hoffman and L. Hoffman (Eds.), *Child development research*. New York: Russell Sage Foundation, 1964, pp. 89–136.
23. Rogers, *Client-centered therapy*, pp. 150, 488.
24. Combs and Snygg, *Individual behavior*, p. 246.
25. C. R. Rogers. *Freedom to learn*. Columbus, OH: Merrill, 1969, p. 286.
26. E. C. Kelley. The fully functioning self. In A. W. Combs (Ed.), *Perceiving, behaving, becoming*. Washington, DC: National Education Association, 1962, pp. 9–20.
27. A. H. Maslow. Self-actualizing people: A study of psychological health. In C. E. Moustakas (Ed.), *The self: Explorations in personal growth*. New York: Harper & Row, 1956, pp. 160–194.
28. *Ibid.*, pp. 161–162.
29. *Ibid.*, p. 176.
30. B. F. Skinner. *Science and human behavior*. New York: Macmillan, 1953, p. 445.
31. B. F. Skinner. *Walden two*. New York: Macmillan, 1948, p. 101.
32. A. H. Maslow. Self-actualizing people: A study of psychological health. In C. E. Moustakas (Ed.), *The self: Explorations in personal growth*. New York: Harper & Row, 1956, pp. 160–194.
33. S. Maddi. Ethics and psychotherapy. Remarks stimulated by White's paper. *The Counseling Psychologist*, 1973, 4(2), 26–29.
34. S. Maddi. Creativity is strenuous. *The University of Chicago Magazine*, September–October, 1973, pp. 18–23.
35. E. G. Williamson. *Vocational counseling*. New York: McGraw-Hill, 1965, p. 185.
36. E. G. Williamson. The social responsibilities of counselors. *Illinois Guidance and Personnel Association Newsletter*, Winter 1963, pp. 5–13.
37. E. G. Williamson. A concept of counseling. *Occupations*, 1950, 29, 182–189.

38. E. G. Williamson. Values orientation in counseling. *Personnel and Guidance Journal*, 1958, *37*, 520–528.
39. M. B. Smith. Comment on White's paper. *The Counseling Psychologist*, 1973, *4*(2), 48–50.
40. R. W. White. The concept of the healthy personality. *The Counseling Psychologist*, 1973, *4*(2), 3–12, 67–69.
41. C. R. Rogers. A theory of therapy, personality, and interpersonal relationships, as developed in the client-centered framework. In S. Koch (Ed.), *Psychology: A study of a science. Vol. 3: Formulations of the person and the social context*. New York: McGraw-Hill, 1959, p. 235.
42. C. R. Rogers. *On becoming a person*. Boston: Houghton Mifflin, 1961, p. 194.
43. Rogers, *A theory of therapy*.

PART TWO

The Therapeutic Process

CHAPTER 4

The Therapeutic Conditions: Responsive Dimensions

The theme of this book is that psychotherapy is a relationship. It is assumed that providing a facilitative or therapeutic relationship is the necessary and sufficient condition for helping those persons who are failing to develop or progress toward self-actualizing behavior. Such individuals, it is assumed, are not in need of direct instruction, skill training, control, and guidance. Rather, it is assumed, if they are provided with the appropriate kind of relationship, their inherent capacity to grow, develop, and become a self-actualizing person will manifest itself. They will be capable of making necessary choices and decisions and of implementing them in action. If they have these capacities, then they have the right to exercise them, and should be given the freedom to do so.

Concern with the nature of the therapeutic relationship has been evident in every theory or approach to psychotherapy. There have been many attempts to identify the characteristics of effective therapists. As you will recall from Chapter 1, Carl Rogers presented in 1957, as hypotheses, three necessary and sufficient conditions for therapeutic personality change: empathy, respect, and genuineness.[1] These three conditions involving the therapist have become the focus of considerable writing and research since then[2] and have come to be known as the core conditions for facilitative interpersonal relationships. Truax and Carkhuff review the evidence for the recognition and acceptance of these conditions by a wide variety of therapists from Freud to the behaviorists.[3] This and more recent evidence is evaluated in Chapter 13.

Truax, Carkhuff, and Berenson have proposed several additional conditions, some of which have been designated as action dimensions, in contrast with responsive dimensions. One of the action dimensions, concreteness of expression, is also included among the responsive dimensions.

In this chapter we deal in more detail than we did in Chapter 1 with the three basic core dimensions and with concreteness; in the next chapter, we consider the action dimensions.

EMPATHIC UNDERSTANDING

In English, the word *understanding* has come to mean knowledge *of,* or understanding *about,* something. One of the goals of science is understanding—understanding of objects and the results of their manipulation. This is not the kind of understanding we refer to when we use the word in counseling or psychotherapy. Here we are concerned not with knowing *about* clients but knowing how they feel and think and perceive things—themselves and the world about them. It is understanding from the internal frame of reference, rather than from the external or so-called objective frame of reference. Some languages, for example French and German, have two verbs for *to know,* one meaning to know from the external frame of reference and the other simply to know, subjectively. Because English does not make this distinction, we need a modifier for the word *understanding; empathic* is used for this purpose.

Empathic understanding has long been recognized as an important element in psychotherapy. In this section we discuss its nature, how it can be measured, and what it looks like in action.

The Nature of Empathy

Empathy should not be confused with sympathy. It does not involve identification with the client. This is clear in Rogers's definition: "[Empathy is] an accurate, empathic understanding of the client's world as seen from the inside. To sense the client's private world as if it were your own, but without losing the 'as if' quality— this is empathy."[4] Colloquially, it is expressed, at least in part, by the phrase "I know where you're coming from." A phrase in the language of some American Indians expresses it: "to walk in his moccasins." Great novelists are experts in empathic understanding, leading their readers to empathize with their characters. The theme of one novel, *To Kill a Mockingbird,* is dependent on the concept of empathy. At one point in the story Atticus Finch, the lawyer, trying to help his two young children to understand people's behavior toward him, says: "If . . . you can learn a simple trick . . . you'll get along a lot better with all kinds of folks. You never really understand a person until you consider things from his point of view—until you climb into his skin and walk around in it."[5]

Empathy, of course, is not a trick, nor is it simple. Our society is externally oriented; we do not normally or easily see things from another person's point of view. We are too preoccupied with our own frame of reference. On the other hand, once we know what it means, most of us can relatively easily assume temporarily another's point of view. Students in counseling or psychotherapy seem to have relatively little difficulty in understanding the nature of empathy and putting themselves in the place of another person—at least momentarily. It seems that the capacity for empathy is present, to some extent at least, in many people in our society, certainly in most of those who are seriously interested in becoming counselors or psychotherapists.

But it is difficult to persist in this frame of reference, since it is not our usual behavior in everyday human relationships. Students easily pop out of the internal into the external frame of reference, and it takes considerable time to overcome the habits of everyday interactions with others. Students are also often bothered by the apparent subjectivity of empathic understanding. They are obsessed with the need to obtain "objective facts." But the so-called facts are nothing more than the subjective perceptions and impressions of other observers, usually with added evaluative or judgmental aspects. The real "facts" in counseling or psychotherapy are the perceptions, ideas, beliefs, attitudes, and feelings of the client; he or she is the expert on these facts, and the counselor must attempt to see and understand them.

The question is sometimes raised regarding discrepancies between the client's perceptions and those of others—shouldn't the counselor check the client's perceptions against those of his or her associates, family, or teachers? If the client's perceptions are greatly out of line with others', this will usually be apparent; often it will be brought to the counselor's attention by those in the client's environment. In cases where the discrepancies are less evident, the counselor will usually become aware of them as counseling continues. The real question is what counselors should or can do about such discrepancies. Usually they should do nothing about them immediately, since there is nothing effective they can do until a relationship is established. When this is achieved, it is likely that the client will recognize, or admit, discrepancies that he or she has been aware of, or will become aware of them, and then therapy can deal with them. Or, if they are apparent, and the client does not seem to be progressing toward awareness of them, the counselor can respond to them through confrontation. (See Chapter 5.)

Empathy involves at least three aspects or stages. Assuming that the client is willing to allow the counselor to enter his or her private world and attempts to communicate perceptions and feelings to the counselor, the counselor must be receptive to the communication. Second, counselors must understand the communication of the client. To do this they must be able to put themselves in the place of the client, to take the role of the client. Third, the counselor must be able to communicate his or her understanding to the client.

Since we cannot actually be another person, we are inevitably outside, in an "as if" situation. This is not necessarily a negative situation, but can be positive if we responsively engage in an exploration with the client of his or her perceptions, emotions, and experiences. It is also a protection against too close an identification and against empathy becoming sympathy. "Being empathic, we assume the role of the other person, and in that role initiate ourselves the process of self-exploration as if we were the other person himself."[6] In trying to understand clients and in feeling and experiencing with them, we help them in the process of expressing, exploring, and understanding themselves.

Differences between counselors and their clients are barriers to empathy. Differences in sex, age, religion, socioeconomic status, education, and culture impede the development of empathic understanding. Of course, no one can completely understand another person. Everyone is unique, a product of a unique series of experiences. The wider a person's background, the more varied his or her experiences, the greater the understanding of a wider variety of other people. Yet it is impossible for any one individual to have the variety of experiences necessary for understanding all other persons, if identical or similar experiences were necessary for empathy. No male can really experience what it is like to be a female; no White can really experience what it is like to be Black. But it is not necessary for one to be exactly like another or to have had similar experiences to understand another. It may help in understanding a psychotic to have been psychotic oneself, but it is not necessary.

We can empathize to some extent at least, and sometimes to a great extent, with any other person on the basis of our commonalities as human beings. As Sullivan put it, "We are all much more simply human than otherwise."[7]

Fortunately, it is not necessary that we understand or empathize completely with another to be able to help the other person through relationship therapy. If we are really trying to understand, with at least occasional success in the beginning of therapy, therapy has a chance of continuing and of being successful. Indeed, clients will try to help the therapist understand them and sometimes will show remarkable persistence with an obtuse therapist.

It is certainly desirable that counselors should prepare themselves in any way they can to understand potential clients. A counselor who wants to work with a particular age, sex, social, or ethnic group should make some effort to gain an understanding of the particular group. It is frequently recommended that such persons take a course in the social and behavioral sciences, particularly anthropology, for this purpose. However, such courses are not particularly helpful, and they may be harmful. Anthropology is, or strives to be, a science. It is the hallmark of science that it is objective—that is, it studies objects or makes objects out of what it studies. Thus, the approach of anthropology, as it is usually taught, does not lead to a human understanding but to the viewing of other peoples as curious objects, sometimes barely human. To be sure, some anthropologists do develop a deep understanding of the peoples they study, but this is not usually conveyed in an anthropology course. In addition, anthropology is concerned with commonalities of cultures, with groups, rather than with individuals. It thus is in danger of fostering stereotypes, particularly in the minds of students, who are taking only a course or two. Stereotypes are harmful rather than helpful in dealing with or understanding individuals. A counselor who has had a course on the poor Whites of Appalachia or the Blacks in the deep rural South is likely to be hindered rather than helped when he encounters a poor Appalachian White or a southern rural Black as a client.

There are two useful ways in which counselors can prepare themselves, to some extent at least, to work with clients from other groups than their own. One is to acquire as much vicarious experience as possible. People who really know the other group can be of help. One widely available source is literature. Students should steep themselves in the literature—poetry, novels, biographies, and autobiographies—of the group. The second way in which the serious student can develop understanding of another group is to live with them—not as a visitor or as a professional person but as a person without any special identity except perhaps as a worker of some kind with them. Perhaps it is not too much to require that prospective counselors have some such experience for from six months to a year.

Measuring Empathic Understanding

In 1961, Truax developed a Tentative Scale for the Measurement of Accurate Empathy. This is a nine-point scale with definitions of each point and examples.[8] Carkhuff revised the scale and converted it into a five-level system for measuring empathic understanding in interpersonal processes.[9] Carkhuff's scale is as follows.

Level 1

The verbal and behavioral expressions of the first person either *do not attend to* or *detract significantly* from the verbal and behavioral expressions of the second person(s) in that they communicate significantly less of the second person's feelings than the second person has communicated himself.

EXAMPLES: The first person communicates no awareness of even the most obvious, expressed surface feelings of the second person. The first person may be bored or uninterested or simply operating from a preconceived frame of reference which totally excludes that of the other person(s).

In summary, the first person does everything but express that he is listening, understanding, or being sensitive to even the feelings of the other person in such a way as to detract significantly from the communications of the second person.

Level 2

While the first person responds to the expressed feelings of the second person(s), he does so in such a way that he *subtracts noticeable affect from the communications* of the second person.

EXAMPLES: The first person may communicate some awareness of obvious surface feelings of the second person, but his communications drain off a level of the affect and distort the level of meaning. The first person may communicate his own ideas of what may be going on, but these are not congruent with the expressions of the second person.

In summary, the first person tends to respond to other than what the second person is expressing or indicating.

Level 3

The expressions of the first person in response to the expressed feelings of the second person(s) are essentially *interchangeable* with those of the second person in that they express essentially the same affect and meaning.

EXAMPLE: The first person responds with accurate understanding of the surface feelings of the second person but may not respond to or may misinterpret the deeper feelings.

In summary, the first person is responding so as to neither subtract from nor add to the expressions of the second person; but he does not respond accurately to how that person really feels beneath the surface feelings. Level 3 constitutes the minimal level of facilitative interpersonal functioning.

Level 4

The responses of the first person add noticeably to the expressions of the second person(s) in such a way as to express feelings a level deeper than the second person was able to express himself.

EXAMPLE: The facilitator communicates his understanding of the expressions of the second person at a level deeper than they were expressed, and thus enables the second person to experience and/or express feelings he was unable to express previously.

In summary, the facilitator's responses add deeper feeling and meaning to the expressions of the second person.

Level 5

The first person's responses add significantly to the feeling and meaning of the expressions of the second person(s) in such a way as to (1) accurately express feelings levels below what the person himself was able to express or (2) in the event of ongoing deep self-exploration on the second person's part, to be fully with him in his deepest moments.

EXAMPLE: The facilitator responds with accuracy to all of the person's deeper as well as surface feelings. He is "together" with the second person or "tuned in" on his wave length. The facilitator and the other person might proceed together to explore previously unexplored areas of human existence.

In summary, the facilitator is responding with a full awareness of who the other person is and a comprehensive and accurate empathic understanding of his deepest feelings.

Examples of Empathy

Carkhuff and Berenson describe the movement from low to high empathy:

> The emphasis, then, is upon movement to levels of feeling and experience deeper than those communicated by the client, yet within the range of expression which the client can constructively employ for his own purposes. The therapist's ability to communicate at high levels of empathic understanding appears to involve the therapist's ability to allow himself to experience or merge in the experience of the client, reflect upon this experience while suspending his own judgments, tolerating his own anxiety, and communicating this understanding to the client.[10]

At low levels of empathy counselors are obtuse to the client's expressions, and are responding to, or with, their own feelings and perceptions. They are not in the client's frame of reference, but may be evaluating and judging the client and his or her behavior, reacting with suggestions, advice, moralizations, and so on. Their responses are irrelevant to the feelings and perceptions of the client.

CLIENT: Sometimes I get so depressed I don't know where I'm going.
THERAPIST: Well, you know, it's around exam time and lots of kids get feeling a little down at this time of year.
CLIENT: Yes, but this has nothing to do with exams. That's not even bothering me.
THERAPIST: You mean none of the exams is bothering you? Surely one of them must be bothering you![11]

At a minimally facilitative level the counselor is with the client and the client feels this.

CLIENT: Sometimes I get so depressed I just don't know what to do.
THERAPIST: Sometimes you feel like you're never going to get up again.
CLIENT: Right. I just don't know what to do with myself. What am I going to do?[12]

At a highly facilitative level, therapists go beyond the words or even expressed feelings of the client to the implications of his or her statements. The therapist is still responding to the client and not intruding feelings or perceptions. The client's feelings may be blurred and confused so that he or she does not recognize all their meanings or implications, which are clarified by the therapist.

CLIENT: Gee, those people! Who do they think they are? I just can't stand interacting with them any more. Just a bunch of phonies. They leave me so frustrated. They make me so anxious. I get angry at myself. I don't even want to be bothered with them anymore. I just wish I could be honest with them and tell them all to go to hell! But I just can't do it.
THERAPIST: Damn, they make you furious! But it's not just them. It's with yourself too, because you don't act on how you feel.[13]

It is impossible for a therapist to maintain the highest level of empathy continuously. And it is unnecessary. In fact, it is probably undesirable. At the beginning of therapy an extremely high level of empathy can be threatening and inhibit the communications of clients. Clients may well feel that the counselor understands them better than they do themselves and that it is unnecessary for them to continue to express themselves. Carkhuff suggests that in the early stage the therapist is most effective if he or she focuses on level 3 (the minimal level) of the facilitative conditions.[14]

Discrimination versus Communication

Carkhuff makes an important distinction between the ability to discriminate an accurate empathic response and the ability to communicate empathically. If one is presented with a number of responses at various levels of empathy, one is able relatively easily, or with relatively little training, to recognize or identify the better or best responses. It is much more difficult to construct or compose a good response. Discrimination is a necessary but not sufficient condition for communication. Individuals who are able to make accurate discriminations are not necessarily able to communicate accurately. Those who can communicate accurately can also discriminate accurately, however.[15]

RESPECT

In his 1957 article, Rogers included unconditional positive regard as one of the conditions for constructive personality change. Rogers credited Standal with originating this term.[16] Positive regard is unconditional when it doesn't depend on the client's behavior. The client is regarded as a person, not as a collection of behaviors. Rogers has used other terms to describe this condition, including acceptance of the client as a person, with negative as well as positive aspects. Here we call it respect. In this section we look at the nature of respect as well as how it is measured and manifested.

The Nature of Respect

Caring about, prizing, valuing, and *liking* are other terms for the respect condition. It is a nonpossessive caring. The client is regarded as a person of worth; he or she is respected. The counselor's attitude is nonevaluative, nonjudgmental, without criticism, ridicule, depreciation, or reservations. This does not mean that the counselor accepts as right, desirable, or likeable, all aspects of the client's behavior or that he or she agrees with or condones all the client's behavior. "In the nonjudgmental attitude the [therapist] does not relinquish his own sense of values, his personal or social ethics."[17] Yet clients are accepted for what they are, as they are. There is no demand or requirement that they change or be different in order to be accepted, or that they be perfect. Imperfections are accepted, along with mistakes and errors, as part of the human condition.

Respect is expressed in the therapist's listening to the client and in the effort to understand the client, as well as in his or her communication of that understanding. On the other hand, respect increases with understanding. While there should be a basic respect for the client simply as a person, a human being, respect is augmented with understanding of his or her uniqueness.

Nonpossessive warmth is another term that has been applied to the respect condition. There is a real interest in the client, a sincere concern for him or her, a trust, a love. It "does not imply passivity or unresponsivity; nonpossessive warmth is an outgoing positive action involving active, personal participation."[18] Although initially respect is expressed by communicating "in at least minimally warm and modulated tones" the potential for warmth,[19] respect can be communicated in many different ways.

We must emphasize that it is not always communicated in warm, modulated tones of voice; it may be communicated, for example, in anger. In the final analysis, it is the client's experience of the expression that counts, and the client may experience the therapist's attempt to share his own experience fully as an indication of the therapist's respect for the client's level of development.[20]

Being open and honest—real and genuine—with the client is also often a manifestation of respect for him or her.

The question of whether respect must be unconditional has been raised. Rogers has expressed some doubt about this, on the basis of a study by Spotts, which indicated that unconditionality contributed no variance apart from positive regard.[21] Barrett-Lennard has developed a relationship inventory for completion by clients that contains separate scales for positive regard and unconditional positive regard.[22] However, they do not appear to be independent. This does not resolve the issue of unconditionality, however; unconditionality may be the basic factor in both.

Carkhuff and Berenson feel that *unconditional positive regard,* as well as *nonpossessive warmth,* are misnomers. "Unconditionality would, instead, appear to be nothing more than the initial suspension of potentially psychonoxious feelings, attitudes, and judgments."[23] It would appear, however, that the nonjudgmental and nonevaluative attitude and the distinction between acceptance of the client as a person worthy of respect regardless of (unacceptable) behaviors constitute what is indicated by the word *unconditional.*

Measuring Respect

Truax developed a five-point Tentative Scale for the Measurement of Nonpossessive Warmth in 1962.[24] The variable of unconditionality is defined as an acceptance of the experience of the client without imposing conditions. Warmth involves a nonpossessive caring for the client as a separate person and, thus, a willingness to share equally his or her joys and aspirations as well as depressions and failures. It involves valuing the patient as a person, separate from any evaluation of his or her behavior or thoughts.[25] Carkhuff's revision of the scale to measure the communication of respect in interpersonal processes[26] follows.

Level 1

The verbal and behavioral expressions of the first person communicate a clear lack of respect (or negative regard) for the second person(s).

EXAMPLE: The first person communicates to the second person that the second person's feelings and experiences are not worthy of consideration or that the second person is not capable of acting constructively. The first person may become the sole focus of evaluation.

In summary, in many ways the first person communicates a total lack of respect for the feelings, experiences, and potentials of the second person.

Level 2

The first person responds to the second person in such a way as to communicate little respect for the feelings, experiences, and potentials of the second person.

EXAMPLE: The first person may respond mechanically or passively or ignore many of the feelings of the second person.

In summary, in many ways the first person displays a lack of respect or concern for the second person's feelings, experiences and potentials.

Level 3

The first person communicates a positive respect and concern for the second person's feelings, experiences and potentials.

EXAMPLE: The first person communicates respect and concern for the second person's ability to express himself and to deal constructively with his life situation.

In summary, in many ways the first person communicates that who the second person is and what he does matter to the first person. Level 3 constitutes the minimal level of facilitative interpersonal functioning.

Level 4

The facilitator clearly communicates a very deep respect and concern for the second person.

EXAMPLE: The facilitator's responses enable the second person to feel free to be himself and to experience being valued as an individual.

In summary, the facilitator communicates a very deep caring for the feelings, experiences, and potentials of the second person.

Level 5

The facilitator communicates the very deepest respect for the second person's worth as a person and his potentials as a free individual.

EXAMPLE: The facilitator cares very deeply for the human potentials of the second person.

In summary, the facilitator is committed to the value of the other person as a human being.

Examples of Respect

In this first example it is obvious that the therapist shows complete lack of respect and warmth for the client but is evaluative:

CLIENT: I just can't wait to get out of school—I'm so excited. I just want to get out and get started on my career. I know I'm going places.
THERAPIST: What's the matter, don't you like school?[27]

The next example also involves disapproval of the client's behavior as well as evaluation and lack of warmth:

THERAPIST: . . . another part here too, that is, if they haven't got a lot of schooling, there may be a good argument, that, that they—are better judges, you know.
CLIENT: Yeah . . .
THERAPIST: Now, I'm not saying that that's necessarily true, I'm—just saying that's *reality*.
CLIENT: Yeah.
THERAPIST: And you're in a *position* that you can't argue with them. Why is it that these people burn you up so much?
CLIENT: They *get by with* too many things . . .
THERAPIST: Why should that bother you?
CLIENT: 'Cause I never got by with anything.
THERAPIST: They're papa figures, aren't they?[28]

Now contrast these with the following dialogue, in which the words can only give an indication of the warmth present:

CLIENT: . . . ever recovering to the extent where I could become self-supporting and live alone. I thought that I was doomed to hospitalization for the rest of my life and seeing some of the people over in the main building, some of those old people who are, who need a lot of attention and all that sort of thing, is the only picture I could see of my own future. Just one of (Therapist: Mhm) complete hopelessness, that there was any . . .
THERAPIST: (Interrupting) You didn't see any hope at all, did you?
CLIENT: Not in the least. I thought no one really cared and I didn't care myself, and I seriously—uh—thought of suicide; if there'd been any way that I could end it all *completely* and not become a burden or an extra care, I would have committed suicide, I was that low. I didn't want to live. In fact, I hoped that I—I would go to sleep at night and not wake up, because I, I really felt there was nothing to live for. (Therapist: Uh huh. [very softly]) Now I, I truly believe that this drug they are giving me helps me a lot, I think, I think it is one drug that really does me *good*. (Therapist: Uh hm.)
THERAPIST: But you say that, that during that time you, you felt as though no one cared, as to what (Client: That's right.) what happened to you.
CLIENT: And, not only that, but I hated *myself* so that I didn't *deserve* to have anyone care for me. I hated myself so that I, I, I not only felt that no one did, but I didn't see any reason why they *should*.
THERAPIST: I guess that makes some sense to me now. I was wondering why it was that you were shutting other people off. You weren't *letting* anyone else care.

CLIENT: I didn't think I was *worth* caring for.

THERAPIST: So you didn't ev—maybe you not only thought you were—hopeless, but you wouldn't allow people . . . (Therapist's statement drowned out by client).[29]

THERAPEUTIC GENUINENESS

One of the conditions postulated by Rogers in 1957 was congruence, or integration in the relationship. By this he meant that "within the relationship [the therapist] is freely and deeply himself, with his actual experiences accurately represented by his awareness of himself."[30] This condition has since become known as genuineness. In this section we examine the nature of genuineness, how it can be measured, and some examples of how it works in a counseling relationship.

The Nature of Genuineness

Therapists who are genuine are "for real," open, honest, sincere. They are involved in the relationship and not simply mirrors, sounding boards, or blank screens. They are real people in real encounters. And that is the reason why the exact nature of the relationship cannot be predicted or controlled in advance. They are freely and deeply themselves, without facades, not phony. They are not thinking and feeling one thing and saying something different. They are, as the existentialist would say, authentic, or, to use Jourard's term, transparent.[31] They are not playing roles. Berne writes:

> If the therapist plays the role of a therapist, he will not get very far with perceptive patients. He has to *be* a therapist. If he decides that a certain patient needs Parental reassurance, he does not play the role of a parent; rather he liberates his Parental ego state. A good test for this is for him to attempt to "show off" his Parentalism in the presence of a colleague, with a patient toward whom he does not *feel* parental. In this case he is playing a role and a forthright patient will soon make clear to him the difference between *being* a reassuring Parent and playing the role of a reassuring parent. One of the functions of psychotherapeutic training establishments is to separate trainees who want to play the role of therapist from those who want to be therapists.[32]

Genuineness appears to have become the major emphasis of many approaches to psychotherapy. The major theories have given it a more important place. Even psychoanalysis, in which the therapist is a rather ambiguous figure, a blank screen, has moved from this position to the acceptance of the therapist as a real person. If there is one thing that unites many of the apparently extremely diverse innovations in psychotherapy, it is the concept of genuineness—of doing one's own thing.

There is a real danger here, however, involving a misinterpretation of genuineness as supporting an "anything goes" policy. Genuineness is not always therapeutic. It is unlikely that a highly authoritative, dogmatic person is therapeutic. Carkhuff and Berenson comment on this problem:

> However, a construct of genuineness must be differentiated from the construct of facilitative genuineness. Obviously, the degree to which an individual is aware of his own experience will be related to the degree to which he can enable another person to become aware of his experience. However, many destructive persons are in full contact with their experience; that is, they are destructive when they are genuine. The potentially deleterious effects of genuineness have been established in some research inquiries. Hence the emphasis upon the therapist's being freely and deeply himself in a nonexploitative relationship incorporates one critical qualification. When his only genuine responses are negative in regard to the second person, the therapist makes an effort to employ his responses constructively as a basis for further inquiry for the therapist, the client and their relationship. In addition, there is evidence to suggest that whereas low levels of genuineness are clearly impediments to client progress in therapy, above a certain minimum level, very high levels of genuineness are not related to additional increases in client functioning. Therefore, while it appears of critical importance to avoid the conscious or unconscious facade of "playing the therapeutic role," the necessity for the therapist's expressing himself fully at all times is not supported. Again, genuineness must not be confused, as is so often done, with free license for the therapist to do what he will in therapy, especially to express hostility. Therapy is not for the therapist. . . . Under some circumstances, the honesty of communication may actually constitute a limitation for the progress of therapy. Thus, with patients functioning at significantly lower levels than the therapist, the therapist may attend cautiously to the client's condition. He will not share with the client that which would make the client's condition the more desperate.[33]

Genuineness does not require that therapists always express all their feelings; it only requires that whatever they do express is real and genuine and not incongruent. And at a minimal level, genuineness is not being insincere, dishonest, phony, or incongruent. Genuineness is not impulsiveness, though the two appear to be equated in the minds of many, instructors as well as students.

Truax and Mitchell make an important point (and Carkhuff and Berenson would appear to agree in their comment just quoted):

> From the research evidence and an examination of the raw data itself relating genuineness to outcome, as well as collateral evidence, it is clear that what is effective is an absence of defensiveness and phoniness—a lack of evidence that the therapist is not genuine. In other

words, it is not the positive end of the genuineness scale that contributes to therapeutic outcome. Instead it is a lack of genuineness which militates against positive client change. The highest levels of the genuineness scale do not discriminate between differential outcomes. The scale itself and the evidence concerning genuineness would be more precise if we dropped the term genuineness and call[ed] it instead by some negative term that would include both defensiveness and being phony.[34]

This is an important point, in view of the increasing emphasis on being genuine. It would appear that the great effort to be genuine is leading to the phenomenon of phony genuineness. This may be an explanation for inconsistent results with the genuineness scale in some studies (such as Bergin and Garfield's[35]).

This caution has apparently not been heeded, especially in group therapy or encounter groups. Genuineness has been distorted to condone therapists who react off the tops of their heads. Gendlin discusses the facilitating of therapy with nonverbal schizophrenics through the expression of the therapist's feelings. But he emphasizes the need for therapists to take "a few steps of self attention" before expressing themselves as well as to clearly identify their feelings as their own. Genuineness, then, does not mean uninhibited expression of feelings. The therapist doesn't unthinkingly blurt out such things as "You bore me," as seems to be encouraged and practiced in the name of genuineness. Rather, if therapists feel bored, they look at themselves and the relationship to see if they are contributing to the feeling. They might end up by saying: "Somehow I feel rather bored by your emotionless recital of events," or something similar.[36]

This confusion is probably related to some of the puzzling and inconsistent results of research. The three basic core conditions are usually positively correlated, often quite highly. But in some instances genuineness has shown no correlation or even a negative correlation with the other two. Garfield and Bergin, in a study that led them to question the applicability of the three core conditions to other than client-centered therapy, found that genuineness correlated negatively with empathy $(-.66)$ and with warmth $(-.75)$.[37] None of the three correlated significantly with several outcome measures, so while it is not possible to say that empathy and warmth were therapeutic, it is obvious that genuineness was not therapeutic in this study.

Measuring Therapeutic Genuineness

Truax constructed a five-point Tentative Scale for the Measurement of Therapist Genuineness or Self-Congruence in 1962.[38] He stated that this was the most difficult scale to develop. Examination of the scale suggests that a high rating would not necessarily represent therapeutic genuineness. It was this scale that Garfield and Bergin used in their 1971 study. Carkhuff's revision of the scale to measure facilitative genuineness in interpersonal processes[39] appears to correct this deficiency.

Level 1

The first person's verbalizations are clearly unrelated to what he is feeling at the moment, or his only genuine responses are negative in regard to the second person(s) and appear to have a totally destructive effect upon the second person.

EXAMPLE: The first person may be defensive in his interaction with the second person(s) and this defensiveness may be demonstrated in the content of his words or his voice quality. Where he is defensive he does not employ his reaction as a basis for potentially valuable inquiry into the relationship.

In summary, there is evidence of a considerable discrepancy between the inner experiencing of the first person and his current verbalizations. Where there is no discrepancy, the first person's reactions are employed solely in a destructive fashion.

Level 2

The first person's verbalizations are slightly unrelated to what he is feeling at the moment, or when his responses are genuine they are negative in regard to the second person; the first person does not appear to know how to employ his negative reactions as a basis for inquiry into the relationship.

EXAMPLE: The first person may respond to the second person(s) in a "professional" manner that has a rehearsed quality or a quality concerning the way a helper "should" respond in that situation.

In summary, the first person is usually responding according to his prescribed role rather than expressing what he personally feels or means. When he is genuine his responses are negative and he is unable to employ them as a basis for further inquiry.

Level 3

The first person provides no "negative" cues between what he says and what he feels, but he provides no positive cues to indicate a really genuine response to the second person(s).

EXAMPLE: The first person may listen and follow the second person(s) but commit nothing more of himself.

In summary, the first person appears to make appropriate responses that do not seem insincere but that do not reflect any real involvement either. Level 3 constitutes the minimal level of facilitative interpersonal functioning.

Level 4

The facilitator presents some positive cues indicating a genuine response (whether positive or negative) in a nondestructive manner to the second person(s).

EXAMPLE: The facilitator's expressions are congruent with his feelings, although he may be somewhat hesitant about expressing them fully.

In summary, the facilitator responds with many of his own feelings, and there is no doubt as to whether he really means what he says. He is able to employ his responses, whatever their emotional content, as a basis for further inquiry into the relationship.

Level 5

The facilitator is freely and deeply himself in a nonexploitative relationship with the second person(s).

EXAMPLE: The facilitator is completely spontaneous in his interaction and open to experiences of all types, both pleasant and hurtful. In the event of hurtful responses the facilitator's comments are employed constructively to open a further area of inquiry for both the facilitator and the second person.

In summary, the facilitator is clearly being himself and yet employing his own genuine responses constructively.

Examples of Genuineness

In the first example, the therapist is clearly being evasive, rather than open and honest.[40]

CLIENT: . . . So that's how I got home from C——. I was kind of lucky.
THERAPIST: Yeah, that is, that's quite a story. (Long pause)
CLIENT: Can I ask you a question?
THERAPIST: Yeah, I guess so.
CLIENT: Do you think I'm crazy?
THERAPIST: Oh no—not in the sense that *some* of the patients you see out in the ward, perhaps.
CLIENT: I don't mean *mentally*, not—where I don't know anything, but I mean, am I out of my head? Do I do things that are foolish for people to do?
THERAPIST: Well, I'd say you do things that you might say are—foolish, in a sense. You do things that aren't . . . (Pause)
CLIENT: (Filling in for therapist) *Normal.*
THERAPIST: Yeah, well, they aren't usual by any means, of course.

Contrast this with the following dialogue:

CLIENT: I'm so thrilled to have found a counselor like you. I didn't know any existed. You seem to understand me so well. It's just great! I feel like I'm coming alive again. I have not felt this in so long.
THERAPIST: Hey, I'm as thrilled to hear you talk this way as you are! I'm pleased that I have been helpful. I do think we still have some work to do yet, though.[41]

CONCRETENESS

These three basic core conditions—empathy, respect, and genuineness—have been recognized for some time and subjected to considerable study. There is research evidence for their effectiveness, which will be reviewed in Chapter 13. In 1964, Truax and Carkhuff proposed another variable, concreteness, as an important facilitative condition.[42] As we did for the other conditions, we look into its nature, its measurement, and how it looks in action.

The Nature of Concreteness

Concreteness, or specificity, involves the use of specific and concrete terminology, rather than general or abstract terminology, in the discussion of feelings, experiences, and behavior. It avoids vagueness and ambiguity. It leads to differentiation of feelings and experiences rather than generalization. Concreteness or specificity is not necessarily the same as practicality, nor is it objectivity. It does not apply to impersonal material—it is *personally relevant* concreteness. It is "the fluent, direct and complete expression of specific feelings and experiences, regardless of their emotional content."[43]

Specificity is the opposite of much of the verbalization of many counselors, who attempt to generalize, categorize, and classify with broad general labels the feelings and experiences of the client. Many interpretations are generalizations, abstractions, or higher-level labeling (or the inclusion of a specific experience under a higher-level category). Concreteness is the opposite of such labeling. It suggests that such interpretation is not useful but harmful. In addition to being threatening, abstract interpretations cut off client exploration. Rather than permitting an analysis of a problem into its specific aspects, labeling leads to the feeling that the problem is solved and the issue closed. A simple, though perhaps extreme, example would be applying the label *Oedipus complex* to a male client's description of his feelings and attitudes regarding his father and mother. The client might well feel that this solves his problem, that he has insight, and that nothing further need be done—or can be done.

Concreteness serves three important functions: (1) it keeps the therapist's response close to the client's feelings and experiences; (2) it fosters accurateness of understanding in the therapist, allowing for early client corrections of misunderstanding; and (3) it encourages the client to attend to specific problem areas.[44]

By responding in specific and concrete terms to long, general, vague ramblings of the client, the therapist helps the client to sift out the personally significant aspects from the irrelevant aspects. Although it might appear that questions of the who, what, when, where, and how type would be useful, Carkhuff believes that

> such questions should serve the function of entry and follow-through in an area only when the helpee cannot himself implement entry and follow-through in that area. In no way should questions and probing dominate helping because of the stimulus response contingencies that it develops. . . .[45]

In other words, questions should perhaps be limited to situations where the therapist doesn't understand or cannot follow the client and must ask for clarification.

It is possible that the level of concreteness should vary during different phases of the therapy process. It should be high in the early stages, but later, when the client moves into deeper and more complex material, a high level may be undesirable or even impossible until confused and mixed feelings and emotions are expressed and become clearer. Later, in the ending phases when the client is planning and engaging in action, high levels would again be desirable. In the early stages, concreteness can contribute to empathic understanding.

Measuring Concreteness

Carkhuff's revision of the scale for measuring concreteness or specificity of expression in interpersonal processes[46] follows.

Level 1

The first person leads or allows all discussion with the second person(s) to deal only with vague and anonymous generalities.

EXAMPLE: The first person and the second person discuss everything on strictly an abstract and highly intellectual level.

In summary, the first person makes no attempt to lead the discussion into the realm of personally relevant specific situations and feelings.

Level 2

The first person frequently leads or allows even discussions of material personally relevant to the second person(s) to be dealt with on a vague and abstract level.

EXAMPLE: The first person and the second person may discuss the "real" feelings but they do so at an abstract, intellectualized level.

In summary, the first person does not elicit discussion of most personally relevant feelings and experiences in specific and concrete terms.

Level 3

The first person at times enables the second person(s) to discuss personally relevant material in specific and concrete terminology.

EXAMPLE: The first person will make it possible for the discussion with the second person(s) to center directly around most things that are personally important to the second person(s), although there will continue to be areas not dealt with concretely and areas in which the second person does not develop fully in specificity.

In summary, the first person sometimes guides the discussions into consideration of personally relevant specific and concrete instances, but these are not always fully developed. Level 3 constitutes the minimal level of facilitative functioning.

Level 4

The facilitator is frequently helpful in enabling the second person(s) to fully develop in concrete and specific terms almost all instances of concern.

EXAMPLE: The facilitator is able on many occasions to guide the discussion to specific feelings and experiences of personally meaningful material.

In summary, the facilitator is very helpful in enabling the discussion to center around specific and concrete instances of most important and personally relevant feelings and experiences.

Level 5

The facilitator is always helpful in guiding the discussion, so that the second person(s) may discuss fluently, directly and completely specific feelings and experiences.

EXAMPLE: The first person involves the second person in discussion of specific feelings, situations, and events, regardless of their emotional content.

In summary, the facilitator facilitates a direct expression of all personally relevant feelings and experiences in concrete and specific terms.

Examples of Concreteness

The first example is of a general, abstract response that clearly will not help the client to focus upon the specifics of the problem:

CLIENT: I don't know just what the problem is. I don't get along with my parents. It's not that I don't like them, or that they don't like me. But we seem to disagree on so many things. Maybe they're small and unimportant, but . . . I don't know, we never have been close . . . there has never, as far as I can remember, been a time when they gave me any spontaneous affection . . . I just don't know what's wrong.

THERAPIST: It seems that your present situation is really of long standing and goes back to a long series of difficulties in your developmental process.

Compare this with the following concrete response to the same client statement:

THERAPIST: Although you say you don't know what's wrong, and although you say your parents like you, they never seem to have given any specific evidence of love or affection.

HOW THE CONDITIONS INTERRELATE

The four conditions of empathy, respect, genuineness, and concreteness interrelate with each other, both in terms of contributing to each other in the therapy process and in being statistically correlated (in most studies). Rogers and Truax suggest that genuineness is basic, since warmth and empathy can be threatening or meaningless without it. In turn, empathy must be based upon warmth and respect.[47] However, warmth and respect are known to increase with the depth of understanding of another, and the attentiveness and listening characterizing the attempt to understand another is evidence of respect for the client. Truax and Carkhuff write: "We begin to perceive the events and experiences of his life 'as if' they were parts of our own life. It is through this process that we come to feel warmth, respect and liking for a person who in everyday life is unlikeable, weak, cowardly, treacherous, vile, or despicable."[48]

More recently, Rogers has suggested that each of the conditions may be the primary or most important element in different situations or kinds of relationships. In everyday relationships in the home, school, and at work, genuineness is probably most important as "a basis for living together in a climate of realness." In special situations of nonverbal relationships—parent and infant, therapist and mute psychotic, doctor and seriously ill patient—warmth or caring may be most important. But when the other person is troubled, hurt, anxious, confused—the situation in which clients find themselves—then empathy "has the highest priority."[49]

SUMMARY

Three basic conditions of a facilitative or therapeutic interpersonal relationship have been implicit if not explicit in most if not all theories or approaches to counseling or psychotherapy. In the currently accepted terminology, they are empathic understanding, respect or warmth, and therapeutic or facilitative genuineness. Considerable evidence for their effectiveness in facilitating a variety of client personality and behavior changes has been accumulated. A fourth condition is described by Truax and Carkhuff: personally relevant concreteness. Some evidence of its effectiveness has been obtained. These four conditions are grouped by Carkhuff and Berenson under the term *core facilitative conditions.* They are the conditions that appear to be the common elements in all or most existing systems or approaches to counseling or psychotherapy. Their definitions or description, together with scales that enable their measurement, were presented in this chapter.

Empathy, respect and warmth, and therapeutic genuineness create an accepting climate in which threat is minimized and trust is maximized. This climate makes it possible for clients to relinquish the defensiveness that characterizes their usual interpersonal relationships, and that also keeps them from facing themselves. It enables clients to engage in those activities described in Chapter 7 that lead to changes in attitudes, feelings, and behaviors.

While these three conditions have been widely recognized and accepted as important if not necessary in psychotherapy, concreteness has been widely neglected. Yet it may be as important and as necessary for client progress as the other conditions. Experienced therapists, as well as beginners, engage in labeling and generalizing, often in the form of interpretations, which take clients away from dealing with the unique specifics of their situations. So-called insight may appear to result, but this is not accompanied by changes in the client's attitudes or behaviors; the process ends with insight, rather than continuing to deal with the specific attitudes and behaviors of the client.

It is likely that the core conditions interact to facilitate or increase each other. Some degree of all the core conditions is necessary to begin with and then they grow together, each one contributing to the increase in level of the other conditions.

NOTES

1. C. R. Rogers. The necessary and sufficient conditions of therapeutic personality change. *Journal of Consulting Psychology*, 1957, *21*, 95–103.
2. C. B. Truax and R. R. Carkhuff. *Toward effective counseling and psychotherapy.* Chicago: Aldine, 1967; R. R. Carkhuff and B. G. Berenson. *Beyond counseling and therapy.* New York: Holt, Rinehart & Winston, 1967; R. R. Carkhuff. *Helping and human relations.* Vol. I, *Selection and training.* Vol. II, *Practice and research.* New York: Holt, Rinehart & Winston, 1969. Reprinted by Human Resource Development Press, Amherst, MA, 1984. Page numbers are for 1969 printing.
3. Truax and Carkhuff, *Toward effective counseling*, pp. 23–43.
4. C. R. Rogers. *On becoming a person.* Boston: Houghton Mifflin, 1961, p. 284.
5. H. Lee. *To kill a mockingbird.* Philadelphia: Lippincott, 1960, p. 24.

6. C. B. Truax and K. M. Mitchell. Research on certain therapist interpersonal skills in relation to process and outcome. In A. E. Bergin and S. L. Garfield (Eds.), *Handbook of psychotherapy and behavior change: An empirical analysis.* New York: Wiley, 1971, pp. 299–344.

7. H. S. Sullivan. *Conceptions of modern psychiatry.* Washington, DC: William Allanson White Psychiatric Foundation, 1947, p. 7.

8. Truax and Carkhuff, *Toward effective counseling,* pp. 46–58.

9. Carkhuff, *Helping,* Vol. II, pp. 315–317.

10. Carkhuff and Berenson, *Beyond counseling,* p. 27.

11. *Ibid.,* p. 32. This and following illustrations from this source are excerpts from actual initial interviews.

12. *Ibid.,* p. 31.

13. Carkhuff, *Helping,* Vol. I, p. 119.

14. *Ibid.,* pp. 202, 216.

15. *Ibid.,* pp. 113–132.

16. Rogers, *On becoming a person,* p. 283.

17. F. P. Biestek. The nonjudgmental attitude. *Social Casework,* 1953, *34,* 235–239.

18. Truax and Mitchell, Research on interpersonal skills, p. 317.

19. Carkhuff, *Helping,* Vol. I, p. 205.

20. Carkhuff and Berenson, *Beyond counseling,* p. 28.

21. C. R. Rogers. The interpersonal relationship: The core of guidance. *Harvard Educational Review,* 1962, *32,* 416–429.

22. G. T. Barrett-Lennard. Dimensions of therapist response as causal factors in therapeutic change. *Psychological Monographs,* 1962, *76* (43, Whole No. 562).

23. Carkhuff and Berenson, *Beyond counseling,* p. 28.

24. Truax and Carkhuff, *Toward effective counseling,* pp. 58–68.

25. *Ibid.,* p. 58.

26. Carkhuff, *Helping,* Vol. II, pp. 317 318.

27. Carkhuff and Berenson, *Beyond counseling,* p. 34.

28. Truax and Carkhuff, *Toward effective counseling,* p. 61.

29. *Ibid.,* p. 67.

30. Rogers, Necessary and sufficient conditions, p. 97.

31. S. Jourard. *The transparent self.* Princeton, NJ: Van Nostrand Reinhold, 1964.

32. E. Berne. *Transactional analysis in psychotherapy.* New York: Grove Press, 1961, p. 233.

33. Carkhuff and Berenson, *Beyond counseling,* pp. 29, 81.

34. Truax and Mitchell, Research on interpersonal skills, p. 316.

35. S. L. Garfield and A. E. Bergin. Therapeutic conditions and outcome. *Journal of Abnormal Psychology,* 1971, *77,* 108–114.

36. E. T. Gendlin. Client-centered developments in work with schizophrenics. *Journal of Counseling Psychology,* 1962, *9,* 205–211.

37. Garfield and Bergin, Therapeutic conditions.

38. Truax and Carkhuff, *Toward effective counseling,* pp. 68–72.

39. Carkhuff, *Helping,* Vol. II, pp. 319–320.

40. Truax and Carkhuff, *Toward effective counseling,* p. 69.

41. Carkhuff, *Helping,* Vol. I, p. 121.

42. C. B. Truax and R. R. Carkhuff. Concreteness: A neglected variable in the psychotherapeutic process. *Journal of Clinical Psychology,* 1964, *20,* 264–267.

43. Carkhuff and Berenson, *Beyond counseling,* p. 29.

44. *Ibid.*, p. 30.
45. Carkhuff, *Helping*, Vol. I, p. 207.
46. Carkhuff, *Helping*, Vol. II, pp. 323–324.
47. Truax and Carkhuff, *Toward effective counseling*, p. 32. But see also p. 42 where the order understanding, respect, and genuineness is suggested. Truax and Mitchell (Research on interpersonal skills, p. 314) also state this order but say that in practice empathic listening results in understanding, leading to liking, which then leads to genuineness on the part of the therapist.
48. Truax and Carkhuff, *Toward effective counseling*, p. 42.
49. C. R. Rogers. Empathic: An unappreciated way of being. *The Counseling Psychologist*, 1975, *5*(2), 2–10.

CHAPTER 5

The Therapeutic Conditions: Action Dimensions

Carkhuff and Berenson distinguish two phases of the counseling or therapy process—the inward and downward phase, or the responsive phase, and the outward and upward phase, or the initiative and action phase. According to them, most traditional therapies consist of only the first phase. It is in this phase, characterized by the responsiveness of the therapist to the client, that the basic core conditions are essential and the therapeutic relationship firmly established. In the second phase, the therapist, on the basis of the understanding developed in the first phase, assumes more initiative in helping the client make and act upon choices and decisions. In the first phase, the client achieves insights; in the second phase, the therapist attempts to change the client's behavior toward more effective functioning.[1]

The second phase involves conditions in addition to those of the first phase. Chapter 4 explains that concreteness is involved in both the responsive phase and the action, or problem-solving, phase. In addition to concreteness, three other conditions are needed to facilitate the second phase. These conditions are confrontation, therapist self-disclosure, and immediacy of the relationship. We discuss these action conditions in depth in this chapter, and then consider how they relate to the responsive conditions. We examine the essence of all the conditions and find it to be love.

CONFRONTATION

Confrontation is one of the action dimensions considered by Carkhuff and Berenson as needed to facilitate the second phase of the counseling process. In this section, we discuss its nature and how it is measured, and give some examples of its use in therapy.

The Nature of Confrontation

There appears to be some confusion regarding the nature of confrontation in psychotherapy. The primary dictionary definition includes an element of hostility. Moreover, it implies a confrontation between two persons. This is not the kind of confrontation of concern here. It is not a personal confrontation of the client by the therapist. The kind of confrontation we are considering is that indicated by a secondary aspect of the dictionary definition: to set side by side for comparison, or to place before.

Confrontation is an expression by the therapist of his or her experience of discrepancies in the client's behavior. Carkhuff distinguishes three broad categories of discrepancy: (1) discrepancy between the clients' expressions of what they are and what they want to be (real self, or self-concept, versus ideal self); (2) discrepancy between clients' verbal expressions about themselves (awareness or insight) and their behavior as it is either observed by the therapist or reported by the clients; and (3) discrepancy between clients' expressed experience of themselves and the therapist's experience of them.[2] A fourth category might be added to cover discrepancy between clients' experiences of themselves and others as reported at different times, either in the same session or in different sessions.

Confrontation can be viewed as the attempt to bring to awareness the presence of cognitive dissonance or incongruence in the client's feelings, attitudes, beliefs, perceptions, or behaviors. It consists of reflecting discrepancies or inconsistencies between or among client statements relating to these areas. Confrontation does not create these discrepancies—it simply sets out or places before the client discrepant statements the client has made. The confrontation is between inconsistent communications of the client, not between the therapist and the client. Often these communications relate to ambivalent feelings and attitudes toward persons in the client's life. But always the sources for the confrontation come from the client; they are not interpretations deriving from the therapist. The therapist remains in the client's frame of reference, and does not take the initiative from the client.

In the early stages of therapy, the therapist is tentative in his or her confrontations, usually formulating them as questions since he or she is not too confident about them. "Premature direct confrontations may have a demoralizing and demobilizing effect upon an inadequately prepared helpee."[3] The therapist may say something like, "You seem to be saying two different things" or "Now you say this, but earlier you seemed to be saying that."

Later in the therapy, more direct confrontations may focus specifically upon discrepancies. "The increasing specificity will lead to the development of an understanding of the distortions in the helpee's assumptive world and, hopefully, to a reconstruction of that world."[4] Direct confrontations precipitate an awareness of a crisis in the client that, when faced, leads to movement to higher levels of functioning. The goal is to enable clients to confront themselves and, when desirable, others. *"Confrontation of self and others is prerequisite to the healthy individual's encounter with life."*[5] An important use of confrontation is to point out to clients that insight is not enough and that, although they have insight, their behavior has not changed. Confrontation enables clients to go beyond insight and to recognize the need to change their behaviors.

Confrontation is not limited to negative aspects of clients or to facing them with their limitations. It also includes pointing out discrepancies involving resources and assets that are unrecognized or unused.

Research on confrontation suggests that high-facilitative therapists, during the first therapy session and even during the first 15 minutes of the session, used more confrontations focused on the therapy relationship, and within the first 30 minutes used more confrontations focused on resources than on pathology and on client actions rather than personality, than did low-facilitative therapists. Low-facilitative therapists focused on client limitations.[6]

All confrontation runs the risk of threatening the client. The association of confrontation with high levels of the core conditions, including empathy, suggests that confrontation may be useful or effective only in the context of high levels of empathy and respect. This further suggests that since high levels of these conditions may not be present or perceived by the client in the first interview or early interviews, confrontation would better not be employed until the relationship has been well established. However, the fact that confrontation in the first interview in the studies referred to above often focused on the therapist and his or her relationship with the client suggests that such confrontation may be useful in structuring the relationship and correcting misconceptions or misperceptions of the client about the nature of the relationship. Mitchell[7] suggests that those confrontations that are most threatening are those that force clients to question certain myths about themselves and their families.

There has been an avoidance of confrontation among therapists of most of the major approaches. Direct confrontation has been limited to clients who are aggressive, manipulative, or confronting themselves; thus, the therapist reacts to rather than initiates confrontation. In addition to the possible dangers when it is not associated with empathy and warmth or concern, confrontation, like genuineness, can be used to vent the therapist's aggressiveness and internal anger, frustration, and other negative feelings. The word itself is perhaps not a felicitous one, with its connotations of aggressiveness and face-to-face conflict. It would be helpful if a more appropriate word could be found.

It is possible that confrontation should not be considered as a separate condition or dimension of psychotherapy. Perhaps it could be included in empathic understanding. The recognition and communicating of discrepancies in the client's verbalizations and behaviors does seem to be an aspect of empathy.

Measuring Confrontation

Carkhuff has developed a scale for measuring confrontation, one in which there is no differentiation between levels 1 and 2. This could be taken as supporting the idea that confrontation is an aspect of high empathy and should be incorporated into the empathy scale. Carkhuff's scale for measuring confrontation in interpersonal processes[8] follows.

Level 1

The verbal and behavioral expressions of the helper disregard the discrepancies in the helpee's behavior (ideal versus real self, insight versus action, helper versus helpee's experiences).

EXAMPLE: The helper may simply ignore all helpee discrepancies by passively accepting them.

In summary, the helper simply disregards all of those discrepancies in the helpee's behavior that might be fruitful areas for consideration.

Level 2

The verbal and behavioral expressions of the helper disregard the discrepancies in the helpee's behavior.

EXAMPLE: The helper, although not explicitly accepting these discrepancies, may simply remain silent concerning most of them.

In summary, the helper disregards the discrepancies in the helpee's behavior, and, thus, potentially important areas of inquiry.

Level 3

The verbal and behavioral expressions of the helper, while open to discrepancies in the helpee's behavior, do not relate directly and specifically to these discrepancies.

EXAMPLE: The helper may simply raise questions without pointing up the diverging directions of the possible answers.

In summary, while the helper does not disregard discrepancies in the helpee's behavior, he does not point up the directions of these discrepancies. Level 3 constitutes the minimum level of facilitative interpersonal functioning.

Level 4

The verbal and behavioral expressions of the helper attend directly and specifically to the discrepancies in the helpee's behavior.

EXAMPLE: The helper confronts the helpee directly and explicitly with discrepancies in the helpee's behavior.

In summary, the helper specifically addresses himself to discrepancies in the helpee's behavior.

Level 5

The verbal and behavioral expressions of the helper are keenly and continually attuned to the discrepancies in the helpee's behavior.

EXAMPLE: The helper confronts the helpee with helpee discrepancies in a sensitive and perceptive manner whenever they appear.

In summary, the helper does not neglect any potentially fruitful inquiry into the discrepancies in the helpee's behavior.

Examples of Confrontation

In the following dialogue, the therapist avoids a confrontation with the client. This dialogue also illustrates lack of openness and honesty on the therapist's part, which suggests that instances of avoidance of client confrontations may be included in a consideration of genuineness.

THERAPIST: I think it is very important to be completely open and honest with each other.
CLIENT: Well, how do I seem to you, how do I come across when you listen to me?
THERAPIST: Well, er umm . . . I like you. You're a nice woman.
CLIENT: Don't equivocate!
THERAPIST: Maybe we need to get to know each other better.
CLIENT: Maybe.[9]

The next example illustrates a high level of confrontation, but it is difficult to distinguish this from a high level of empathy.

CLIENT: I now understand what my father has done to me. It's all very clear to me. I think I've got the situation licked.
THERAPIST: But you're still getting up at 5 o'clock in the morning for him when he could get rides from a lot of other men.
CLIENT: Well, uh, he is still my father.

THERAPIST: Yeah, and you're still scared to death of him . . . scared that he'll beat you up or disapprove of you and you're thirty-five years old now. You still fear him like you were a kid.

CLIENT: No, you're wrong, because I don't feel scared of him right now.

THERAPIST: You're scared right now—here—with me—he's here . . .

CLIENT: (Pause) I guess I understand him better for what he is, but when I'm around him, I'm still scared, and always think of standing up to him after I leave him. Then I talk myself out of doing what I really want to do.[10]

The following dialogue illustrates a positive confrontation, facing the client with an unrecognized or unaccepted strength.

CLIENT: I know I sound weak and mousy. My question is—am I?

THERAPIST: I get your question, but you don't really come across as being this upset over it, and I don't experience you as a weak person.

CLIENT: I don't really feel weak, but somehow. . . .

THERAPIST: You don't like being seen as a weak person.

CLIENT: I know people like me better when I act weak.

THERAPIST: Maybe you're afraid people won't like you if you come on strong.[11]

Again, it would appear that positive confrontation involves empathy, with an aspect of immediacy.

THERAPIST SELF-DISCLOSURE

O. H. Mowrer has for some time emphasized self-disclosure on the part of the therapist, leader, or facilitator in groups. In this section we consider the nature of self-disclosure, how it is measured, and how it looks in practice.

The Nature of Self-Disclosure

What the effects of self-disclosure are is not clear from the research available. Yet there are those who advocate therapist self-disclosure. Beutler states that "the degree either of experimenter or therapist self-disclosure precipitates a similar disclosure level in subjects and patients."[12] But Strong and Claiborn write that "therapist disclosure to encourage patient disclosure does not seem like a good use of the therapist's power unless some specific disclosure is needed."[13] A study by Derlega, Lovell, and Chaiken[14] found that therapist self-disclosure increased client self-disclosure only when the client was informed before therapy that therapist self-disclosure was appropriate. Analogue studies suggest that relatively few therapist self-disclosures, and disclosures of only moderate personal material, are most facilitative of client self-disclosure.

Self-disclosure early in therapy as a model for client self-disclosure is unnecessary if the client understands the nature of therapy. Most clients expect to talk about themselves; indeed, they usually come to therapy for that purpose. If clients do not understand this, then simple structuring of the client's role is more efficient and effective than modeling, since the client can misunderstand or fail to understand the modeling. Clients don't expect therapists to talk about themselves, and may be embarrassed, puzzled, or mystified when they do. Clients are not really interested in the therapist's personal life when they come for therapy.

Therapist disclosure of similarities with the client in the effort to increase his or her attractiveness may reduce the client's perception of the therapist's competence and expertise, or may be perceived as reassurance that the client's problems are not as serious as he or she had thought, with the possible result of decrease in motivation for therapy or desire to change. On the other hand, therapist disclosure of differences in background, education, and experience from client's may lead to negative feelings, reduced attractiveness, or feelings that his or her problems are more serious than he or she had thought.

Strong[15] has suggested that therapist self-disclosures provide social comparison data and thus increase or decrease patients' evaluations of themselves, the severity of their problems, the validity of their ideas, and even their self-esteem. There is almost a complete lack of research on the effects of therapist self-disclosure on client improvement, however. Dickenson[16] found no relationship between therapist self-disclosure and client improvement in individual therapy. And Hayward[17] also found no relationship.

Therapists disclose themselves in everything they say and do, and clients form a picture or perception of the therapist from these disclosures. The question is how much disclosure, particularly verbal disclosure of specific personal information and experiences, especially those not related to the therapy or the therapy relationship, the therapist should engage in. It would appear that the therapist should be very cautious about such disclosures. Disclosure of the therapist's present feelings or thoughts during the therapy is essentially a matter of genuineness.

Therapist self-disclosure must be for the benefit of the client. It is the client who must engage in self-disclosure for therapy to occur, not the therapist. Therapists shouldn't engage in self-disclosure for their own benefit or therapy. Therapy is for the client, not the therapist.

As therapy nears ending, however, clients become less focused upon themselves. Resolution of their own problems no longer requires all their attention. They become more aware of the therapist as a person, become more interested in the therapist as an individual, and may express this interest by questions about the therapist as a person. The occurrence of this in therapy is an indication that the therapy is nearing, or is at, its end.

Just as there is some question about whether confrontation is not a part of empathy (with perhaps an aspect of genuineness), so there is some question as to whether therapist self-disclosure is not a part of honesty and genuineness (with perhaps an aspect of empathy). Carkhuff notes that "the dimension of self-disclosure is one facet of genuineness. . . . Spontaneous sharing on the part of both parties is the essence of a genuine relationship."[18]

Measuring Self-Disclosure

Carkhuff has developed a scale to measure facilitative self-disclosure in interpersonal processes[19] based upon Dickenson's scale.

Level 1

The first person actively attempts to remain detached from the second person(s) and discloses nothing about his own feelings or personality to the second person(s), or if he does disclose himself, he does so in a way that is not tuned to the second person's general progress.

EXAMPLE: The first person may attempt, whether awkwardly or skillfully, to divert the second person's attention from focusing upon personal questions concerning the first person, or his self-disclosures may be ego shattering for the second person(s) and may ultimately cause him to lose faith in the first person.

In summary, the first person actively attempts to remain ambiguous and an unknown quantity to the second person(s), or if he is self-disclosing, he does so solely out of his own needs and is oblivious to the needs of the second person(s).

Level 2

The first person, while not always appearing actively to avoid self-disclosures, never volunteers personal information about himself.

EXAMPLE: The first person may respond briefly to direct questions from the client about himself; however, he does so hesitantly and never provides more information about himself than the second person(s) specifically requests.

In summary, the second person(s) either does not ask about the personality of the first person, or, if he does, the barest minimum of brief, vague, and superficial responses are offered by the first person.

Level 3

The first person volunteers personal information about himself which may be in keeping with the second person's interests, but this information is often vague and indicates little about the unique character of the first person.

EXAMPLE: While the first person volunteers personal information and never gives the impression that he does not wish to disclose more about himself, nevertheless, the content of his verbalizations is generally centered upon his reactions to the second person(s) and his ideas concerning their interaction.

In summary, the first person may introduce more abstract, personal ideas in accord with the second person's interests, but these ideas do not stamp him as a unique person. Level 3 constitutes the minimum level of facilitative interpersonal functioning.

Level 4

The facilitator freely volunteers information about his personal ideas, attitudes, and experiences in accord with the second person's interests and concerns.

EXAMPLE: The facilitator may discuss personal ideas in both depth and detail, and his expressions reveal him to be a unique individual.

In summary, the facilitator is free and spontaneous in volunteering personal information about himself, and in so doing may reveal in a constructive fashion quite intimate material about his own feelings and beliefs.

Level 5

The facilitator volunteers very intimate and often detailed material about his own personality, and in keeping with the second person's needs may express information that might be extremely embarrassing under different circumstances or if revealed by the second person to an outsider.

EXAMPLE: The facilitator gives the impression of holding nothing back and of disclosing his feelings and ideas fully and completely to the second person(s). If some of his feelings are negative concerning the second person(s), the facilitator employs them constructively as a basis for an open-ended inquiry.

. In summary, the facilitator is operating in a constructive fashion at the most intimate levels of self-disclosure.

Examples of Self-Disclosure

Examples of facilitative therapist self-disclosure are difficult to come by. Low levels of self-disclosure simply do not need to be illustrated—they represent the absence of the therapist's discussion of himself or herself. However, low levels would also be represented by refusal of the therapist to reveal himself or herself when it would be therapeutic. Thus:

CLIENT: After I left here the last time I began to feel depressed and to wonder if I would ever get better. I guess I began to doubt your ability to help me. After all, you're so much younger than I am—you can't have had much experience. . . . What about your training and experience? Do you have medical training or a doctor's degree?

THERAPIST: I don't think that my training or experience is relevant here. Your doubts are probably related to your own inadequacies and problems.

A simple self-disclosure is illustrated in the following dialogue:

CLIENT: I just don't think anyone can understand what I am going through unless he has gone through the same thing—or something close to it. I'm not sure you understand—or that I should expect you to. Do you at all know how I feel?

THERAPIST: Yes, I do; as a matter of fact I went through something very similar when my mother died.

A very different kind of self-disclosure is reconstructed by one of Carkhuff's clients:

THERAPIST: Last hour you wondered why I'd make myself available for counseling you. Now I know. Now I can say it. I think I can learn from you.

CLIENT: I honor you for saying that. It makes you more vulnerable.

THERAPIST: You don't know *how* vulnerable.

CLIENT: I know. (I tried to make an intellectual discussion about it.)

THERAPIST: Let's just leave it at what I said.

CLIENT: O.K., we'll do it your way.[20]

IMMEDIACY OF RELATIONSHIP

Immediacy refers to the current interaction of the therapist and the client in the relationship. We look more closely at immediacy in this section, and consider how it can be measured. We also look at some examples of the presence of immediacy in the counseling situation.

The Nature of Immediacy

Concern with immediacy is significant because the client's behavior and functioning in the therapy relationship are indicative of his or her functioning in other interpersonal relationships. Gestalt therapy recognizes this in a concern with the here and now.[21] The Adlerians also focus on immediate behavior in the counseling situation. Kell and Mueller emphasize what they call the eliciting behaviors of clients in the counseling relationship, particularly self-defeating behaviors.[22] If the essence of counseling is a relationship, and we are concerned about the functioning of the client in interpersonal relationships—indeed, it is because of inadequate functioning in interpersonal relationships that most clients come to a counselor—then the client's functioning in the counseling relationship should be important.

> The way he relates to the counselor is a snapshot of the way he relates to others. . . . Clients come to counseling manipulating, hostile, rejecting, testing. They invest or do not invest; they are afraid; they present weakness; they attempt to seduce; they stay in a shell; they hide; they try to force the counselor to be responsible; they try to force punishment from the counselor; they apologize for being human. If the counselor does not focus on trying to understand these things, growth possibilities for clients can be missed.[23]

The counselor has the opportunity to deal directly with the client's problem behavior, and the client has the opportunity to learn and to change his or her behavior.

Carkhuff suggests that immediacy bridges the gap between empathy and confrontation, making possible

> a translation in the immediate present of the helper's insights into the helpee's expressions. The helper in responding immediately to his experience of the relationship with the helpee not only allows the helpee to have the intense experience of two persons in interaction but also provides a model of a person who understands and acts upon his experience of both his impact upon the other and the other's impact upon him.[24]

The therapist must be sensitive toward the feelings of the client about him or her and deal with them rather than ignore them. It is particularly difficult for the therapist to recognize negative feelings as related to himself or herself or, if he or she does recognize them, to respond to them. The difficulty is increased by the fact that the client's message may be, and often is, indirect; that is, it is concealed in references to other persons than the therapist. Carkhuff gives as an example the statement by a client that she has difficulty relating to her physician, which is a way of stating that she has difficulty relating to the therapist.[25] It is obvious that this is an inference, or even an interpretation, that is based upon the therapist's feeling or intuition—or, if the inference is accurate, on his or her sensitivity. There is the danger that the therapist may be mistaken, that he or she is imposing his or her own interpretation, or projecting, rather than being sensitive to the client. In addition to depending on his or her own experiencing of the client, the therapist is going beyond, or ignoring, the content of the client's communication to respond to the unspoken message. "Usually when the helpee cannot express himself directly, it is not so much a function of his inability to express himself as it is of the attitudes he holds about the helper in relation to himself."[26] While an accurate response by the therapist can facilitate progress, an inaccurate response can be threatening and damaging.

While the relationship at every moment can be examined in terms of its immediacy, it is not always appropriate to respond to this, and it is, of course, impossible for the therapist to focus continuously on the immediacy of the relationship. It is perhaps most appropriate to focus on immediacy when the therapy seems to be stalled or going nowhere—though this may be simply the result of the client "taking a rest." But it may be because of factors in the immediate relationship, and focusing upon the relationship may help. If the counselor is unable to identify precipitating factors, he or she can ask the client for help—to say what he or she feels is impeding the relationship. It is possible that the impasse involves feelings, attitudes, or behavior of the counselor of which he or she is unaware. But it is also useful to look specifically at the relationship in terms of immediacy when things seem to be going well—that is, to look at its positive aspects.

Immediacy, while involving the relationship of the client to the therapist, is not a transference relationship. It involves the therapist as he or she really is, rather than simply, or mainly, as a representative of some other important figure in the client's experience. However, the client's relationship with the therapist is related to and influenced by his or her habits or methods of relating to others, though not necessarily in the manner of the psychoanalytic transference.

As in the case of the other action dimensions, therapist responses of immediacy at a high level are not suddenly presented to the client. Before the therapist knows and understands the client, he or she cannot be too certain of his or her experience of the client. And before the client has developed a good relationship with the therapist, he or she is not prepared for the disclosure. Therefore, the therapist's expression of immediacy is tentative: "Are you trying to tell me how you feel about me and our relationship?" As the relationship develops, the therapist becomes more sure of his or her inferences, and the client more ready to accept them. But also, as the client improves and functions at higher levels, he or she becomes more open in his or her communications, and interpretations of immediacy are then unnecessary.

As in the cases of confrontation and self-disclosure, it may be questioned whether immediacy is independent of or qualitatively different from the conditions considered in Chapter 4. To be sensitive to clients' perceptions, feelings, and attitudes toward the therapist or to how they are relating to the therapist would appear to be a part of empathy. Carkhuff refers to immediacy as "one of the most critical variables in terms of communicating a depth of understanding of the complex interactions between the parties in the relationship."[27] The expression of the therapist's experiences of the client appears to be an aspect of genuineness. The pointing out of the meaning of the client's words or behavior in terms of his or her relationship with the therapist appears to be similar to confrontation. Thus immediacy may be empathy and/or genuineness and/or confrontation that involves a particular content—the relationship between the therapist and the client. Since empathy, warmth, and genuineness are no doubt complex variables, it is probably desirable to attempt to analyze them into components. How this can best be done is a problem: Is it desirable to do so in terms of content areas, such as the client's behavior in therapy as distinguished from his behavior outside the relationship?

As in the cases of confrontation and therapist self-disclosure, there has been very little research on immediacy. Referring to a study[28] that found that clients of therapists who were significantly higher in immediacy than in empathy, warmth, and genuineness showed significant deterioration in therapy, Mitchell, Bozarth, and Krauft note that it is possible that

> immediacy is related strongly to *positive* outcome only within the context of high levels of the interpersonal skills. It may be that high levels of immediacy so enhance the potential of the here-and-now therapist-client relationship for *therapeutic benefit or harm* that such therapist demands to intensify the alliance must be accompanied by high levels of empathy, warmth and genuineness. On the other hand, clinical wisdom suggests to us that a therapist who demands an intense relationship in the context of nonfacilitative levels of the interpersonal skills moves his client toward an intimacy with a person who is unable (or unwilling) to understand him, who remains unconcerned about him and lacking in respect, and who deals with him in a caricature of the professional relationship in a distant, stereotyped, and phony relationship.[29]

Measuring Immediacy

Carkhuff's scale for measuring immediacy of relationship in interpersonal processes[30] is a revision of scales by the Mitchells and by Leitner and Berenson.[31] It is as follows.

Level 1

The verbal and behavioral expressions of the helper disregard the content and effect of the helpee's expressions that have the potential for relating to the helper.

EXAMPLE: The helper may simply ignore all helpee communications, whether direct or indirect, that deal with the helper-helpee relationship.

In summary, the helper simply disregards all of those helpee messages that are related to the helper.

Level 2

The verbal and behavioral expressions of the helper disregard most of the helpee expressions that have the potential for relating to the helper.

EXAMPLE: Even if the helpee is talking about helping personnel in general, the helper may, in general, remain silent or just not relate the content to himself.

In summary, the helper appears to choose to disregard most of those helpee messages that are related to the helper.

Level 3

The verbal and behavior expressions of the helper, while open to interpretations of immediacy, do not relate what the helpee is saying to what is going on between the helper and the helpee in the immediate moment.

EXAMPLE: The helper may make literal responses to or reflections on the helpee's expressions or otherwise open-minded responses that refer to no one specifically but that might refer to the helper.

In summary, while the helper does not extend the helpee's expressions to immediacy, he is not closed to such interpretations. Level 3 constitutes the minimum level of facilitative interpersonal functioning.

Level 4

The verbal and behavioral expressions of the helper appear cautiously to relate the helpee's expressions directly to the helper-helpee relationship.

EXAMPLE: The helper attempts to relate the helpee's responses to himself, but he does so in a tentative manner.

In summary, the helper relates the helpee's responses to himself in an open, cautious manner.

Level 5

The verbal and behavioral expressions of the helper relate the helpee's expressions directly to the helper-helpee relationship.

EXAMPLE: The helper in a direct and explicit manner relates the helpee's expressions to himself.

In summary, the helper is not hesitant in making explicit interpretations of the helper-helpee relationship.

Examples of Immediacy

In the following example, the therapist ignores the client's feelings about him, focusing instead on the client's general reaction of discouragement.

CLIENT: I'm not sure I should continue these sessions. I don't feel I'm getting anywhere. You—they don't seem to be helping me. I don't get the feeling you are very concerned.

THERAPIST: You're pretty discouraged and feel like quitting and giving up trying.

CLIENT: Yeah . . . it doesn't seem worthwhile to continue.

Contrast this with the following dialogue, where the therapist responds with a high level of immediacy (as well as confrontation) to the client's (implicit or explicit) feelings of aggression toward the therapist:

THERAPIST: John, you really want to destroy our relationship here.

CLIENT: It's more than that.

THERAPIST: You want to kill me.

CLIENT: No, not really, I. . . .

THERAPIST: John, you want to kill me.

CLIENT: Yes, I want to kill you. I know you haven't earned it, but I want to kill you, maybe for everyone I hate.

THERAPIST: That's too easy.

CLIENT: All I know is I want to kill you.

THERAPIST: You can't.

CLIENT: I can! I can! One way or another I will. So I can't take you this way but I'll find another. I'll fail you. I'll lead you astray. You'll think I'm improving but I'll fail. I'll be your failure case. You'll be responsible.

THERAPIST: You'll do anything you have to, to undermine me, to destroy me, even something that hurts you.

CLIENT: Yes, yes.

THERAPIST: If you can in some way defeat me, you won't have to change your way of living. You do stupid things to protect a stupid way of life, and that's stupid.

CLIENT: Oh, I want to change. I do, I can't help it. I can't help it. God, I've been wrong to hurt you.

THERAPIST: You had to find out whether you could take me. If you could, I couldn't help you, and I can.[32]

The following dialogue illustrates the therapist's inference that the client's statement about others also applies to the therapist:

CLIENT: I'm never sure where I stand with anyone.

THERAPIST: That applies here as well, right, Jim?

CLIENT: Yeah, I guess it does. I've been thinking of bringing it up—guess I was afraid to learn that you, too, would give some meaningless bunch of words.

THERAPIST: You're telling me you're not sure you trust me enough to go further—even though we have shared a great deal.

CLIENT: Guess I was sure you'd think I was crazy—earlier I felt I might shock you.

THERAPIST: Look—at this moment I experience this: Whatever Jim fears most does not cause me *any* anxiety—I'm not sure I can get it all into words—but your impulses don't scare me—and I trust that. I feel good with you, Jim, and when our meetings are over I do not feel drained of energy. Damn it, you have your own strength—have it, for crying out loud—then you will know.[33]

THE INTEGRATION OF RESPONSIVE
AND ACTION DIMENSIONS

The separation of the therapeutic conditions into two groups—the understanding or responsive conditions and the initiating or action conditions—is not a hard and fast separation. To some extent all the conditions are or can be present throughout the therapy process. Concreteness can be a responsive or an action dimension. Genuineness can be a responsive or an action dimension. Understanding or empathy is essential for confrontation and immediacy. Warmth or respect also is essential as a base for the action conditions. The action conditions must have a context of warmth and understanding. This is important, particularly for the beginning counselor, who may be tempted (or encouraged by a misunderstanding of the place of the action conditions) to quickly move into high levels of action conditions without adequate understanding or without the basis of empathy and warmth or respect.

The division of therapy into dimensions or conditions that lead to insight and dimensions or conditions that lead to action is probably not warranted.[34] The understanding conditions, in addition to providing the basis for insight, also may contribute directly to action or make action possible for the client whose therapeutic relationship lacks high levels of the action conditions. On the other hand, the action conditions can stimulate and contribute to client insight. It is possible, as has been indicated earlier, to consider the action conditions not as new or different conditions but as extensions of the understanding conditions to new areas. Thus, therapist self-disclosure is genuineness or openness applied to the therapist's personal life. Immediacy is empathy applied to the therapist-client relationship of the moment. In addition, the action conditions may be to some extent, if not entirely, essentially high levels of the understanding conditions. That this is the case seems to be recognized, implicitly, by Carkhuff.[35]

The deliberate use of the action dimensions—particularly by the beginning counselor or therapist, who is apt not to be particularly high in the responsive dimensions—should be cautious. Confrontation inherently has the possibility of being threatening to the client, and self-disclosure and immediacy can also be threatening, in which case they can hold up or slow down rather than facilitate client progress. In fact, it is my view that all therapists should focus on providing the highest levels of the responsive dimensions, and appropriate expression of the action dimensions will follow as the therapy relationship develops. This view is supported by the fact that there is an almost total absence of research to support the effectiveness of the action dimensions in therapy, while there is some indication that these dimensions can lead to client deterioration rather than improvement.

THE ESSENCE OF THE CONDITIONS

When one brings together the various aspects of the facilitative conditions—empathy, warmth, respect, concern, valuing and prizing, openness, honesty, genuineness, transparency, intimacy, self-disclosure, confrontation—it becomes apparent that they constitute love in the highest sense, or *agape,* to use the Greek term. A loving relationship is the therapy for all disorders of the human spirit and of disturbed interpersonal relationships. It is not necessary to wait for a "breakthrough" or a discovery of new methods or techniques in psychotherapy or human relations. We already have, in essence, the answer—the answer that has been reached through thousands of years of human experience and recognized by the great philosophers of various times and cultures.

The therapist is not a technician, operating objectively on the client. He cannot be detached or disengaged but must be involved in a personal, human encounter. If the therapist is to help clients, he or she must feel for them, love them in the sense of *agape.* It is perhaps a basic fact of human relationships that you can't really help people without becoming involved with them, without caring for them or liking them. Arthur Burton notes that "after all research on psychotherapy is accounted for, psychotherapy still resolves itself into a relationship best subsumed by the word 'love.'"[36] As the popular song puts it, "You're nobody until somebody loves you." Then you can become a self-actualizing person.

It is relevant to recall here the discussion in Chapter 3 on the self-actualizing person and society. There it was pointed out that self-actualizing persons are necessary for the survival of society. The conditions we have been discussing are characteristics of self-actualizing persons and thus are the conditions necessary for the survival of society. They are not limited to a single culture. They are the characteristics of self-actualizing persons in all cultures, and the conditions for the development of self-actualizing persons in all cultures. Love is not culture-specific or culture-bound.

Psychotherapy is a human relationship involving two unique individuals. Thus, each relationship is unique. Since this is so, the nature or outcome of the relationship cannot be predicted in detail. But it is not necessary to predict the specifics of the relationship. The therapist need only begin, enter the encounter, without concern about its exact nature or outcome. The therapist must commit to the client and to the relationship without knowing just what will develop or just what it will mean.

If the therapist must have assurance about what will happen and how the relationship will go, he or she will be unable to commit to it. If the therapist can't trust himself or herself in the relationship, he or she can't help the client. The relationship must be free to develop spontaneously. If the therapist has preconceived notions about its nature, he or she will control and restrict the relationship. The need for control, for predictability of the specifics, represents a lack of tolerance for ambiguity and is an indication that the individual is unsuitable for the practice of psychotherapy. The therapist must have confidence in himself or herself as a person. Too many counseling students are seeking for *something to do to their clients,* rather than being concerned about how *to be somebody with them.*

This does not mean that the therapy process is unpredictable in its general nature and ultimate outcome. Not at all. *If* the conditions for therapeutic personality change are present in the therapist as a person, *then* a relationship will develop that will lead to the client becoming a more self-actualizing person and, in the process and/or as a result, changing in specific ways or achieving those specific goals that he or she desires and that are aspects of or by-products of a self-actualizing process.

Is Love Conditional?

There has been considerable discussion about the conditionality of the therapeutic conditions. Rogers used the term *unconditional positive regard.* Yet an analysis of a therapy interview conducted by Rogers indicated that Rogers's responses were not noncontingent but varied with the statements of the client.[37] Thus, the level of the conditions varies during therapy and in relationship to the behavior of the client. Yet love, it would probably be generally agreed, is unconditional. It is given without demanding something in return. It is bestowed on a person not for *what* he or she is but for *who* he or she is.

The solution to the problem would appear to relate to distinguishing between the client as a person—the *who*—and the client's behavior—the *what*. The client is unconditionally accepted and respected as a person. The therapist manifests a basic respect, concern, and warmth regardless of *what* the client is or of the client's behavior in or out of the therapy relationship. This basic, minimum level of love, of respect and warmth, is unconditional.

But one who loves and respects another is, of course, affected by the behavior of the other. He or she is pleased by some things and displeased by others, satisfied by some characteristics and behaviors and dissatisfied by others. In addition, love has great expectations. Real love expects—in a sense, demands—the best in others. Therapists who care deeply about their client are affected by the client's behavior, both in and out of therapy. They are pleased or disappointed, happy or sad, approving or disapproving, depending on how the client behaves. Therapists are more interested in some things the client talks about than in others. And they express these feelings, whether they are aware of it or intend to or not. As we note in our discussion of relevance (Chapter 6), therapists respond to what they think is relevant and do not respond to what they think is irrelevant. The therapist's responses are contingent upon the client's behavior.

But throughout all this differential responsiveness, there is a basic respect, concern, caring, or love for the client as a person. Without it the therapist could not help the client. The client would not continue the relationship. Without it the therapist would not be a significant person to the client, and if he or she were not a significant person, his or her responses would not be meaningful or important to the client and would have no effect on the client.

But when one really cares about another, one wants to help the other to be a better person and to prevent him or her from making mistakes. Thus, there is the temptation to intervene actively in the life of the other. If one loves another, one cannot allow the other to make a mistake, to fail, to do something that clearly seems to be bad or wrong. Or can one? Doesn't a real love, a greater love, respect the right of the other to make his or her own decisions, even to make mistakes or to fail? And how is one to know what is a mistake or what actions will lead to failure, what is good or bad, right or wrong, for another? And even where certain actions are clearly wrong, or bad, can or should one, even on the basis of love, intervene, thus indicating lack of faith in the other? Possibly so, in extreme instances where irreparable damage seems sure to be done. But it might be maintained that under the conditions of real love, which include faith and confidence in the other person, the other will not choose to act in a way that is clearly bad, wrong, or harmful to self or others. The question perhaps revolves around the extent of the love or caring one has for the other, the respect one has for his or her integrity, the faith one has in the other, and the relationship he or she is providing for the other.

Love must allow the loved one to make his or her own choices and, in the extreme case, must leave open the possibility that death rather than life may be chosen, because it has such confidence that the power of love will lead to the choice of life. But the risk that death might be chosen must be taken because love requires that the loved one have the freedom of choice.

Is Love Controlling?

There is a final aspect of the conditions—or of love—that is significant for the problem of control. In reinforcement terms, the most potent reinforcer of human behavior is a good human relationship. The conditions—or love—are not effective, in the long run, unless they are real or genuine. When it is real and genuine, love prevents one from using or exploiting another for one's own purposes. It would thus appear that there is an inbuilt protection in the conditions against excessive control or manipulation.

Yet this does not appear to eliminate the possibility of control by misguided persons of good intentions. Possessive love, as is well known, can be harmful. Is there then no protection against influence by those who can offer love and understanding? It appears that brainwashing is most effective where there is real belief in what is being imposed and where there is real concern for the person being influenced—a desire to "save his soul," so to speak. In Orwell's *1984,* Winston, even though tortured by his inquisitor, O'Brien, felt love for him because O'Brien understood him.[38]

It has been pointed out that we should take comfort "in the knowledge that the behavior of those who exercise control is generally governed more by the behavior of those controlled than by anything else."[39] But is it? History, and *Walden Two,*[40] do not demonstrate this. It is only true on the assumption that behavior is mainly controlled by automatic reinforcement.

Perhaps here is the key, as Skinner himself has suggested. When there is awareness that one is being controlled—even by the loving and understanding of another—then one is not in the position of responding automatically to reinforcement. Looking at it in another way, if respect is not a part of love, it is not real love. Or, if respect as well as empathic understanding and genuineness are not present, the individual responds differently. And if respect is present, then there is no attempt to control in a manipulative sense, or in terms of what the controller thinks is best. It is our ability to be aware of being controlled that is our protection. Respect for another prevents the controller from manipulating another, and the awareness of lack of respect prevents the other from being manipulated by a possessive love and understanding.

The Conditions and the Goal

It should be apparent to you that there is a particular kind of relationship between the ultimate goal of counseling and the conditions of the therapeutic relationship (or for the development of self-actualizing persons). The description of the self-actualizing person (Chapter 3) includes acceptance of and respect for others, openness, honesty, and genuineness, and the capacity for deep interpersonal relations with others. The conditions are thus aspects of the goal; the goal includes the conditions. *The condition for self-actualizing persons is an environment of other self-actualizing persons.* The therapist, then, must be a self-actualizing person.

OTHER CONDITIONS

Are the conditions described in Chapters 4 and 5 the only conditions included in the psychotherapy relationship? We don't know. These conditions account for only part of the variance in therapy outcomes. But it must be remembered that neither the conditions nor the outcomes are measured with a high degree of reliability, so that any measured relationship would be attenuated. And there are, of course, conditions in the client that affect outcome (Chapter 7).

There may be other important therapist variables. For example, there is good reason to believe that the expectations of the therapist exert a great influence upon the client's behavior.[41] All therapists expect their clients to change; otherwise they would not be engaged in psychotherapy. Furthermore, they believe that they and/or their methods are instruments of such change. The degree of confidence in themselves and their methods may vary, but it would appear that some such confidence must exist or therapists would leave the profession or change to other methods. The minimum level of confidence for some effectiveness may be relatively low, however; I have had students who were skeptical about the efficacy of the core conditions, but who found, somewhat to their surprise, that their clients did improve or change. On the other hand, the confidence in a method may be so strong that therapists can be successful with any method in which they believe. This, of course, makes it difficult, if not impossible, to evaluate methods apart from therapist confidence in the method. We face the paradox that no method can be successful unless the therapist has confidence in it, yet a method may be successful only because the therapist (and the client) has confidence in it.

These factors have been given little attention in research. Most research comparing different methods of counseling or psychotherapy has not controlled for the therapists' belief in or confidence in themselves and their methods. Research that attempts to control for therapist personality differences by having the same therapists utilize different methods fails to control for the factor of relative belief in or confidence in the different methods (and also for different levels of experience and competence in different methods).[42]

SUMMARY

In this chapter we continued consideration of the conditions for the development of self-actualizing persons, or for the therapeutic process. Several conditions other than the core facilitative dimensions discussed in Chapter 4 have been identified or described and rating scales developed for their measurement. The three considered in this chapter are designated by Carkhuff as action-oriented or initiative conditions, as distinguished from the understanding or responsive conditions. These three conditions or dimensions are confrontation, therapist self-disclosure, and immediacy of the relationship.

We emphasized that no sharp line can be drawn separating the two types of conditions. The understanding conditions lead to, and may be sufficient for, client action, while the initiative conditions facilitate understanding and client insight. We suggested that the action-oriented conditions can be considered extensions of the responsive conditions or can represent high levels of these conditions.

The essence of the conditions, we suggested, is love or agape. Whether love or the conditions are conditional or unconditional was discussed. We concluded that a basic level of respect, warmth, and caring, or love for the client as a person is unconditional. But since therapists do care for the client, the client's behavior does make a difference to them and they respond positively or negatively. From the clients' standpoint, unless they feel the basic unconditional respect and concern of the therapist for them, they will not be affected by the therapist's differential responding. Thus, both unconditional and conditional elements are present and necessary for the therapist to have any influence upon the client.

NOTES

1. R. R. Carkhuff and B. G. Berenson. *Beyond counseling and therapy*. New York: Holt, Rinehart & Winston, 1967, Chap. 9.
2. R. R. Carkhuff. *Helping and human relations*. Vol. I, *Selection and training*. Vol. II, *Practice and research*. New York: Holt, Rinehart & Winston, 1969, Vol. I, p. 191. Reprinted by Human Resource Development Press, Amherst, MA, 1984. Page numbers are for 1969 printing.
3. *Ibid.*, Vol. II, p. 93.
4. *Ibid.*, Vol. I, p. 211.
5. *Ibid.*, Vol. II, p. 93.
6. K. M. Mitchell and B. G. Berenson. Differential use of confrontation by high and low facilitative therapists. *Journal of Nervous and Mental Disease*, 1970, *151*, 303–309; K. M. Mitchell and L. A. Hall. Frequency and type of confrontation over time within the first interview. *Journal of Consulting and Clinical Psychology*, 1971, *37*, 437–442; S. Anderson. Effects of confrontation by high- and low-functioning clients. *Journal of Counseling Psychology*, 1969, *16*, 299–302.
7. K. M. Mitchell. Confrontation: Some redefinitions. Unpublished manuscript, New Jersey Medical School, 1975.
8. Carkhuff, *Helping*, Vol. II, pp. 324–325.
9. Carkhuff and Berenson, *Beyond counseling*, pp. 176–177. This and the following examples from this source are excerpts from actual interviews.
10. *Ibid.*, p. 173.
11. *Ibid.*, p. 174.
12. L. E. Beutler. Psychotherapy and persuasion. In L. E. Beutler and R. Greene (Eds.), *Special problems in child and adolescent behavior*. Westport, CT: Technomic, 1978, pp. 119–159.
13. S. R. Strong and C. D. Claiborn. *Change through interaction: Social psychological processes of counseling and psychotherapy*. New York: Wiley, 1982, p. 157.
14. V. J. Derlega, R. Lovell, and A. L. Chaiken. Effects of therapist disclosure and its perceived appropriateness on client self-disclosure. *Journal of Consulting and Clinical Psychology*, 1976, *44*, 866.
15. S. R. Strong. Social psychological approach to psychotherapy research. In S. L. Garfield and A. E. Bergin (Eds.), *Handbook of psychotherapy and behavior change* (2nd. ed.). New York: Wiley, 1978, pp. 101–136.
16. W. A. Dickenson. Therapist self-disclosure as a variable in psychotherapeutic process and outcome. *Dissertation Abstracts International*, 1969, *30*, 2434B.
17. R. H. Hayward. Process and outcome consequences of therapist self-disclosure. *Dissertation Abstracts International*, 1974, *34*, 6210B–6211B.
18. Carkhuff, *Helping*, Vol. I, pp. 208, 209.
19. *Ibid.*, Vol. II, pp. 321–322.
20. *Ibid.*, p. 110.
21. F. S. Perls. *Gestalt therapy verbatim*. Moab, UT: Real People Press, 1969.
22. B. L. Kell and W. J. Mueller. *Impact and change: A study of counseling relationships*. New York: Appleton-Century-Crofts, 1966.

23. M. R. Cudney. The use of immediacy in counseling. In J. C. Heston and W. B. Frick (Eds.), *Counseling for the liberal arts campus.* Yellow Springs, OH: Antioch Press, 1968, pp. 135, 136.

24. Carkhuff, *Helping*, Vol. I, p. 192.

25. *Ibid.,* p. 194.

26. *Ibid.,* p. 212.

27. *Ibid.,* p. 192.

28. R. M. Mitchell. Relationship between therapist response to therapist-relevant client expressions and therapy process and client outcome. *Dissertation Abstracts International,* 1971, *32,* 1853B.

29. K. M. Mitchell, J. D. Bozarth, and C. C. Krauft. A reappraisal of the therapeutic effectiveness of accurate empathy, nonpossessive warmth, and genuineness. In A. S. Gurman and A. M. Razin (Eds.), *Effective psychotherapy: A handbook of research.* New York: Pergamon Press, 1977, pp. 482–502.

30. Carkhuff, *Helping*, Vol. II, pp. 326–327.

31. R. Mitchell and K. M. Mitchell. The therapist immediate relationship scale. Unpublished research scale, Michigan State University, 1966; L. Leitner and B. G. Berenson. Immediate relationship scale: A revision. Unpublished research scale, State University of New York at Buffalo, 1967.

32. Carkhuff and Berenson, *Beyond counseling,* p. 149.

33. *Ibid.,* p. 189.

34. *Ibid.,* pp. 139, 229.

35. Carkhuff, *Helping*, Vol. I, p. 218.

36. A. Burton. *Modern humanistic psychotherapy.* San Francisco: Jossey-Bass, 1967, pp. 102–103.

37. C. B. Truax. Reinforcement and non-reinforcement in Rogerian psychotherapy. *Journal of Abnormal and Social Psychology,* 1966, *71,* 1–9.

38. G. Orwell. *1984.* New York: Harcourt Brace Jovanovich, 1949.

39. W. F. Day. Review of B. F. Skinner, *Beyond freedom and dignity. Contemporary Psychology,* 1972, *17,* 465–469.

40. B. F. Skinner. *Walden two.* New York: Macmillan, 1948.

41. R. Rosenthal. *Experimenter effects in behavioral research.* New York: Appleton-Century-Crofts, 1966.

42. See, for example, G. Paul. *Insight versus desensitization in psychotherapy.* Stanford, CA: Stanford University Press, 1966.

CHAPTER 6

Implementing the Conditions: The Therapist in the Process

The immediate goal of counseling or psychotherapy is the initiation and continuation of the therapeutic process. This is achieved, on the part of the counselor, by providing the basic core conditions. The client also has a contribution to the process, which is not one-sided but a relationship. In this chapter we consider the implementation of the conditions by the counselor and in the next chapter we view the process from the client's standpoint.

The conditions of a good therapeutic relationship are not techniques. They are often referred to as skills, which is a somewhat better term, though still not adequate. They are attitudes, but they are more than attitudes. They involve behavior, especially verbal behavior. But behind the words are the attitudes and feelings of the therapist. The expression of the attitudes and feelings is not, for the beginning counseling student, natural or spontaneous. It is therefore desirable, if not necessary, to offer some suggestions to the student about the implementation of the conditions. As students gain experience, they become less aware of their implementing the conditions or of different ways of responding to the client. Their behavior becomes spontaneous.

It is essential that counselors first recognize the basic attitude or frame of reference from which they must operate if they are to understand clients. This is the internal frame of reference of the client. It is not too much to say that if the student does not or cannot assume or adopt the internal frame of reference, he or she can never understand clients and thus can never become a counselor or therapist. Yet I have seen students who have not achieved this at the end of their practicum experience. In many cases it may be that this requirement was never pointed out to them by their instructors—who themselves may not operate on this basis—since it is my experience that students who are made aware of this requirement can learn to operate from the client's internal frame of reference during practicum.

THE THERAPIST'S RESPONSIBILITY

The beginning counselor may enter the practice of counseling or psychotherapy with unrealistic expectations or with dreams of quickly achieving far-reaching, even miraculous, changes in clients. He or she may anticipate the glowing satisfaction from grateful clients attributing their new lives to the counselor.

This is an unrealistic expectation. Counselors who hold such an expectation are doomed to disappointment and frustration, as well as anxiety, which will interfere with their effectiveness as counselors. Counseling or psychotherapy is no profession for anyone who is dependent upon spectacular results for the satisfaction of a need for accomplishment. It is no place for the impatient person, who must see immediate results, or the person dependent upon rapid, steady, and easily observable progress in clients for his or her own professional satisfaction and self-esteem.

It is only reasonable not to expect sudden, miraculous changes in psychotherapy. Clients have behind them years of living and experience, usually of unhappy, disturbed living under adverse conditions and detrimental interpersonal relationships. Attitudes and habits built up and practiced during this long period of time do not usually change easily or quickly. Counseling or psychotherapy, for an hour a week or at most several hours, constitutes but a small part of the client's life. Freud was well aware of the difficulties and limitations of psychotherapy and cautioned against unrealistic expectations; he expected therapy to take several years. It was only when psychoanalysis came to America that brief psychoanalytic therapy was developed, under the pressure in America to speed things up, to become more efficient (without always being more effective). But Wyatt notes that "it does not make biological sense that an organism molded into a certain pattern under innumerable influences over many years, should be changed profoundly through an influence within a few months. A therapist who insists on the rebirth of his patients may have missed his calling."[1] Therapy involves the development of a relationship, which takes time. The counselor must avoid impatience with clients for taking time to enter the relationship and for slowness in trusting the therapist. There is no such thing as instant intimacy. As the popular song puts it, "You can't hurry love."

Few therapists have claimed much more than 50 percent success in their cases. The claims of Ellis, Wolpe, and others of up to 90 percent success are of doubtful validity. Few therapists would maintain that complete cures are possible for all emotionally disturbed persons. Studies of clients seldom find more than two thirds of them improved. Indeed, the discouraging early research on the outcomes of psychotherapy suggested no evidence that psychotherapy results in better than chance improvement or is better than no therapy.[2]

Actually, the results of psychotherapy are both better and worse than the early surveys indicated. Although, on the average, clients may not appear to be any better off following therapy (at least on our inadequate and imperfect criterion measures), analysis of the data has shown that some clients improve considerably, while others get worse. Psychotherapy may be for the better or for worse.[3] In addition, there is evidence that people improve "spontaneously," that is, without psychotherapy. Since improvement cannot actually be spontaneous (that is, without some influence or cause), it appears that people who are not treated by professional counselors or psychotherapists receive help from other persons in their environment. Again, this is both encouraging and discouraging. It is encouraging in that it indicates that the conditions for therapeutic change are present in many nonprofessional people. It is discouraging in that it indicates that, on the average, psychotherapists apparently possess no greater degree of these conditions than does the population in general. It also suggests that all the special methods and techniques in which therapists engage, beyond the basic relationship, add little if anything to the outcome of the therapeutic relationship.

But recent research does show that positive change and improvement is possible and that this improvement is related to the existence of high levels of the basic core conditions. Thus, the counselor or therapist, while being patient and reasonable, should not be pessimistic. Positive change can and does occur, occasionally dramatically. And each therapist has a great responsibility to be among those therapists who help their clients rather than make them worse. By not expecting quick and extensive changes or expecting that every client will improve, the counselor is relieved of one source of anxiety that can impair his or her functioning. On the other hand, since at least some of the variables or conditions leading to therapeutic change are now known, *the counselor cannot evade the responsibility for providing at least minimal necessary levels of these conditions to his or her clients.* While this is an awesome responsibility, the fact that we know what these conditions are and that they can be learned or acquired means that the counselor or psychotherapist can do something to meet this responsibility. This knowledge also means that educators of counselors and trainers of psychotherapists have the responsibility and obligation of teaching their students about these conditions. This is not always done successfully—as should be obvious from research indicating that many experienced, practicing therapists have clients who become worse.[4]

  While no book or didactic instruction alone can teach counseling or psychotherapy, they can contribute to such teaching. Students need to know what they should do before they can be expected to do it. In the preceding chapters we discussed the nature of the conditions for therapeutic personality change. Here we attempt to assist the student in applying or implementing these conditions through listening, structuring, and responding.

It should be emphasized that this is only a beginning, an orientation, and that it is only through supervised practicum training and then continuing experience in the practice of counseling or psychotherapy that high levels of the conditions can be achieved and maintained. It is important also for the student to recognize that the responsive or understanding conditions come first and that it is only in the context of these conditions that the initiative or action conditions are helpful or therapeutic.

LISTENING

If therapists are to reach any understanding of clients, they must allow clients to present themselves. Only clients can tell the therapist how they feel, what they think, how they see themselves and the world. Only by listening to clients can the therapist enter their worlds and see things as they do. The first rule of therapy is to listen to the client.

It should be obvious that one cannot listen if one is talking. Yet beginning counselors seem to find it extremely difficult not to talk. Perhaps they have been trained to initiate conversation in social situations. Many of them have had experience in teaching or preaching, where they have assumed the initiative and have taken responsibility for directing or guiding conversations or discussions, so that they are unable to relinquish the initiative to another. Or perhaps they have read something somewhere about the necessity for the counselor to establish rapport by finding some common experience, acquaintance, or activity with the client. At any rate, the problem is so common that I begin students in the counseling practicum with a simple, concrete rule: Keep your mouth shut. This is an objective, easily observed criterion for the instructor and the counseling student to evaluate in a tape recording. Someone has suggested that with beginning counselors adhesive tape might be more useful than recording tape.

The difficulty created by counselors taking the initiative in the early part of counseling is that they impose their frames of reference on clients. Rather than presenting themselves from their own frames of reference, clients present themselves as they think the counselor wants them to. There are those who feel that if the counselor is to understand clients, he or she needs certain kinds of information about them, which should be obtained in the initial interview. But such an approach does two things: (1) it sets the structure of counseling as one in which the counselor leads and the client follows; and (2) it may lead to knowledge *about* or understanding *about* the client, but not to an empathic understanding from the client's frame of reference. Such an approach meets the counselor's needs, such as inability to tolerate ambiguity and the fear of an unstructured encounter, rather than being helpful to the client or to the progress of therapy.

Listening to other persons, allowing them to present themselves freely without forcing them into one's own frame of reference, is a difficult thing to do. One must really be interested in the other person and what he or she has to say. In most social conversation, listening is only the necessary waiting for one's turn to speak, and rather than listeners focusing attention on what another is saying, they are thinking about what they are going to say when their turn comes. Too many counselors engage in this kind of listening. Real listening is difficult. The listener must not be preoccupied with himself or herself. Real listening is not a passive but an active process. The listener's complete attention must be given to the speaker. While he or she is listening to the client—indeed during the entire therapy process—the therapist must be totally committed to the client. Real listening is hard work. Some years ago I saw a cartoon in which two psychiatrists were in an elevator. One was impeccably neat and fresh; the other looked bedraggled, with tie askew and suit rumpled. The second psychiatrist asked the first: "How can you listen to people's problems all day and still look so fresh?" To which the other replied: "Who listens?"

Frieda Fromm-Reichmann writes:

What then are the basic requirements as to the personality and professional abilities of a psychiatrist? If I were asked to answer this question in one sentence, I would reply, "The psychotherapist must be able to listen." This does not appear to be a startling statement, but it is intended to be just that. To be able to listen to another person in this other person's own right, without reacting along the lines of one's own problems or experiences, of which one may be reminded, perhaps in a disturbing way, is an act of interpersonal exchange which few people are able to practice without special training. To be in command of this act is by no means tantamount to actually being a good psychiatrist, but it is a prerequisite of all intensive psychotherapy.[5]

The therapist in listening must not only suspend thinking about his or her own experiences and problems but must also suspend all evaluation and judgment of the client. The suspension of concern for his or her own experiences and problems does not mean, however, that the therapist represses all the feelings that arise in response to what the client is saying. These feelings and associations are useful in understanding what the client is saying.

Listening to another is a manifestation of respect. We all like those who really listen to us. It is not uncommon for someone to remark upon what a nice person and good conversationalist another person is, when observation would indicate that the other person is a good listener and seldom dominates the conversation. Listening is a potent reinforcer. It reinforces verbal productiveness in the client, and without such verbal productiveness therapy could not progress.

STRUCTURING

Many clients do not know how to act or what to do in psychotherapy. They may have misconceptions about the nature of psychotherapy and its practice. The counselor or psychotherapist is a professional person, and people often have certain conceptions of their relationships with professional persons. Professional persons are experts and authorities. Therefore, one listens to them and is passive or subordinate in the relationship. Students often identify counselors with teachers. Thus, they often remain silent, waiting for permission to speak, or expect the counselor to interrogate them. Adults often equate the psychotherapist with the physician. Thus they may begin by stating their complaints or problems. But then they wait for the therapist to question them. They expect the therapist to give them advice or solutions to their problems.

Structuring is orienting clients to their role and responsibility in the relationship and to the role and responsibility of the therapist. Overt or verbal structuring may not be necessary. If clients enter the relationship by taking the responsibility for presenting themselves and their problems and concerns, it is not necessary for the therapist to engage in formal structuring. The therapist informs the client of his or her own role by behavior, by modeling rather than by verbal discussion. Formal verbal structuring is necessary only where (1) clients have no idea about what they are expected to do or what the therapist's role is; and (2) clients have misconceptions of what they are expected to do or what the therapist's role is.

In the early period of client-centered therapy, structuring was often routinely practiced by many counselors, and many instructors taught their students to structure routinely. Structuring was probably necessary in most cases since the approach was new and different from that used by most counselors. Now, the educated public knows what to expect. Popular magazines have carried articles on how to behave when seeing a psychotherapist. They have indicated that the client is expected to do the talking, that the therapist listens —and probably will not even ask many questions. However, many segments of the public, and many clients, including perhaps most students, at least below the college level, do not know what psychotherapy is really like.

Thus, the therapist should be prepared to structure when necessary. One of the problems regarding the practice of client-centered therapy has occurred here. There are those who have claimed that the client-centered approach is not appropriate for counseling in the public schools because students are dependent and not able to take responsibility for themselves in the counseling process. This opinion has arisen at least in part from a misconception by many would-be client-centered counselors about the client-centered approach. In this misconception, to be client-centered is to be passive. Thus, when students come to see the counselor, they wait for permission to speak or, not knowing what they should do, remain silent. The counselor does not structure. As a result, no relationship is established, and the student leaves, does not return, and is not helped. And the blame is placed on "client-centered counseling." The counselor may conclude that client-centered counseling is not appropriate for students, abandon all its principles, and become directive in approach. But all that may be necessary is to give the student permission to speak and to define counseling as different from the classroom situation. Simply saying, "Can you tell me why you are here?" may be sufficient to enable the student to enter a relationship.

Where structuring is called for, it should be provided only to the extent necessary. It is undesirable and unnecessary for counselors to go into a long lecture on the nature of their approach—probably saying that they are not going to do much of the talking or to dominate the relationship, at the same time as they are doing exactly that! Structuring should be brief, given only to the extent necessary at the moment, and provided more explicitly later as needed. As the relationship gets started, the behavior of the therapist provides the necessary structure.'

To engage in structuring when it is not necessary, after clients have engaged in the appropriate behavior of talking about themselves, can disrupt the process, at least temporarily. The following dialogue illustrates this. The client had begun talking about himself, but at a pause, the counselor, a practicum student who had been taught in a prepracticum course to structure routinely, did so.

THERAPIST: You see, you have an hour, your appointment, and of course we can give you the tests, but, you know if you want to talk more, I'll be glad to listen, you know, so I can help you. So feel free, and relax . . . it's your time and just use it as you want to.
CLIENT: Well, I don't know what to say, exactly . . . ah . . . well . . . do you think it would help if I tell you a lot about my background and things like that?

One can easily imagine the thoughts of the client, who had been doing what he thought he was supposed to do but now must feel that what he was doing was not right. Rather than facilitating the process, structuring interfered with the client's progress in expressing himself spontaneously.

RESPONDING

The function of the therapist, at least in the beginning of therapy (and, essentially, throughout the process), is to respond to the client. Interviews in which the client is responding to the therapist are not therapy interviews but interrogations, usually. A simple rule for beginning students in counseling that avoids the development of a situation where the client is responding to the counselor is: Never ask a question—except when you don't understand what the client is saying. Again, this provides a very simple, objective criterion for the beginning student. It is very easy to determine from a tape recording who is responding to whom.

If the client is responding to the counselor, it is clearly the counselor's interview. The counselor is leading and guiding the talk of the client, usually along his or her own preconceived lines of what is important, relevant, or interesting. The counselor is placing his or her own structure and frame of reference on the client. The counselor is not likely to be able to enter the client's frame of reference and develop an empathic understanding of him or her.

A question that always arises in discussions of therapist listening and responding is what to do with a silent or inarticulate client. Can one listen to or respond to silence? To some extent one can. Sensitive therapists can sometimes feel or intuit what a client is thinking or can sometimes hazard a guess. They can then respond, perhaps in a tentative way. The client may display or communicate discomfort, uncertainty, hesitation, or confusion. The counselor may respond with "You don't know where to start" or "You find it hard to decide what to say first" or "You find it hard to talk" or "You don't know what you are supposed to do?" If clients are completely inarticulate, or say they are, the counselor is in a dilemma. Presumably the counselor wants the client to take responsibility for therapy and wants to avoid a relationship in which the client is responding. Even though clients are dependent at the beginning, the counselor presumably wants them to move toward independence and does not want to reinforce dependent behavior.

There is a possible way out of this dilemma. If it is necessary for counselors to initiate interaction, they can do so in a way that will ensure that *at least 50 percent of the time they will be responding to the client.* They can do this by simply responding to every response they elicit from the client, before going on, if necessary, with another initiating action. Fifty percent reinforcement is perhaps not too effective, but with most clients it will be greater than this, and the client is taught that the counselor responds to him or her. If counselors assume and continue the initiative, they are reinforcing the client in responding and make it difficult if not impossible for a therapy relationship to develop.

Another question is what to do when the client engages in irrelevant talk. Here we must first ask: What is irrelevant talk? How does the therapist know what is relevant or irrelevant? What are the criteria for irrelevance?

In one respect, everything the client says is relevant, in some way, to the counseling interaction. That is, there is a reason for everything he or she says. The counselor can never be sure that what the client is saying is irrelevant, from the client's point of view. Fromm-Reichmann refutes the claim that therapists who fall asleep during the therapy hour only fall asleep when the client is producing irrelevant material and wake up as soon as the client's talk becomes pertinent.[6] Some things, of course, are more relevant than others, and the counselor has some feeling for relative relevance. In fact, counselors are always acting upon, or responding on the basis of, their perceptions of what is relevant or most relevant.

There are several reasons why clients may engage in irrelevant talk. First, they may be encouraged to do so by the therapist's misconceived attempts to develop rapport. Second, they may not yet trust the therapist. Third, they may not be ready to move into emotionally significant or threatening material. Fourth, they may be "taking a rest" before attacking their problems again. In any case, for the therapist to charge the client with being irrelevant and to insist that he or she move into more relevant material does not help the situation; because it may be threatening, it leads to resistance and delays the client's return to relevant talk.

When the counselor does feel that the client is engaging in irrelevant talk, the counselor simply does not respond but remains quiet, ready to respond when the client moves into relevant material. The lack of response withholds encouragement. In effect, by not responding the counselor tends to extinguish the client's talk. This is an important point to recognize in relation to those who recommend that the counselor engage the client in "small talk" or social talk at the opening of the interview, particularly the first interview, supposedly to put the client at ease or to establish rapport. Such talk is a waste of time. If clients have come voluntarily, they do not come to discuss the weather or some other irrelevant material. And if clients have not come voluntarily, they know damn well they were not referred to discuss the weather. Counseling is not a social conversation, and for the counselor to begin it as such is misleading in terms of structuring and reinforces such an approach by the client. A study of therapeutic interviews found that the shift from conventional pleasantries to the work of therapy hindered the therapeutic process. The investigators concluded that "the absence of such pleasantries, with an immediate approach to the work of the interview, in itself seems to indicate a more conjunctive integration of therapist and patient."[7] The comments of Fromm-Reichmann are relevant here:

> I strongly advise against any attempt on the part of the psychiatrist to make things seemingly easier for the patient by pretending that the professional doctor-patient relationship is a social one. Deep down in his mind, no patient wants a nonprofessional relationship with his therapist, regardless of the fact that he may express himself to the contrary. . . . Moreover, the psychiatrist who enters into a social relationship with his patient may easily become sufficiently involved himself in the nonprofessional aspects of the relationship to be rendered incapable of keeping control over the professional aspect of the doctor-patient relationship.[8]

I have seen this happen with counseling students and their clients.

Counselors thus influence clients' verbalizations by their responsiveness or lack of responsiveness. Whatever they respond to is reinforced. The counselor selects from the client's productions those (or elements of those) he or she feels are most relevant and responds to them, ignoring others. One of the functions of the therapist's responses, then, is to influence the content and manner of the client's talk.

There is an aspect of the counseling process that fits in here, though it may be considered as a part of structuring. This is the tendency—nay, the need—of many counselors to make of counseling a logical problem-analysis and problem-solving process. This is an occupational handicap of therapists who have been trained in a program that emphasizes logic and research. Counselors working in college or university settings often seem to suffer from this problem-solving tendency.

But counseling or psychotherapy—as life—is a psychological, not a logical, process. To try to force clients to be logical is to lead them to intellectualize and to ignore their feelings—or to talk *about* their feelings rather than to express them. The counselor's insistence that the client talk about various aspects of his or her life, usually in an order determined by the counselor, is a manifestation of this tendency toward logical analysis. The chronological approach also imposes a structure on the client's thinking and talking.

Counseling or psychotherapy must take clients where they are and deal with their logic or apparent lack of logic. It must allow them to deal with their problems and their lives as they see them, in the order that is psychologically relevant to them.

TYPES OF RESPONSES

Another basic function of therapists' responses, at least in the early phases of therapy, is to communicate to the client their understanding of what the client is saying or trying to say. There are a number of ways in which counselors can respond to clients to communicate their understanding as well as their interest in and concern about what the client is saying.

Acceptance Responses

Acceptance responses tell clients that the therapist is there, listening, with them, following them. They are simple indications of understanding: "Uh huh," "Yes," "I see," "I understand," "I follow you." Silence may also convey acceptance.

Reflection Responses

Reflection responses go somewhat beyond simple acceptance responses. Reflection of content, or restating what the client is saying in different words, lets the client know that the therapist is hearing what he or she is saying and that the therapist understands the content, if not what is behind it. Reflections of feelings go beyond or behind the content. They are responses to the more obvious or clear feelings that the client has about the content. They let the client know that the counselor recognizes and is aware of what he or she is feeling. Simple acceptance and reflection of content responses need not represent empathic understanding. The therapist can emit such responses as a technique. They are easily faked. But reflection of feeling is more difficult to fake and requires some real, or empathic, understanding. Beginning students often find it difficult to respond to feelings rather than simply to content. I have sometimes suggested to students that they begin a response, to themselves if not overtly, with the words "You feel . . ." to help them focus on just what the client is feeling.

Clarification Responses

The client's verbalizations, especially when he or she is disturbed and feeling deeply, are not always clear and obvious. They may be confused, jumbled, hesitant, incomplete, disordered, or fragmentary. In clarification responses, the counselor attempts to put together what the client is saying or trying to say, to put into words vague ideas or feelings that are implicit if not explicit in the client's talking. What is confused to the client may not be clear to the therapist either, so that clarification responses are not easy to formulate, and the therapist often is not sure of their accuracy. This kind of response, therefore, is often tentative or phrased in the form of a question: "Are you saying . . . ?"; "I hear you saying. . . . Is that it?"; "You seem to be saying . . ."; or "You seem to be feeling. . . ."

Specific or Concrete Responses

The counselor attempts to make concrete and specific what may be general and abstract in the client's verbalizations. Concrete and specific responses help clients become more specific, help them move from vagueness to clarity and focus upon reality, upon the practical; thus they are helped to move from feeling to action.

Specificity, by avoiding abstractions and generalizations, helps clients analyze their problems in detail. Generalizations and abstractions give them the feeling that their problems are resolved because they can give them names and labels. Labeling has often been advocated to help the client discriminate and avoid overgeneralization. This may be true if the labeling is specific and discriminating in nature. But much labeling is general, often overgeneralized. It consists of assigning a specific problem to a higher category or concept.

The effect of such labeling or generalization on the client is to discourage further discussion or exploration of the problem.

In Chapter 5, an example of lack of concreteness was discussed. A male client talks about his early relationships with, and feelings about, his parents. The counselor, who has some familiarity with psychoanalytic theory, has an "insight"—the client has an Oedipus complex. He is unable to refrain from communicating this insight to the client, so he tells the client: "You seem to have an Oedipus complex." The client, who also has some familiarity with psychoanalytic theory, agrees: "You're right. I guess I do have an Oedipus complex." Then he discontinues his discussion of his relationship with his parents. What point is there in continuing? The problem is solved—it has been labeled. Thus, generalization discourages further client activity in analyzing problems.

Silence

Silence on the part of the therapist has varying effects, depending upon how it is perceived by the client. To vocal clients, silence on the part of the therapist may be welcome—as long as they know the counselor is listening. But silence can be ambiguous. Silence on the part of the psychoanalyst is probably one of the bases for transference, encouraging the client to project onto the therapist. Therapists are sometimes warned about the dangers of catharsis in the beginning of therapy. While I have never observed the dire results that are sometimes predicted, it is possible that clients who do not return after a first interview in which they have disclosed themselves with little if any response from the therapist may fail to return because of uncertainty about whether the therapist really was listening, was interested, or understood them. Fear that the therapist did not understand or accept them, because of their exposure of undesirable thoughts or behavior, may lead them not to return. Therefore, it is desirable that the therapist respond to let clients know they are heard, understood, and accepted, even if this means breaking in occasionally.

When clients pause in their talk, they usually (though not always) expect and desire a response from the therapist. Not to receive a response may be perceived by clients as rejection. Or, it may be seen as an indication that they were not talking about what they should be talking about. Silence on the part of the counselor, it will be recalled, is a method of extinguishing irrelevant talk. But it can also extinguish talking in general by the client. Responsiveness on the part of the therapist facilitates deeper exploration on the part of the client, avoiding a one-way recital.

Thus, therapist silence has different effects, and the therapist must be aware of the possible effects and allow or break silence depending upon his or her sensitivity to how the client perceives the silence. Therapy can occur during long silences. But long silences in the first interview should usually be avoided.

Interpretation Responses

Clarification responses deal with what is explicitly or implicitly in the client's behavior, verbal and/or nonverbal. Interpretations go beyond this, involving a contribution by the therapist. In interpretation, the therapist adds to what the client is saying, going beyond the client's verbalizations and putting in something of his or her own.

The line between clarification and interpretation is a fine one. They would appear to be on a continuum. There will often be disagreement on whether a therapist's response is a clarification or an interpretation. Whether it is classified as one or the other will depend, in part, on the sensitivity of the observer. What is clarification to a highly sensitive observer (or therapist) may appear to be interpretation to one who is less sensitive to what is implicit in what the client is saying. The highest level of empathy (level 5) may appear to be interpretation. Carkhuff talks about the "additive" element of the counselor beyond level 3. Carkhuff and Berenson state that the therapist who is functioning at level 3

> does not provide the level of empathic communication in which one person anticipates another. He does not facilitate the client's movement to a deeper level except insofar as he has understood the previous level. . . . In order for the therapy process to move effectively, the therapist must add something to the client's responses, and we might add, something which the client at his present level of development can use constructively. This brings us into the area of what we term depth reflections or moderate interpretations all of which, if accurate, enable the client to go a level deeper in his explorations.[9]

Yet a reading of the definition of level 5 makes it clear that the therapist is responding to what he or she senses is there, behind or below the words of the client. Rogers writes: "When the client's world is clear to the counselor and he can move about in it freely, then he can communicate his understanding of what is vaguely known to the client and he can also voice meanings in the client's experience of which the client is scarcely aware."[10] Martin states: "The therapist's task is to hear *what is implicit in the client's current experiencing*—what the client is trying to say and can't quite say."[11]

The counselor who thoroughly enters into the client's frame of reference, who perceives as the client does, can often speak *for* the client when the client is not able to speak adequately for himself or herself. "The whole therapist can see the world through the eyes of his client, *sometimes better than the client who is functioning at low levels. . . .*"[12] But it is important to emphasize that the counselor is operating *in the client's frame of reference.* It would perhaps be as well to make the distinction between reflective and empathic responses on the one hand, and interpretive responses on the other, on this basis. Interpretation is based on the counselor's frame of reference, or an external frame of reference. The counselor views the client from the outside and attempts to fit him or her into a system, theory, or structure. In addition to the classification—or neglecting the uniqueness of the client—and generalization, or higher-order labeling, that may be involved, interpretative responses depart from the client's frame of reference and are thus less meaningful and helpful to the client.

A reading of the literature on so-called interpretative psychotherapies, including psychoanalysis, makes it clear that in most cases interpretation is actually clarification. It is one of the misconceptions of psychoanalysis that the analyst interprets from the beginning of therapy. Orthodox analysts usually don't venture what they call interpretation until well along in therapy—often only after months of listening to the client—and then their interpretations are tentative. In fact, such interpretations are usually clarifications. Interpretations that go beyond clarification are called "wild interpretations." Yet students who want to become psychoanalytically oriented counselors can hardly wait to interpret, often beginning early in the first interview, before they can possibly have any real understanding of the client. If an interpretive therapy is to be used, it is necessary for the therapist to thoroughly understand the client first.

E. H. Porter makes an interesting distinction between reflection and interpretation.

> The difference is not in what the therapist says. The difference is in the therapist's *purpose* when he says it. . . . When the therapist utters some words which are a construing of what the client or patient has expressed and it is the therapist's purpose to be asking of the client or patient whether or not the construction put on the client's expression was the meaning intended—that's a reflection.
>
> When the therapist utters some words which are a construing of what the client or patient has expressed and it is the therapist's purpose to be informing the patient what meaning his expression holds regardless of his, the patient's, intended meaning—that's an interpretation.[13]

Interpretations—that is, responses that go beyond what is explicit or implicit in the client's behavior—retard therapy rather than facilitate it. Interpretations are threatening and often lead to resistance. They give clients the impression that the therapist knows more about them than they do about themselves and thus lead to less client talk and self-analysis. And interpretations that are abstractions or generalizations, as suggested in the discussion of specificity, lead to the inhibition of client activity and exploration.

Questioning

Little has been said so far about questioning as a technique (except in regard to the silent client), although textbooks on counseling and psychotherapy often give extensive space to the discussion of this topic. The reason is simple—questioning by the therapist has little place in counseling or psychotherapy. The topic would be omitted here except that counseling students must be explicitly warned against the use of questioning because so many of them fall into the trap of engaging in question and answer sessions with their clients. I have heard tapes of students nearing the end of an intensive practicum that are nothing but question and answer sessions. Interviews in which the client does little but respond to questions by the therapist are not therapy interviews. They are more like interrogations. Counseling should not be modeled after Sgt. Friday or Perry Mason interviews.

There are a number of reasons for avoiding questioning in therapy interviews.

1. Questions in therapy interviews can be threatening to the client, who may not be ready for the self-disclosure they demand.

2. The client may not know the answers to the questions, particularly early in the therapy process, when the questions may involve dynamics of which the client is not aware.

3. Questioning sets the stage for client dependency. Questioning places the initiative and the responsibility with the therapist. The message to the client is: "If you will only answer these questions, I will know what your problem is and will be able to give you the solution." The result is that the client does not take responsibility for the process and is discouraged from taking the initiative and prevented from engaging in the process of self-exploration.

4. Questioning frames the therapy as an externally oriented process, rather than one in which the therapist is attempting to assume the internal frame of reference of the client in the process of empathic understanding.

5. Questions raise the level of discussion from the affective to the cognitive. A favorite question of therapists, encouraged by many writers and instructors, is of the kind: "How did you feel?" or "How did that make you feel?" Answers to such questions are not

expressions of feelings, but expressions of how the client *thinks* he/she felt; that is, the response is a cognitive one.

Anything of significance for therapy can be achieved by the therapist without the use of direct or probing questions. The therapist must have the patience to wait for clients to disclose relevant material at their own time and pace. Therapist responses involving clarification of client statements may be framed in the form of questions when the therapist is not sure that he or she understands what the client is saying. Such questions as "Is this what you are saying . . . ?" or "Are you saying . . . ?" are of course appropriate. They leave the initiative with the client and avoid the problems of direct, probing questions.

Ornston and his associates found that beginning therapists ask more questions than experienced therapists.[14] Friel, Berenson, and Mitchell in a study of high-functioning and low-functioning counselors found one major factor for the low-functioning group. Carkhuff refers to it as the "stupid question" factor.[15]

It is relatively easy to get counseling students to avoid this nontherapeutic activity by simply instructing them not to ask questions. My statement to beginning practicum students includes three simple rules: (1) Keep your mouth shut—you can't listen to the client when you are talking; (2) Never ask a question, except when you do not understand what the client is saying, or when you have a silent client; and (3) Respond to the client—don't have the client responding to you.

TWO PROCESSES OR ONE?

As I mentioned in Chapter 5, Carkhuff and Berenson have suggested that there are two distinct phases of counseling, different enough to be considered as two separate processes. The first is characterized by such terms as facilitative, understanding, passive, nondirective, and responding, while the second is characterized by such terms as action, active, directive, assertive, and initiating.

In the first phase, characterized by Carkhuff and Berenson as the downward and inward phase, the counselor is relatively passive, concentrating on gaining an understanding of the client and assisting the client to gain an understanding of himself or herself, or to achieve insight. In this phase, the therapist conditions of empathic understanding, respect or warmth, concreteness, and genuineness are most important. The emphasis is on the minimal condition level (level 3 on the 5-point scales). Empathic understanding does not move greatly beyond the client's clear or obvious communication.

Respect is unconditional. The emphasis in genuineness is on not being phony or inauthentic, rather than on the therapist's openness or expressiveness. Concreteness is directed toward helping the client become more specific in his or her communications. But the achievement of insight by the client is not enough; Carkhuff and Berenson criticize traditional therapies because they do not go beyond insight. They say that "most therapists conclude therapy where we conclude the first phase."[16]

The second phase, the upward and outward phase, or "the period of emergent directionality,"[17] moves from the facilitative conditions to the action conditions. Genuineness continues, but as an open sharing. Therapist self-disclosure enters into the relationship, though it diminishes as the process proceeds. The therapist "actively interprets with immediacy his experience of the helpee's motives and attitudes toward the helper that present obstacles to progress, both in terms of internal understanding and external action" (levels 4 and 5 on the immediacy scale).[18] Confrontation is used to present the client with discrepancies and inconsistencies in his or her behavior. Concreteness is directed toward specific alternatives in problem solution and action. Empathy must still be present but is now subordinated to the action dimensions, serving to keep the therapist's understanding current. The therapist acts upon the understanding achieved in the first phase to encourage and guide or direct the client toward action. Respect, or unconditional positive regard, becomes conditional.

Carkhuff and Berenson recognize that there can be no sharply divided phases. There is no specific point at which the therapist moves from one phase to another. The facilitative conditions continue throughout the second, or action, phase. In some cases the action conditions may precede the facilitative conditions: "Frequently, . . . it is necessary for the person to act in the absence of understanding. . . . the helper directs the activities of those who cannot initiate either meaningful communication or action on their own."[19] However, these instances involve clients—or individuals—at such a low level of functioning that they are unable to enter a relationship, and the helping process would not be called psychotherapy.

While it may be useful to think in terms of stages or phases in the total therapeutic process, there is a danger that the phases or stages will be considered as separate and discrete steps, particularly by counseling students and beginning counselors. It is probably better to think in terms of a single, but developing, process. In the case of the phases described by Carkhuff and Berenson, it would appear that they reflect a single continuing, developing process, or a growing, deepening relationship between the therapist and the client. The process is a natural development of an interpersonal relationship. In beginning such a relationship, it is natural and necessary that the therapist, or helper, be more responsive—listening, following the client, providing a warm atmosphere—in order to get to know and understand the client. As the relationship develops and the therapist increases his or her understanding, he or she can respond at higher levels of empathy—levels that may appear to be more active, even interpretative. With this increased understanding, the therapist can respond to the client's behavior in the interview in the ways that are encompassed under the concept of immediacy. The therapist's greater understanding also enables him or her to make statements or responses that we define as confrontations. The therapist also becomes more relaxed, at ease, and spontaneous, so that he or she becomes more open, honest, and genuine, engaging in higher-level therapeutic genuineness and self-disclosure. Carkhuff himself notes that "the dimension of self-disclosure is one facet of genuineness. . . ."[20]

In fact, then, it appears that the action conditions are essentially high levels of the facilitative or understanding conditions. The difference is perhaps one of degree or depth of response, of specificity, clarity, certainty, strength, and openness of the therapist's responses.

A second question can be raised regarding the two phases described by Carkhuff and Berenson. Their second, or action phase, seems to be based on the assumption that the client, under the influence of the facilitative relationship and on the basis of self-understanding and insight, is unable to determine and undertake appropriate action on his or her own—rather, he or she must be directed or guided by the therapist. Yet clients of traditional, or client-centered, therapists have made decisions and engaged in actions without such direction and guidance, under the influence of only (although at high levels) the facilitative conditions. Perhaps the assumption that clients on their own can move into action needs to be tested, with each client, before the therapist enters with direction and guidance. No client should be deprived of the satisfaction of acting on his or her own if he or she is capable, even if it may take longer. The reluctance to wait for clients, or the abandonment of the assumption that they can do it on their own, may be an indication of lack of patience on the part of the therapist or lack of confidence in clients rather than inability of clients to move into action on their own.

If the development of autonomy or independence is one of the goals of psychotherapy, then active direction or guidance by the therapist is inconsistent with this goal. Every effort should be made to allow clients to initiate their own actions. To the extent that they do so they become independent; moreover, the satisfaction involved in doing it themselves reinforces independence and thus increases the probability of continuing independence.

Carkhuff recognizes that some clients are able to act upon their discriminations and insights. These are apparently clients functioning at level 3. The level 3 client is a client who, though distressed, is functioning at a minimally effective level. Carkhuff and Berenson state that

> The level 3 client, having established that the counselor is functioning at minimally facilitative levels, continues with his self-exploration and problem expression independent of the counselor. . . . Once the high-level functioning client is aware that his counselor is functioning at high levels and is genuinely sensitive and respectful, the client can continue on his own independently, whether or not the counselor continues to function at high levels.[21]

And again, they suggest that during the second phase the therapist must be guided by the client; "Indeed he may discern the client's readiness and ability to determine his own direction."[22] Perhaps more clients would be able to act upon their discriminations and insights if permitted to do so by a patient, discerning therapist who had confidence in the client's ability. Carkhuff's statement is important here: "The helper does not commit too much of himself in the interest of offering the helpee as much opportunity as possible to develop himself as fully as possible."[23]

SUMMARY

In this chapter we considered how the therapist implements the facilitative conditions and the initiative or action conditions in the therapy process. The responsibility of the therapist for providing at least minimal conditions was emphasized, since counseling or psychotherapy can be for better or worse, depending on whether the counselor provides high or low levels of the conditions.

Although, for purposes of discussion, the conditions were divided into two phases, the usefulness, or the existence, of such a division was questioned. It is probably better to think in terms of a single process, which develops as the relationship between the therapist and the client grows and becomes more intimate and intense. Thus, the therapist, as he or she comes to know and deeply understand the client, becomes more involved and more active in the sense that he or she is more genuine and spontaneous and responds more in the way indicated by the so-called action conditions of self-disclosure, immediacy, and confrontation. It was suggested that these conditions are essentially high levels of the so-called facilitative or understanding conditions; and that the therapist should act on the assumption that most clients, under these high-level conditions, can and will make their own choices and decisions and translate their self-understanding and insights into action without specific direction or guidance by the therapist.

While this chapter may have appeared to emphasize technique, we are concerned not with the impersonal application of techniques as a means of manipulating the client's behavior. We are concerned with the implementation of the basic attitudes or conditions of psychotherapy. Therapy is more dependent on who the therapist *is* than on what he or she *does*. Counselors must be more concerned about *being someone* with their clients than in *doing something to them*. Methods or techniques cannot be separated from their user or the user's personality. And users cannot be separated from their theories, beliefs, and values and attitudes. Relationship therapy is, as Burton notes of existential therapy, the technique of no technique.[24] It is the therapist's attitudes "rather than the therapist's technical knowledge and skill, which are primarily responsible for therapeutic change."[25]

NOTES

1. F. Wyatt. The self-experience of the psychotherapist. *Journal of Consulting Psychology*, 1948, *12*, 83–87.
2. H. J. Eysenck. The effects of psychotherapy: An evaluation. *Journal of Consulting Psychology*, 1952, *16*, 319–334; E. E. Levitt. The results of psychotherapy with children. *Journal of Consulting Psychology*, 1957, *21*, 189–196.
3. C. B. Truax and R. R. Carkhuff. For better or for worse: The process of psychotherapeutic personality change. In Academic Assembly on Clinical Psychology (Ed.), *Recent advances in the study of behaviour change*. Montreal: McGill University, 1963, Chap. 8. See also A. E. Bergin. The effects of psychotherapy: Negative results revisited. *Journal of Counseling Psychology*, 1963, *10*, 244–250; A. E. Bergin. Some implications of psychotherapy research for therapeutic practice. *Journal of Abnormal and Social Psychology*, 1966, *71*, 235–246; A. E. Bergin. An empirical analysis of therapeutic issues. In D. Arbuckle (Ed.), *Counseling and psychotherapy: An overview*. New York: McGraw-Hill, 1967, pp. 175–208; A. E. Bergin. Further comments on psychotherapy research and therapeutic practice. *International Journal of Psychiatry*, 1967, *3*, 317–323; A. E. Bergin. The evaluation of therapeutic outcomes. In A. E. Bergin and S. L. Garfield (Eds.), *Handbook of psychotherapy and behavior change: An empirical analysis*. New York: Wiley, 1971, pp. 217–270; H. H. Strupp, S. W. Hadley, and B. Gomes-Schwartz. *Psychotherapy for better or worse: The problem of negative effects*. New York: Aronson, 1977; M. J. Lambert, A. E. Bergin, and J. L. Collins. Therapist induced deterioration in psychotherapy. In A. S. Gurman and A. M. Razin (Eds.), *Effective psychotherapy: A handbook of research*. New York: Pergamon Press, 1977, pp. 452–481.

4. R. R. Carkhuff and B. G. Berenson. *Beyond counseling and psychotherapy.* New York: Holt, Rinehart & Winston, 1967, Chap. 1.

5. F. Fromm-Reichmann. *Principles of intensive psychotherapy.* Chicago: University of Chicago Press, 1950, p. 7.

6. *Ibid.,* p. 10. She is apparently referring to Ferenczi's statement: "The danger of the doctor's falling asleep . . . need not be regarded as grave because we awake at the first occurrence of any importance for the treatment." (S. Ferenczi. Missbrauch der Assoziansfreiheit. In *Bausteine zur Psychoanalysis,* II. Vienna: International Psychoanalysis, Verlag, 1927, p. 41. Quoted by H. Racker. The meaning and uses of countertransference. *Psychoanalysis,* 1957, *26,* 303–357.)

7. S. H. Eldred et al. A procedure for the systematic analysis of psychotherapeutic interviews. *Psychiatry,* 1954, *17,* 337–346.

8. Fromm-Reichmann, *Principles,* p. 46.

9. Carkhuff and Berenson, *Beyond counseling,* p. 136.

10. C. R. Rogers. The interpersonal relationship: The core of guidance. *Harvard Educational Review,* 1962, *32,* 416–429.

11. D. G. Martin. *Learning-based client-centered therapy.* Monterey, CA: Brooks/Cole, 1972, p. 81.

12. Carkhuff and Berenson, *Beyond counseling,* p. 184.

13. E. H. Porter. In S. W. Standal and R. J. Corsini (Eds.), *Critical incidents in psychotherapy.* Englewood Cliffs, NJ: Prentice-Hall, 1959, p. 57. Carl Rogers, independently commenting on the same incident, suggests that what was labeled an interpretation by the therapist was actually not an interpretation since its intent was to be empathic (p. 58).

14. P. S. Ornston, D. V. Cuchetti, J. Levine, and L. B. Fierman. Some parameters of verbal behavior that reliably differentiate novice from experienced psychotherapists. *Journal of Abnormal Psychology,* 1968, *73,* 240–244.

15. T. Friel, B. G. Berenson, and K. M. Mitchell. Factor analysis of therapeutic conditions for high- and low-functioning therapists. *Journal of Clinical Psychology,* 1971, *27,* 291–293. R. R. Carkhuff. *Helping and human relations.* Vol. II, *Practice and research.* New York: Holt, Rinehart & Winston, 1969, Vol. II, p. 32.

16. Carkhuff and Berenson, *Beyond counseling,* p. 135.

17. *Ibid.,* p. 141.

18. Carkhuff, *Helping,* Vol. II, p. 99.

19. *Ibid.,* pp. 37, 44.

20. *Ibid.,* Vol. I, p. 208.

21. Carkhuff and Berenson, *Beyond counseling,* pp. 57, 138.

22. *Ibid.,* p. 142.

23. Carkhuff, *Helping,* Vol. II, p. 97.

24. A. Burton. *Modern humanistic psychotherapy.* San Francisco: Jossey-Bass, 1967, p. 6.

25. C. R. Rogers. *On becoming a person.* Boston: Houghton Mifflin, 1961, p. 63.

CHAPTER 7

The Client
in the Process

In Chapter 6 we considered the counselor's or therapist's contribution to the therapy process. Therapy is a relationship that involves the client. The client is not, and cannot be, a passive recipient. Change in attitudes and behavior—or learning—requires some activity on the part of the person who is being changed—the learner. In this chapter we consider the process from the standpoint of clients—the nature of their involvement or participation in the process. First, however, it is necessary to view clients as they present themselves for help.

CLIENT CHARACTERISTICS

There has been considerable discussion about whether it is necessary that clients come voluntarily to counseling or psychotherapy to be helped. There has been some confusion regarding the use of the words *voluntary* and *involuntary*. There is general agreement that psychotherapy is not, and cannot be, imposed upon an unwilling client. Counseling or psychotherapy is concerned with voluntary change in the client. Of course it is possible to change a person's behavior without his or her consent or voluntary involvement. This can be achieved through the use of drugs and psychosurgery, through coercion or threats or through physical force, and to some extent through conditioning. But these methods of change are not counseling or psychotherapy.

People may be compelled to submit themselves to an exposure to the counselor or therapist, but they cannot be forced to become involved in the therapy relationship. Many counselors or psychotherapists will accept persons who are referred to them but who are unwilling to come, as in the case of a person required to "have psychotherapy" by the courts. These referrals sometimes become clients through voluntarily entering into a therapy relationship when it is offered by the therapist. They are not, then, involuntary clients.

Thus, one of the requirements of therapy is that clients voluntarily enter a relationship that they expect will lead to some kind of change in themselves. They want to change, expect to change, and believe that the therapist and the therapy relationship will effect that change.

Why do people want to change, and seek psychotherapy? Such people are often labeled mentally ill, neurotic, or emotionally disturbed. But these labels tell us little, even though clients may accept them as applying to themselves. From their own point of view, however, clients present themselves for psychotherapy because they "hurt" or suffer in some way, to a greater or lesser degree. They are unhappy, discouraged, depressed, anxious, dissatisfied. They have feelings of inadequacy and of failure, they have unfulfilled desires and aspirations, their lives lack meaning, goals, or a sense of direction. They want to be different, and they realize that they are not what they want to be or what they can be. They recognize the discrepancy between what they could be and what they are, a discrepancy between their self-concept and their ideal self-concept. In short, whether they think of it in these terms or not, *they are not self-actualizing persons* or not as highly self-actualizing as they want to be or could be. The drive for self-actualization is frustrated or not satisfied, and this motivates them to want to change.

Not all persons who are not self-actualizing can benefit from psychotherapy or are open to the possibility of benefiting from psychotherapy. Some persons are functioning at such a low level that they are no longer open to the establishment of the interpersonal relationship of psychotherapy. This is the case with many of the regressed patients in mental hospitals. Perhaps they are "unmotivated"; that is, they have given up hope. They may have been hurt so much that the drive for self-actualization has been repressed or even killed; all that is left is the minimal drive for physical self-preservation. Sometimes even that is lost in patients who refuse to eat. These persons are inaccessible to psychotherapy and other methods are used to try to help them, including shock treatment, which for unknown reasons sometimes makes them accessible to interpersonal relationships, including psychotherapy. Behavior modification techniques may also reach these otherwise unreachable patients. Persistent offering of a human or therapeutic relationship also may succeed with some of them.[1] Perhaps anything that succeeds in getting such patients to realize or recognize that someone is genuinely and sincerely concerned about them, interested in them, and desperately wants to help them, can be successful in arousing them from their regression. This may be the explanation for the success of any new and different treatment applied with enthusiasm and hope by a committed hospital staff.

The importance of the perception by the client of the interest and concern of the therapist must be recognized in relation to the conditions offered by the therapist. *The offering or providing of the conditions by the therapist is not sufficient; they must be recognized or perceived by the client.* Rogers, in his necessary and sufficient conditions for therapeutic personality change, includes the condition that "the communication to the client of the therapist's empathic understanding and unconditional positive regard is to a minimal degree achieved."[2]

There is another characteristic necessary for initiation of therapy. Clients must be able, in some way and at least to some degree, to communicate their feelings, attitudes, and experiences to the therapist. The most empathic therapist cannot understand clients or enter their frame of reference unless clients let him or her in and in some way communicate how they see themselves and the world. The most common and the most effective way is, of course, through verbalization. The therapist's listening is ineffective unless the client talks. There are other ways of communicating in addition to verbalization, and the therapist must be sensitive to these; for example, sometimes the client's writing or such other expressive activities as art may communicate.[3] These, while helpful in addition to verbalization, are usually not adequate by themselves.

Thus, clients present themselves to the counselor or psychotherapist as persons who are motivated to change, at least to the extent that they are ready to commit time and, often, money to achieve this change. Clients have faith and confidence in the therapist and his or her methods, so that they trust themselves to the relationship. And they are able to perceive, at least to a minimal degree, the therapist's respect, interest, concern, and understanding. These are the conditions in the client that make possible the beginning of therapy. While it would appear that some motivation to seek help is a necessary condition for psychotherapy, belief in the therapist and his or her methods, while desirable, may not be necessary. That this is so is suggested by the fact that some people get help and improve their relationships when working with nonprofessional "therapists" where no strong belief or faith is present (so-called "spontaneous" remission—see Chapter 8).

STRUCTURING THE CLIENT'S WORK

Clients present themselves to the therapist with some uncertainty, doubts, hesitations, anxiety, and even fear connected with the therapy situation and the therapist. They may not know what to expect, or may have misconceptions about the process, about what the therapist will do, and about what they are expected to do. Where this is the case, the therapist clarifies the situation by structuring.

Part of the structuring consists of explaining to clients the nature of the clients' work, which is essentially to talk about themselves, their feelings, attitudes, and experiences. Even though clients recognize and accept this task, it is often not easy for them to do it. They may begin in a perfunctory way, or may only be able to give a general, superficial statement of their problems and then wait, depending upon the therapist for help. The prospect of revealing oneself openly to another is threatening. They may not yet trust the therapist, or may see the therapist as a cold surgeon who is going to open them up without concern for how much it will hurt.

If clients are to engage in their work, they must not feel threatened. The facilitative conditions provided by the therapist minimize threat. Love—real love—is challenging but not threatening. Learning, it is recognized, does not occur under conditions of threat. Behavior becomes restricted and narrowed rather than variable and exploratory, as is necessary for problem-solving. It is important that the therapist communicate these conditions, and that the client perceive them. It is only when the client feels accepted, respected, understood, safe, and secure with the therapist that he or she can begin to make progress. With an anxious, fearful, threatened, and hesitant client, it is difficult to communicate the conditions and to establish a nonthreatening atmosphere. Prolonged silence on the part of the therapist can be highly threatening. On the other hand, profuse verbalization and reassurance can be inhibiting to the client. The process may be slow in beginning. The therapist must have patience and not impose himself too forcefully upon the client. The therapy relationship, like any other human relationship, takes time to develop. There is and can be no such thing as instant intimacy.

CLIENT SELF-EXPLORATION

There have been many discussions of the counseling process in terms of client involvement. But it appears that the basic activity of the client is to engage in a process of self-exploration or intrapersonal exploration. In every approach to psychotherapy, clients talk about themselves, about their beliefs, attitudes, feelings, experiences, thoughts, and actions. Considerable research supports the existence of a relationship between client self-exploration and successful therapy or favorable outcomes.[4] There is also considerable research indicating that the level of client self-exploration is related to and influenced by the level of facilitative conditions provided by the therapist (see Chapter 13). However, there are differences among clients in their levels of self-exploration that are not related to therapist levels of the conditions.[5]

The process of self-exploration is a complex one, involving several aspects or (perhaps) stages. Self-disclosure is the first stage.

Self-Disclosure

Before clients can explore themselves, they must disclose or reveal themselves. In the beginning of counseling, this is most often the disclosure of negative aspects of themselves—problems, failures, inadequacies, and so on. Since these constitute the bases of clients' dissatisfaction and unhappiness, they are the reasons clients have sought counseling. But since they are negative—indicating a low or negative self-concept—they are difficult to express. Self-disclosure at this level represents self-exposure.

The question often arises among students about the desirability of accepting, or listening with acceptance to, extensive disclosures of negative feelings and emotions, self-negation and self-criticism, the expression of feelings of worthlessness, discouragement, depression—even suicide. Isn't this likely to reinforce these feelings and make the client worse? Shouldn't the counselor reassure clients that things aren't as bad as they think they are, that clients aren't as bad as they think they are?

The therapist must remember that clients come just because they have problems, negative feelings, and a negative self-concept. Their low opinions of themselves are not (usually) simply a misperception or unrealistic—there is some basis in reality. They are failing to be their best selves, to be self-actualizing persons. To deny this or feelings that this is the case (even when it is not so bad as clients feel it is) is not to help clients but to prevent them from going on to a recognition of the positive aspects of themselves and their situations. The process of reaching the positive cannot be short-circuited. If clients are to reach a positive self-concept, they must be allowed to express negative feelings. And the counselor must be willing and able to go with them to the depths and face the worst with them; the counselor must not allow his or her own anxiety, fears, and discomfort to prevent this descent. It is only when they have plumbed the depths and seen themselves at their worst, that clients can rise again and, knowing the worst, build a new and positive self.

The assumption is that there is some good in every client, something positive in every situation, but that clients can only recognize this if they are allowed to express the worst:

CLIENT: Things look pretty discouraging.
THERAPIST: It's pretty grim.
CLIENT: It's worse than that—it's hopeless.
THERAPIST: There's just *no* hope.
CLIENT: No—none at all. There's no way out.
THERAPIST: It's the end—a dead end—completely black, without a ray of light or hope.
CLIENT: (Pause) Well—maybe not completely. I'm not ready to give up completely yet.

If a client can see no hope and does give up, it is possible that he or she is right—that it is the end. And reassurance by or optimism on the part of the counselor isn't likely to help.

Clients who are able to disclose themselves are already at stage 4 of Rogers's Scale of Process in Psychotherapy, an elaborate scale Rogers developed to cover the whole course of therapy. Rogers gives this example of a client at stage 4: "I'm not living up to what I am. I really should be doing more than I am. . . ."[6] Rogers notes that successful cases begin at a higher level on the process scale than do unsuccessful cases. At stage 4, the client has perceived that the therapist understands him or her and is able to engage in self-disclosure. It is the difficulty of reaching this level with seriously disturbed clients that is responsible for many drop-outs from therapy and thus the failures with the more severely disturbed.

Rates of Self-Exploration

Once clients have disclosed themselves, or have put themselves out and on view to themselves and the therapist, they are able to look at themselves and to engage in the process of exploring what and who they are. Clients are then "free to explore, experience, and experiment with" themselves.[7] They can *be themselves* in a way they can't in ordinary interpersonal relationships; they can be open, real, and honest with themselves as well as with the therapist. They are able to face themselves as they are.

The process of self-exploration does not proceed simultaneously and at equivalent levels in all areas of the client's life, with all problems, or in all aspects of his or her difficulties. Progress may occur to some extent in one area and then be blocked or slow down. The client shifts to another area only to reach a level beyond which he or she is not ready or able to go. This may repeat itself in still other areas. Eventually the client returns to the first area and to each of the other areas, to progress further. Exploration in each area makes it possible to explore the other areas more deeply. It is not useful or possible to insist that the client stick to one area or problem until it is thoroughly explored before moving on to another. The total process is not a logical one, but a psychological process in which the areas or problems are interrelated and cannot be explored completely as independent problems.

Clients begin where they are able to and usually in areas where they are most conscious of a problem. They move to other relevant areas and problems when they are ready and able to do so in the nonthreatening relationship. To attempt to push clients or to direct them toward other areas the therapist considers important is to introduce threat and to risk retarding rather than facilitating clients' self-exploration. Attempting to introduce the action conditions (confronting, particularly) as the client is beginning the exploration of new areas or problems can be inhibiting because it is threatening. Even moving to high levels of the facilitative conditions

> may have harmful effects at this stage of helping. The minimally facilitative conditions enable the helpee to know that someone can understand him on his terms in addition to providing him with the feedback necessary for later reformulations. The minimally facilitative conditions are sufficient in and of themselves to elicit a depth of self-exploration in all relevant areas.[8]

Measuring Depth of Self-Exploration

In 1963, Truax developed a nine-point Depth of Self-Exploration Scale.[9] Carkhuff revised this into a five-level scale for measuring client self-exploration in interpersonal processes.[10] Carkhuff's scale is as follows.

Level 1

> The second person does not discuss personally relevant material, either because he has had no opportunity to do such or because he is actively evading the discussion even when it is introduced by the first person.
>
> EXAMPLE: The second person avoids any self-descriptions or self-exploration or direct expression of feelings that would lead him to reveal himself to the first person.
>
> In summary, for a variety of possible reasons the second person does not give any evidence of self-exploration.

Level 2

The second person responds with discussion to the introduction of personally relevant material by the first person but does so in a mechanical manner and without the demonstration of emotional feelings.

EXAMPLE: The second person simply discusses the material without exploring the significance or the meaning of the material or attempting further exploration of that feeling in an effort to uncover related feelings or material.

In summary, the second person responds mechanically and remotely to the introduction of personally relevant material by the first person.

Level 3

The second person voluntarily introduces discussions of personally relevant material but does so in a mechanical manner and without the demonstration of emotional feeling.

EXAMPLE: The emotional remoteness and mechanical manner of the discussion give the discussion a quality of being rehearsed.

In summary, the second person introduces personally relevant material but does so without spontaneity or emotional proximity and without an inward probing to discover new feelings and experiences.

Level 4

The second person voluntarily introduces discussions of personally relevant material with both spontaneity and emotional proximity.

EXAMPLE: The voice quality and other characteristics of the second person are very much "with" the feelings and other personal materials that are being verbalized.

In summary, the second person introduces personally relevant discussions with spontaneity and emotional proximity but without a distinct tendency toward inward probing to discover new feelings and experiences.

Level 5

The second person actively and spontaneously engages in an inward probing to discover new feelings and experiences about himself and his world.

EXAMPLE: The second person is searching to discover new feelings concerning himself and his world even though at the moment he may perhaps be doing so fearfully and tentatively.

In summary, the second person is fully and actively focusing upon himself and exploring himself and his world.

Level 1 (which corresponds to points 0 and 1 on the Truax scale) is illustrated by the following dialogue:

THERAPIST: As though you're just feeling kind of down about these things . . .

CLIENT: Tired.
THERAPIST: What?
CLIENT: Tired.
THERAPIST: Tired . . . kind of worn out?
CLIENT: Couldn't sleep last night. (Pause)
THERAPIST: You're just feeling kind of worn out.
  (Client does not respond—silence to end of tape.) [11]

An example of the highest level is the following dialogue:

CLIENT: (She is relating experiences in Germany during World War II) I don't want to exaggerate but, why, you could have killed for some things! And the pendulum was always swinging. You never knew. You'd steal carrots to eat because you were always so dreadfully hungry. There was no clothing, no fuel . . . and the cold. . . . (Voice soft, reflects a great deal of concentration) They had . . . they always announced the dead, those who had been killed in the war. And one always went and read the lists. I don't recall exactly where they were. . . . (Pause) It was conducive to think that life was . . .
THERAPIST: Unendurable, and getting used to the, that way of living.
CLIENT: Yes, yes, uh hum, I had no . . . I was not . . . I have a very close girlfriend who shared my things, but I was not kind and tender with my brothers. I remember one thing that really shames me still. I was to watch out for them, and my younger brother fell and bruised his head one day, and I just pulled his cap over that. Really, really, but . . . but my excuse I think I can say was that nobody ever treated me lovingly. At least I think that.
THERAPIST: It was a hard life and you have to be hard. This is what you knew.
CLIENT: I think I was harder than I really had to be but I was just, ah, hard . . .
THERAPIST: Because you hadn't been taught to be soft and loving.
CLIENT: Yes, ah, yes. I don't know whether you teach somebody to be, to be . . . do you?
THERAPIST: Well, you haven't experienced it?
CLIENT: I feel that way now, toward my family, my husband, and children . . . I can . . . love them. [12]

CLIENT AWARENESS OF THE BASIC SELF

The process of self-exploration leads to self-discovery, self-understanding, and self-awareness, among other things. This is more than what is commonly meant by insight, which is usually an intellectualized statement of a problem in terms of its origins or etiology.

Self-understanding is not limited to intrapersonal processes but includes an understanding of the impact the client has on other people, or the nature of his or her functioning in interpersonal relationships. Clients begin to see themselves, at least to some extent, as others see them.

Self-exploration reveals inconsistencies and contradictions. Attitudes and feelings that have been experienced but denied to awareness are discovered. Experiences inconsistent with the self-concept or self-image, previously denied or distorted, become symbolized in awareness. Clients become more open to their experiences.

With increasing self-awareness, clients' self-concepts become clearer. And with clear self-concepts their vague dissatisfactions with themselves become more specific. They begin to see in what specific respects they are failing to actualize themselves, and in just what ways they fail to measure up to their self-ideals. They begin to reorganize their self-concepts to assimilate all their experiences of themselves; self-concept becomes more congruent with experiences and thus more realistic. In turn, clients' perceptions of their ideal selves become more realistic and more attainable, and their selves become more congruent with their ideal selves. With these changes in the self and self-concept, clients become more accepting of themselves and feel more confident and self-directing. They experience more acceptance from others, both because they perceive more realistically and accurately and because their changed selves elicit more positive reactions from others. They become fully functioning persons, more self-actualizing persons.[13] Their feelings of adequacy and of self-esteem increase.

In the process of developing self-understanding and self-awareness, both positive and negative attitudes about the self arise. Not all that clients discover about themselves is negative or bad. Experiences that at first do not seem to belong to, and cannot be integrated into, the self, become accepted as the self; "the client discovers that he can *be* his experience, with all of its variety and surface contradiction. . . ."[14] As the process continues, negative attitudes toward the self decrease and positive attitudes increase. "The client not only accepts himself—a phase which may carry the connotation of a grudging and reluctant acceptance of the inevitable—he actually comes to *like* himself."[15] The self that emerges—the deep, basic nature of the client—is not bad, antisocial, or destructive. The core of the self "is not bad, nor terribly wrong, but something positive. Underneath the layer of controlled surface behavior, underneath the bitterness, underneath the hurt, is a self that is positive, that is without hate."[16]

In a very significant way, then, therapy does not necessarily require the changing of the basic self. It involves the discovery of the positive core of the self, and its freeing so that the client can be his or her real, basic self. The conditions of therapy provide a non-threatening environment in which the client does not have to respond negatively, aggressively, or defensively, but can be the self that he or she really is or is capable of being. Therapy is, then, a situation in which clients can be themselves—their best selves, the potential selves that have been covered up, or not allowed to develop, by the absence of the conditions of good interpersonal relationships. In terms of the relation of the self-concept and the self-ideal, the discrepancy may be reduced by change in the self-ideal as much as, if not more than, by change in the self-concept. Or, perhaps more accurately, changes in the self-concept may occur without changes in the basic self.

It is important that the process of self-exploration not be confused with client talk *about* themselves. This is often a problem with students beginning practicum. By continued questioning, they get clients to make statements about themselves and mistake this for client self-exploration. But in such talk clients (as well as the counselor) are viewing themselves as objects and are not actually expressing or disclosing themselves. Their talk is externally oriented, abstract, generalized—an intellectual or rational discourse about themselves as objects.

INSIGHT AND ACTION

Insight, it frequently has been stated, is not enough. Self-understanding is not acceptable as a goal of counseling or psychotherapy. There must be action or changes in client behavior, or therapy cannot be considered successful. We have noted that Carkhuff and Berenson have claimed that traditional therapies stop at self-understanding and insight. They have suggested that the core or facilitative conditions lead to insight but not to action, and that new conditions, the action conditions, must be introduced in a second phase of psychotherapy to move the client beyond understanding to action.

In the consideration of the counselor's implementation of the conditions (Chapter 6), I indicated that I prefer to think in terms of a single process rather than two processes, of a continuous process rather than two phases. I questioned whether the so-called action conditions are actually new or different conditions and suggested that they can be incorporated into the facilitative conditions, representing essentially high levels of these conditions. And I do not include a separate action phase in discussing the client's work in the process but end with the development of self-awareness in the client.

The position I take is that action by the client or changes in behavior accompany or follow as a natural consequence the development of self-awareness. In fact, as has been noted by many writers, action or changes in behavior may precede insight, or a clear verbalizable understanding, or self-awareness. Action and understanding are interacting or reciprocal processes. Carkhuff notes that "in healthy people understanding is simultaneous with action. . . ."[17] He suggests, however, that low-functioning persons, including the majority of clients, are unable to act upon their self-understanding and need to be pushed by the therapist. If, in the process of therapy, low-functioning clients develop self-understanding and begin to function in the therapy relationship at a higher level, why cannot they then act upon their understanding? It is possible that the problem is one of time, with an impatient therapist being unable or reluctant to wait for the client to begin acting and changing behaviors.

For it is apparent that *the client's behavior does change in the therapy relationship itself.* Clients disclose themselves and engage in productive self-exploration, which they were not able to do before. They develop and express self-awareness. They become more accepting of themselves. They become more accepting of others, including the therapist. They become more open, honest, and genuine. In other words, they become more like the therapist; they manifest the conditions of a good interpersonal relationship—empathic understanding, respect and warmth, genuineness, concreteness, and self-disclosure. They become, within the therapy relationship, more self-actualizing persons.

The result of therapy, then, is that clients become more self-actualizing persons. The characteristics of the self-actualizing person include the facilitative conditions of a good human relationship. Clients, in becoming more like the therapist, manifest the conditions to which they are exposed. If, as has been indicated earlier (Chapter 5), the essence of these conditions is love, then the client learns to love as a result of therapy. To love others, then, is an aspect of being self-actualizing. Glasser states that one of the two basic psychological needs of humans is to receive love and to give love. "At all times in our lives we must have at least one person who cares about us and whom we care for ourselves. . . . To either love or allow ourselves to be loved is not enough; we must do both."[18]

Now there is no question that the generalization of these changes outside the therapy relationship is a difficult and slow process. But it does occur, and it is facilitated by the fact that, through the principle of reciprocal affect, the persons with whom the client relates become more accepting, understanding, and genuine.

Furthermore, in terms of more specific or more concrete changes in behavior, the client's basic drive toward self-actualization, freed from its frustration by lack of facilitative interpersonal relationships, produces changes in the client. The motivation is there, the self-understanding is present, and, to the extent possible in his or her external environment, the client's behavior changes. In perceptual or phenomenological terms, the client's perceptions have changed, and his or her behavior changes accordingly. With a change in the self-concept, behavior then changes to become consistent with the self-concept, which is a basic determiner of behavior. Specific behavior changes occur as a by-product of self-actualization.

A BEHAVIORAL VIEW OF THE THERAPEUTIC RELATIONSHIP

If learning is defined as those changes in behavior that are not due to native response tendencies, maturation, or temporary states of the organism (as a result of fatigue or drugs, for example),[19] then counseling or psychotherapy must involve learning. But there are different views of the nature of learning, differing descriptions of the learning process, and different theories of learning. When I referred to perceptual or phenomenological changes leading to behavior changes, I was speaking in terms of one theory of learning. The detailed considerations of the therapy process by Carl Rogers are formulated, essentially, in terms of a perceptual theory of learning and behavior.[20] Perceptual theory is not currently popular or influential in psychology, however. The prevailing orientation in the field of learning is toward behavior theory, and discussions of a learning approach to counseling or psychotherapy usually assume this orientation.

To a certain extent at least, behavioral change, or learning, can be described by, or cast into, various theoretical orientations. Each orientation is to some extent a different way of viewing the same phenomena. One orientation may be more restricted or limited than another, but even a restricted viewpoint can be expanded or extended to encompass, at least in a general way, a wide variety of phenomena. In this respect, reinforcement, a basic concept of the behavioral approach to learning and behavior, can be extended to apply to the therapy process, as can other concepts as well. I shall therefore describe the process of counseling of psychotherapy that has been developed in this and the two preceding chapters in terms

of a behavioral approach to learning.[21] The way in which the therapeutic conditions operate can be described—or "explained"—in terms
of this approach. Truax and Carkhuff suggested that there are four
learning modalities or channels by which the basic facilitative conditions operate in psychotherapy: (1) reinforcement of human relating,
(2) reinforcement of self-exploration, (3) elimination of specific
anxieties and fears, and (4) reinforcement of positive self-concepts
and self-valuations.[22] In this section we consider each of these modalities in terms of behavioral theory. We also consider a fifth important
learning modality: modeling.

Reinforcement of Human Relating

Clients have difficulties in interpersonal relations; thus, interpersonal relations are sources of anxiety and fear. Their interpersonal
relations have been associated with painful experiences—rejection,
lack of understanding, hostility, threat, and so on, from others. As
a result, they are hesitant to approach others and are threatened by
the prospect of relating to others. Yet they come for therapy because
the pain or disturbance is so great that they will do almost anything
to seek help. They approach the therapist, though at the same time
they have strong avoidance responses. They suffer from the approach-
avoidance conflict described by Miller.[23]

The therapist responds to the client with warmth, respect, concern, and understanding. These constitute, then, rewards for the
approach responses of the client. The therapist presents a nonthreatening relationship. It is more than a situation in which the
process of extinction operates, where clients find that the therapist
does not act toward them in the negative ways in which others have
acted or continue to act toward them. They are actually rewarded
for efforts to relate to another.

The therapist must begin reinforcement of those behaviors
approaching or approximating the desired behaviors. Even slight,
tentative, or hesitant relating behaviors must be met with warmth
and empathy, with positive responses. Truax and Carkhuff state that,
for most effective results:

> The therapist would tend to offer relatively high levels of warmth and
> empathy to any and all verbalizations by the patient (random con-
> tinuous reinforcement) and also, on a selective basis, provide higher
> levels of warmth more frequently to the patient's attempts toward
> human relating. Thus the effective therapist might respond with em-
> pathy and warmth 40 percent of the time to definite attempts at
> human relating. As in all learning situations, for "shaping" to be effec-
> tive, the reinforcement must begin with the responses currently avail-
> able in the patient. Thus, responses with even the slightest resemblance
> to attempts at human relating would immediately be followed by a

relative increase in empathy and warmth. With some patients this would particularly mean that even negative or hostile reactions to the therapist would be met by heightened expressions of warmth and accurate empathy. Over time, as the patient consequently begins to relate more frequently, more closely and more effectively, the therapist should become more selective in his offering of warmth and empathy. The criterion for reinforcement is gradually raised as the patient is better able to relate. This suggests that the therapist, to be more effective, would offer high levels of warmth and empathy more and more selectively across time in therapy.[24]

This passage suggests that while the therapist begins by being unconditional (providing continuous reinforcement for any client responses), he or she should move toward discrimination, or conditional reinforcement. The implication is that the therapist should consciously and deliberately deliver reinforcements on a contingency basis. However, attempts to do this in research, either in interview situations or counseling analogue studies, indicate that it is not possible for therapists to discriminate and respond to, or to recognize and reinforce, predetermined classes of behavior with accuracy and consistency. Skinner has noted that "the contingencies of reinforcement which are most efficient in controlling the organism cannot be arranged through . . . personal mediation. . . . Mechanical and electrical devices must be used. Personal arrangement and personal observation of results are unthinkable."[25] He is referring to teaching in a class of children, but the same can be said for the individual personal situation. Thus, conscious, deliberate attempts to reinforce specific client responses are not very effective, since to be effective every (or almost every) response must be reinforced, and this is not humanly possible. Moreover, the conscious and deliberate dispensing of predetermined rewards or reinforcements leads to an unnaturalness and lack of spontaneity or genuineness that can dilute or destroy their effectiveness as the client becomes aware of their artificial nature.

However, the therapist is not unconditional in his or her responses, even in the beginning of therapy. The therapist is more concerned about some of the client's verbalizations than about others; he or she is more interested in some topics than others. It is well known that what clients talk about is related to the theoretical orientation of the therapist. If the therapist values dreams, clients dream and report their dreams. If the therapist is interested in sex, clients talk about sex. If the therapist deals with phobias or fears, clients present these to the therapist.

The presence of minimal levels of the facilitative conditions provides a nonthreatening atmosphere in which the client can begin to relate to another person. If the client is to remain in the therapy situation, the lack of threat must continue. Thus, it would appear that minimal levels of the core conditions must continue throughout therapy. In fact, contrary to the implication in the quotation from Truax and Carkhuff that the more effective therapist would be highly conditional, Truax later found that the overall level of facilitative conditions in group therapy was independent of the degree to which the conditions were offered differentially as reinforcers.[26]

While there are those who maintain that an "optimum" level of anxiety (which is never defined) is necessary to keep the client working on his or her problems, I suggest that there is sufficient anxiety present within the client, without the therapist adding to it. The therapist

> must discriminate between those anxiety changes evoked by the patient's self-exploration and those evoked by his own threatening or inept attempts at interpretation or empathic responses. If the therapist fails to make this discrimination it is unlikely that he will prove helpful. It may be best to assume that whenever the patient shows an increase in anxiety and *withdrawal*, the therapist's response (or lack of response) is the source of the anxiety arousal.[27]

Reinforcement of Self-Exploration

The therapist does respond, intuitively, to some activities or verbalizations of the client and not to others. After the relationship begins, and after the opening remarks of the interview sessions, the therapist does not respond to social conversation by the client. As indicated in Chapter 6, such material is considered irrelevant. The therapist does respond to self-talk, since this is assumed to be relevant. At the beginning of therapy, such self-talk is usually of a negative character. The therapist thus is reinforcing negative self-references. But negative self-references are only one subcategory of the self-reference category. So when, as normally happens, positive self-references begin to occur, these also are reinforced. But self-references are themselves only a subcategory of a broader kind of client statements—self-exploratory statements. The therapist, in responding to the several categories of self-exploratory statements, participates in a process known as shaping. In this process, in the absence of the desired behavior (here self-exploration), behaviors that approximate this response (here spontaneous verbalization) are reinforced; when behavior that is closer to the desired behavior occurs (such as self-talk), it is reinforced. Eventually, the client engages in self-exploration, which is then reinforced by the therapist, leading to self-exploration at deeper and deeper levels.

Self-exploration is often a painful or anxiety-arousing process. Thus, even though it is reinforced by specific therapist responses of interest, acceptance, and understanding, clients may become anxious or threatened by the nature of the material they are exploring. The therapist must be careful that his or her responses do not increase threat. Probing questions and interpretations are likely to do this. They cause the client to retreat—to resist, the phenomenon noted by interpretative therapists. It is desirable that the client be helped to explore as deeply as he or she can at the moment. The context of the facilitative conditions maintains a safe nonthreatening atmosphere for this. This atmosphere can be considered "a counterconditioning agent, a pleasant stimulus to be paired with the mildly anxiety-provoking cues associated with the leading edge of the conflict region," or the self-exploratory process.[28] In this respect, the non-threatening therapy relationship is similar to the inducement of relaxation by behavior therapists. In fact, "it seems probable that eliciting warmth and comfort as responses incompatible with anxiety and fear and avoidance produces more potent and adaptive counter-conditioning than deep muscle relaxation."[29]

The warm, accepting, nonthreatening therapy environment would appear to be a more relevant condition for reducing or extinguishing anxieties related to social or interpersonal processes than physical relaxation. However, as Truax and Carkhuff suggest, clients may have developed conditioned anxiety responses to "human warmth" (probably phony or manipulative in nature), so that the therapist should be cautious about offering strong, overwhelming warmth at the beginning of therapy.

The client, then, engages in the process of self-exploration in a warm, relaxing, nonthreatening atmosphere. Nevertheless, the process arouses anxiety as it progresses; the client stops, retreats, rests, takes a breather by moving into irrelevant, or less relevant, areas. Self-exploration is a step-by-step process, or a two-step forward and one backward process—an approach-avoidance situation. If the therapist, by his or her specific responses (including concreteness and confrontation), helps clients explore themselves in the presence of the facilitative conditions, clients progress. The therapist's accepting, warm, empathic responses are rewarding. Clients feel satisfaction in their achievement. Anxiety related to the topic that they are exploring is reduced.

Behavior therapists emphasize that they are systematic in their rewards or reinforcements and, while recognizing that other therapists utilize reinforcement, insist that it is unsystematic.[30] But it has already been suggested that it is extremely difficult, if not impossible, to really be systematic in dispensing rewards in the ongoing complex process of psychotherapy. (The process of systematic desensitization *is* systematic, but this is a process of extinction, not of positive conditioning.) I suggest that the relationship therapist is more systematic in his or her reinforcements intuitively and spontaneously than it is possible to be by taking thought and attempting to provide reinforcements on a conscious, mechanical basis.

Martin describes this intuitive reinforcement process when he says:

> The client is progressing through an "anxiety hierarchy" as he moves to more and more anxiety-provoking cues, and the nature of the hierarchy continually changes as more and more cues become available to increase his understanding. A consequence of this is that an anxiety hierarchy established at any point in therapy will necessarily be at least partially incorrect. The process of therapy I am describing permits the therapist and client to modify continuously the nature of the hierarchy, as correction of it becomes necessary with new knowledge. Clients do indeed progress in therapy along an anxiety hierarchy, but it is a hierarchy that the client and therapist discover together during the therapy process. The client will attempt to take the next step on his hierarchy. The therapist's job is to hear this attempt and to facilitate it by responding to the leading edge of what the client is trying to deal with.[31]

The therapist's empathic responses facilitate self-exploration. Being understood is rewarding. The therapist's empathic responses are conditional. But they vary not by the intent or design of the therapist. They are contingent on the client's success in clarifying his or her self-exploration. While minimal levels of warmth, acceptance, and concern maintain the client in his or her self-exploration, highly empathic responses reward especially successful or clear self-exploratory efforts. The therapist cannot be highly empathic if the client is extremely vague and confused. He can only respond to, or reward, the effort. But when the client engages in clear, specific, highly insightful self-exploration, the therapist is able to respond with high levels of accurate empathy, which is highly reinforcing to the client.

The recognition of the influence of reinforcement provides the counselor with a way of meeting the problem of responding to the silent or highly nonverbal client. Counselor responses of attention, interest, concern, and understanding to the verbalizations of the client are rewarding and encourage the client to continue self-talk and self-exploration. Continuous questioning by the counselor will not accomplish this. In fact, it will teach the client to be responsive to the counselor and to wait for the counselor to continue questioning or initiating the interchange.

Recognizing the principle of reinforcement also suggests that the questions of the counselor should be directed toward eliciting self-talk by the client rather than factual information or personal history material. It is not necessary—or perhaps even desirable—that the questions be of the type frequently recommended by instructors in counseling—that is, questions directed at past or present feelings, such as "How do you feel about that?" or "How did that make you feel?" Contrary to the assumption that these questions lead to the expression of real or basic feelings, it is more likely that they lead to the expression of considered or intellectualized feelings. The direct focusing upon feelings by the client, rather than the unconsidered spontaneous expression of feelings, introduces a cognitive element that leads to talk *about* feelings rather than the *expression of* feelings.

The objection has been raised that encouraging client self-talk and self-exploration would, by generalization, lead to the client imposing such talk on those he or she interacts with outside therapy. However, a moment's thought should lead to the recognition that, if such talk were not responded to positively, it would be extinguished, and clients would learn to discriminate regarding with whom they could engage in such talk. In this regard also, it would be anticipated that the generalization of clients' other learnings in therapy—understanding, respect, warmth and acceptance, and openness, honesty, and genuineness—would be responded to positively by others in their environment and thus be reinforced. Since such characteristics are responded to by the development of the same characteristics in those who are exposed to them, clients would experience an increase in these conditions in their everyday environment, which would enhance the therapy.

Elimination of Specific Anxieties and Fears

If the client has learned specific anxieties or fears in the area of human relating, these may be removed through desensitization or adaptation, reactive inhibition or internal inhibition, and counterconditioning. These processes occur in the traditional psychotherapies as a result of the nonspecific or general nature of the non-threatening, accepting therapy relationship. The shaping process for progress in self-exploration would appear to fall under this learning modality of Truax and Carkhuff, at least insofar as specific anxieties and fears are dealt with. Where the client's problem appears to be an isolated specific fear or anxiety, the use of techniques of behavior modification, such as systematic desensitization, would appear to be appropriate.

Reinforcement of Positive Self-Concepts and Self-Valuations

As clients progress in therapy, their responses become more positive in regard to themselves or their self-concepts. These responses are welcomed by the therapist, who sees them as desirable, as indications of progress. The therapist is thus pleased with the client, and indications of this pleasure and approval are communicated to the client. It is important to emphasize here that such positive client responses come late in therapy, as a result of the process of self-exploration. It is not desirable—or possible—to short-circuit the process by extinguishing negative self-references and reinforcing positive self-references from the beginning of therapy. It might be possible to condition clients to emit positive self-references in a relatively short period of time. However, this would simply be the conditioning of verbal behavior. Efforts to do this with "normal" subjects in analogue studies have not always been successful. Whether this is related to a social set to be self-critical rather than self-praising, or to an innate resistance to glossing over negative feelings, is not known. The ignoring of negative self-references and the reinforcement of positive self-references prevents or inhibits the process of client self-exploration.

Modeling

In addition to the specific behavioral learning process operating in counseling or psychotherapy, a more general learning process occurs. This is the process called modeling. Modeling, of course, is not strictly a behavioristic technique. The behaviorists did not invent it or discover it, and it did not arise from laboratory research, as the behaviorists are so fond of claiming for other techniques. Modeling is a basic and pervasive method of learning and, in primitive societies, constitutes the educational process, or the process by which the young acquire the behaviors necessary for survival. Modeling as a method of teaching and learning has the advantage over reinforcement of specific behaviors, in that it makes possible the learning of complex wholes, the acquisition of patterns of behavior, rather than the piecemeal learning of wholes by the prior learning of parts that must then be integrated. It also often leads to rapid learning, often one-trial learning, without practice being necessary.

Modeling involves the observation and imitation by the subject of another person. The process is a highly complex one, and its effects or results involve numerous factors, in the model, the subject, and the relationship between them.[32] It is not necessary, for modeling to occur, that the model intend to model; he or she becomes a model for others in the appropriate setting.

Thus, the therapist becomes a model for the client. The attitudes of the client toward the therapist make him or her a model. Descriptions of modeling have focused upon nonverbal behaviors. But most of the behaviors in which we are interested in psychotherapy, at least in relationship therapy, are interpersonal behaviors that are verbal, or verbally mediated. The verbal behavior of the therapist in the interpersonal relationship of psychotherapy is a model of interpersonal relationships. Bandura suggests that since change agents model certain attitudes and social behaviors, these activities should be analyzed in terms of the behavior being modeled or its functional value for clients. He then criticizes "conventional interview therapists" because they "mainly exemplify silence and interpretive behaviors that have limited functional value for clients. To the extent that clients emulate these behaviors in their everyday behavior they become pests or bores."[33] This may be the case in psychoanalysis; I have experienced this in groups of persons undergoing analysis. But if we substitute listening for silence and empathic understanding for interpretation, the criticism is inappropriate. Listening to and understanding others are useful and facilitative conditions for all interpersonal relationships. The relationship therapist is modeling the facilitative conditions for good human relationships.

Relationship therapy is thus not a therapy in which clients only talk about their problems—"verbal substitutes," as Bandura calls it— but one in which clients deal directly with problem behavior, with difficulties in interpersonal relationships. Clients are thus actually doing what Bandura says social-learning behavior therapists do— "devoting the major portion of their time to altering the conditions governing deviant behaviors rather than conversing about them."[34] It would appear that relationship therapy fits at least the first part of Bandura's description: "A powerful form of treatment is one in which therapeutic agents themselves model the desired behavior and arrange optimal conditions for clients to engage in similar activities until they can perform the behavior skillfully and fearlessly."[35]

It may be questioned whether, if self-disclosure on the part of the client is desired, the therapist shouldn't model this at the beginning of therapy. The answer, I think, is that this would be inconsistent with other objectives of the therapist—respecting the client, listening to and understanding the client, and not imposing himself or herself on the client. Therapy is for the client, not for the therapist. In his approach to groups, Mowrer does engage in self-disclosure as a model for the group members.[36] Whether this is helpful in individual therapy (it is apparently not necessary) is not known[37] (see pp. 80–84).

It may be helpful or facilitative for the client to have some pretherapy orientation or training in preparation for entering a therapy relationship, and this could include modeling of self-disclosure. Truax and Carkhuff found that such "vicarious therapy pretraining" did facilitate therapy to some extent and resulted in greater improvement.[38] Hoehn-Saric et al. developed a Role Induction Interview to influence clients' expectations about psychotherapy (including the behavior expected of the client and the therapist) and to prepare them for certain developments, such as resistance and the expectation that improvement would occur in four months. The interview appeared to be effective to some extent, including resulting in greater likelihood of the client continuing in therapy.[39]

Modeling is a complex process, and although it no doubt incorporates elements of conditioning, it is not explainable simply in conditioning terms. While vicarious conditioning (observation of the model being rewarded) may be an element, modeling is effective without this. Cognitive elements are certainly present. Truax and Carkhuff discuss the principle of reciprocal affect, referring to the fact that people respond with affect similar to that to which they are exposed. This would appear to be modeling. But the principle is descriptive, not explanatory.

In summary, it is possible to describe the therapy process developed in this book in behavioral learning terms. Conditioning, both classical and operant, is involved in the process. Whether this description is explanatory or sufficient to understand the total process perhaps depends on the point of view of the reader, or the breadth of his or her concept or theory of learning. At any rate, the description given here is incomplete. The process of psychotherapy is complex and cannot be reduced to simple stimulus-response components. Behavior therapists no longer attempt to do this; the inclusion of modeling is an expansion of the earlier, restricted behavioristic approach. Learning is a complex process involving more than stimulus-response elements or conditioning. "Research has begun to make it increasingly clear that the learning in the behavioral therapies involves complex cognitive, emotional and motivational changes operating within a social context."[40]

If the facilitative conditions can be described in behavioral terms, behavior therapy techniques can be described in terms of the facilitative conditions. Thus, Truax has indicated that (unpublished dissertation) studies show that "the level of empathy, etc., of the therapist is the crucial factor in traditional desensitization therapy."[41] This, of course, does not show, or imply, that the process is not a learning process. It is only to say that facilitative conditions are part of the learning or behavior changes that occur in behavior therapy. Certainly, psychotherapy is not a simple conditioning process. The fact that behavior changes follow a reward does not mean that the therapeutic relationship is an automatic sequence of conditioning without awareness on the part of the client. It must be recognized that the extension of the concept of reinforcement beyond the

simple conditioning that occurs in the laboratory leads to the introduction of other variables that influence and change the nature of
the process. In complex situations what is labeled reinforcement may
actually be described in other terms. What is termed a reinforcement
may operate on a cognitive basis, such as providing information regarding the consequences of behavior.

Learning, it is being increasingly recognized, is a complex process,
and a strict behavioristic interpretation is limited. The extension of
the concept of reinforcement as a universal factor in learning appears
to be impressive, but it must be remembered that such usage extends
the term beyond its origins in laboratory situations. "No one will
dispute that reinforcement is important. As Michael Polanyi once
pointed out, since it includes anything that can change behavior, it
must be."[42]

But this is only one way of describing behavior change, and it is
not explanatory. There are different kinds or levels of learning.
Razran describes four evolutionary levels—reactive (nonassociative
or reflexive); connective (conditioning); integrative (perceiving); and
symbolic (thinking).[43] The importance of the last two, or the cognitive aspects of learning, has been neglected by the behaviorists until
recently.

There is a useful way of looking at the relationship between the
core or facilitative conditions and the techniques of behavior modification (such as reinforcement, desensitization, extinction, and
modeling). Rather than viewing them as separate or independent, or
as different approaches or techniques, they can be incorporated in a
single approach, in which the behavioristic techniques are seen as
modes of operation of the conditions. Then it becomes clear that
there is no necessary or inherent contradiction or inconsistency. The
influence of the core conditions is mediated, at least in part, through
the behavioristic conditions. On the other hand, as is being increasingly recognized, the behavioristic techniques operate in the context
of a relationship, and, in fact, their effectiveness depends to a great
extent on the nature and quality of the relationship.

Behavior therapists have rejected the medical or disease model
of psychopathology and psychotherapy.[44] Traditional or psycho-
dynamic psychotherapies, such as psychoanalysis, client-centered
therapy, and existential analysis have been associated with the
disease or medical model by many behavior therapists. But it should
be clear that relationship therapy is not based upon the medical
model. In fact, it could justifiably be claimed that it is based upon
the behavioral or environmental model, since the cause of emotional
disturbance is seen as developing from the nature of the human
environment, and its amelioration requires the modification of the

human environment. However, the description in behavioral or learning theory terms is not necessarily explanatory. Although psychotherapy is a learning process, it is not simply stimulus-response learning or conditioning. Learning is much more complex than these simple theories would imply, involving complex cognitive and affective elements and a social context that influences the process. The client in the process is more than a rat in a Skinner box being taught tricks by operant conditioning.

SUMMARY

In this chapter we considered the client's role and activities in the therapy process. Client characteristics related to client involvement and progress in psychotherapy were suggested, including desire to change and confidence in the therapist as an agent in inducing change. The basic motivation to change is the drive toward self-actualization. While the facilitative conditions must be present in the therapist for therapy to occur, this is not sufficient. They must be perceived by the client. The client who will not or cannot perceive the conditions cannot be helped.

The work of the client consists essentially of self-exploration. This begins with self-disclosure and ends with self-awareness, self-understanding, or insight. The problem of insight versus action was discussed, and it was concluded that action or behavior changes accompany or follow the development of self-awareness as a natural consequence of a change in perceptions, particularly change in perception of the self, or in the self-concept.

The chapter concluded with a section discussing the therapeutic process from a behavioristic learning point of view. It was recognized that the therapist's responses and behaviors act as reinforcers for the client's behavior. In fact, it was suggested that the relationship therapist naturally or intuitively provides more systematic reinforcement than could be provided by a conscious effort to do so. The facilitative conditions that the therapist provides are, in behavioristic terms, the most powerful reinforcers for client self-exploration and for the development of the conditions themselves in the client. This process may also be described as modeling.

NOTES

1. E. T. Gendlin. Client-centered development in work with schizophrenics. *Journal of Counseling Psychology*, 1962, *9*, 205–211.
2. C. R. Rogers. The necessary and sufficient conditions of therapeutic personality change. *Journal of Consulting Psychology*, 1957, *21*, p. 96.

3. L. Pearson (Ed.). *The use of written productions in counseling and psychotherapy.* Springfield, IL: Thomas, 1965.
4. C. B. Truax and R. R. Carkhuff. *Toward effective counseling and psychotherapy.* Chicago: Aldine, 1967; R. R. Carkhuff and B. G. Berenson. *Beyond counseling and therapy.* New York: Holt, Rinehart & Winston, 1967; R. R. Carkhuff. *Helping and human relations.* Vol. I, *Selection and training.* Vol. II, *Practice and research.* New York: Holt, Rinehart & Winston, 1969.
5. Truax and Carkhuff, *Toward effective counseling,* p. 192.
6. C. R. Rogers. *On becoming a person.* Boston: Houghton Mifflin, 1961, p. 139.
7. Carkhuff and Berenson, *Beyond counseling,* p. 7.
8. Carkhuff, *Helping,* Vol. II, p. 41.
9. Truax and Carkhuff, *Toward effective counseling,* pp. 194-208.
10. Carkhuff, *Helping,* Vol. II, pp. 327-328.
11. Truax and Carkhuff, *Toward effective counseling,* p. 196.
12. *Ibid.,* p. 206.
13. Adapted from C. R. Rogers. A theory of therapy, personality, and interpersonal relationships. In S. Koch (Ed.), *Psychology: A study of science.* Vol. III, *Formulations of the person and the social context.* New York: McGraw-Hill, 1959, pp. 218-219.
14. Rogers, *On becoming a person,* p. 80.
15. *Ibid.,* p. 87.
16. *Ibid.,* p. 101.
17. Carkhuff, *Helping,* Vol. II, p. 35.
18. W. Glasser. *Reality therapy.* New York: Harper & Row, 1965, pp. 7, 10.
19. E. R. Hilgard and G. H. Bower. *Theories of learning* (3rd ed.). New York: Appleton-Century-Crofts, 1966, p. 2.
20. See A. W. Combs, A. C. Richards, and F. Richards. *Perceptual psychology.* New York: Harper & Row, 1975.
21. The relevant literature goes back some forty years and is extensive. See, for example, the following: F. J. Shaw. A stimulus response analysis of repression and insight in psychotherapy. *Psychological Review,* 1946, *53,* 36-42; L. F. Shaffer. The problem of psychotherapy. *American Psychologist,* 1947, *2,* 459-467; E. J. Shoben, Jr. A learning theory interpretation of psychotherapy. *Harvard Educational Review,* 1948, *18,* 129-145; E. J. Shoben, Jr. Psychotherapy as a problem in learning theory. *Psychological Bulletin,* 1949, *46,* 366-392; E. J. Shoben, Jr. Some observations on psychotherapy and the learning process. In O. H. Mowrer (Ed.), *Psychotherapy: Theory and research.* New York: Ronald, 1953; Ann Magaret. Generalization in psychotherapy. *Journal of Consulting Psychology,* 1950, *14,* 64-70; J. Dollard and N. E. Miller. *Personality and psychotherapy.* New York: McGraw-Hill, 1950; F. H. Kanfer. Comments on learning in psychotherapy. *Psychological Reports,* 1961, *9,* 681-699; A. Bandura. Psychotherapy as a learning process. *Psychological Bulletin,* 1961, *58,* 143-149; C. B. Truax. Some implications of behavior therapy for psychotherapy. *Journal of Counseling Psychology,* 1966, *13,* 160-170 (also as Chap. 4 in C. B. Truax and R. R. Carkhuff. *Toward effective counseling and psychotherapy.* Chicago: Aldine, 1967); C. H. Patterson. Some notes on behavior theory, behavior therapy and behavioral counseling. *The Counseling Psychologist,* 1969, *1*(4), 44-56; D. G. Martin. *Learning-based client-centered therapy.* Monterey, CA: Brooks/Cole, 1972. The voluminous literature on behavior therapy is also relevant here.

22. Truax and Carkhuff, *Toward effective counseling*, pp. 151–161.
23. Dollard and Miller, *Personality and psychotherapy.*
24. Truax and Carkhuff, *Toward effective counseling*, pp. 152–153.
25. B. F. Skinner. *The technology of teaching.* New York: Appleton-Century-Crofts, 1968, p. 29.
26. C. B. Truax. Therapist interpersonal reinforcement of client self-exploration and therapeutic outcome in group psychotherapy. *Journal of Counseling Psychology*, 1968, *15*, 225–231.
27. Truax and Carkhuff, *Toward effective counseling*, p. 155.
28. Martin, *Learning-based client-centered therapy*, p. 67.
29. Truax and Carkhuff, *Toward effective counseling*, p. 155.
30. L. P. Ullmann and L. Krasner (Eds.). *Case studies in behavior modification.* New York: Holt, Rinehart & Winston, 1965, p. 37.
31. Martin, *Learning-based client-centered therapy*, pp. 69–70.
32. A. Bandura. *Principles of behavior modification.* New York: Holt, Rinehart & Winston, 1969; A. Bandura. Psychotherapy based upon modeling principles. In A. E. Bergin and S. L. Garfield (Eds.), *Handbook of psychotherapy and behavior change: An empirical analysis.* New York: Wiley, 1971, pp. 653–708.
33. Bandura, Psychotherapy based upon modeling principles, p. 654.
34. *Ibid.*, p. 653.
35. *Ibid.*, p. 689.
36. O. H. Mowrer. *The new group therapy.* Princeton, NJ: Van Nostrand Reinhold, 1964.
37. In an experimental interview situation, Powell found that interviewer self-disclosure statements were more effective than approval-supportive statements or reflections in increasing subject self-references, both positive and negative. (W. J. Powell. Differential effectiveness of interviewer interventions in an experimental interview. *Journal of Consulting and Clinical Psychology*, 1968, *32*, 210–215.)
38. Truax and Carkhuff, *Toward effective counseling*, pp. 153, 362–363. See also G. A. Marlatt, E. A. Jacobsen, S. L. Johnson, and D. J. Morrice. Effect of exposure to a model receiving evaluative feedback upon consequent behavior in an interview. *Journal of Clinical and Consulting Psychology*, 1970, *34*, 104–112.
39. R. Hoehn-Saric, J. W. Frank, S. D. Imber, E. H. Nash, A. R. Stone, and C. L. Battle. Systematic preparation of patients for psychotherapy. I. Effects on therapy behavior and outcome. *Journal of Psychiatric Research*, 1964, *2*, 267–281.
40. E. J. Murray and L. I. Jacobson. The nature of learning in traditional and behavioral psychotherapy. In Bergin and Garfield, *Handbook*, p. 723. See also F. H. Kanfer and J. S. Phillips, *Learning foundations of behavior therapy.* New York: Wiley, 1970.
41. C. B. Truax. Personal communication October 26, 1972. See also R. J. Morris and K. R. Suckerman. The importance of the therapeutic relationship to systematic desensitization. *Journal of Consulting and Clinical Psychology*, 1974, *42*, 147; R. J. Morris and K. R. Suckerman. Therapist warmth as a factor in automated systematic desensitization. *Journal of Consulting and Clinical Psychology*, 1974, *42*, 244–250. Relevant here is the study by Vitalo, in which it was found that verbal conditioning occurred only with experimenters who were high on the core conditions. R. Vitalo. The effects of interpersonal functioning in a conditioning paradigm. *Journal*

of Counseling Psychology, 1970, *17*, 141–144. See also A. Sapolsky. Effect of interpersonal relationships upon verbal conditioning. *Journal of Abnormal and Social Psychology*, 1960, *60*, 241–246; D. J. Mickelson and R. R. Stevic. Differential effects of facilitative and non-facilitative behavioral counselors. *Journal of Consulting Psychology*, 1971, *18*, 314–319. Krasner emphasizes the importance of the therapist/client relationship in all forms of behavior therapy (L. Krasner. The operant approach in behavior therapy. In Bergin and Garfield, *Handbook*, pp. 612–652).

42. Quoted by W. R. Thompson. Review of J. P. Scott and S. F. Scott (Eds.), *Social control and social change. Contemporary Psychology*, 1972, *17*, 524–525.

43. G. Razran. *Mind in evolution: An East-West synthesis of learned behavior and cognition.* Boston: Houghton Mifflin, 1971.

44. L. P. Ullmann and L. Krasner. *A psychological approach to abnormal behavior.* Englewood Cliffs, NJ: Prentice-Hall, 1969.

CHAPTER 8

Diagnosis

Emphasis on diagnosis in psychiatry has waxed and waned throughout the history of psychotherapy. Psychiatry, accepting the medical model, has assumed that differential diagnosis followed by differential treatment is its necessary goal. As a result, a tremendous amount of time and effort has been devoted to the development of diagnostic classifications for psychiatric and psychological disturbances. In the field of medicine, the discovery of different etiologies in terms of foreign agents—chemical, bacteriological, or viral—has led to the development of specific differential treatments. By analogy, it is assumed that the discovery of different causes for emotional disorders can lead to differential specific treatments. The classical paradigm was the discovery that the spirochete of syphilis leads to the development of paresis; this model has stimulated the hope that etiological agents (whether biological or psychological) will be discovered for other discrete conditions.

So far, no progress has been made. Yet the attempts to develop classification systems continue. It is recognized that existing systems, which are not based upon different etiologies but upon symptoms or syndromes, are not adequate, and efforts to find a system of classification are continuing. Perhaps the most elaborate diagnostic classification developed to date is Thorne's.[1]

In this chapter we discuss diagnosis: current interest in it; theories that argue against the existence of a basis for classification and diagnosis; the place for diagnosis.

THE RESURGENCE OF INTEREST IN DIAGNOSIS

At present, concern with diagnosis in psychiatry is relatively quiescent. But diagnosis in psychology has experienced a revival. Ford and Urban noted the resurgence of interest in diagnosis and classification of clients and problems in their chapter in the 1967 *Annual Review of Psychology*. They pointed out that both Eysenck and Rachman, and Ban "are pursuing the notion that differential problems require differential treatment"; referring to Angyal's *Neurosis and Treatment,* they noted that he "finds one element, 'universal ambiguity,' at the core of all neurosis. . . . Such over-simplification of the problem seems anachronistic."[2] Ford and Urban discussed the objectives of psychotherapy in the following terms:

> Most of the theories which have guided psychotherapy during the last half century have characterized all behavior disorder as resulting from a common nucleus, whether it was an oedipus complex (Freud), a conflict between strivings for independence and dependence (Rank), strivings to overcome inferiority (Adler), or conflicts between learned and organismic evaluations (Rogers), to name only a few. If the cause of all disorder is basically the same, it follows that one psychotherapeutic approach will suffice for all. *The trend now is clearly to reject this view.* There is growing evidence that disorders may differ in the patterns of behavior which become involved, the antecedents which elicit these patterns, and the consequents to which they lead.[3]

In a later publication, they wrote that the task of the therapy field is "to articulate the conditions under which specific tactics are appropriate for particularized sets of problems . . . the discovery of which set of procedures is effective for what set of purposes when applied to what kinds of patients with which sets of problems and practiced by which sorts of people."[4]

This theme has been echoed by other writers. Paul writes: "In all its complexity, the question toward which all outcome research should ultimately be directed is the following: *what* treatment, by *whom,* is most effective for *this* individual with *that* specific problem, and under *which* set of circumstances."[5] Blocher writes: "The old questions of, 'Is counseling effective?' or 'Which counseling theory is correct?' are seen as largely rhetorical. They give way to questions of 'What treatment in the hands of which counselors can offer what benefit to particular clients?'"[6]

Strupp and Bergin, following their review of research in counseling and psychotherapy, make a similar statement:

> We have become convinced that the therapy of the future will consist of a set of specific techniques that can be applied under specifiable conditions to specific problems, symptoms, or cases. . . . It has become increasingly clear that psychotherapy as currently practiced is not a unitary process and is not applied to a unitary problem. Consequently, the traditional problem "Is psychotherapy effective?" is no longer appropriate.
>
> In the light of these observations, we feel that the problem of psychotherapy research in its most general terms, should be reformulated

as a standard scientific question: what specific therapeutic interventions produce what specific changes in specific patients under specific conditions? [7]

In his introduction to a review of research in psychotherapy, Bergin writes:

> We appear to be beyond the stage of asking the overly general and unanswerable question, 'Is psychotherapy effective?' Instead we are prepared to ask, 'Under what conditions will this type of client with these particular problems be changed in what ways by specific types of therapists?' [8]

And in a later review, Bergin states: "We feel quite strongly that researchers and therapists should begin to think more precisely in terms of *kinds of change* rather than in terms of a general multiform change" and notes that "the development of a general trend toward *specific* rather than global improvements indices." [9]

And Kiesler, who in 1966 wrote about the myths of the uniformity of clients and the uniformity of therapists, declares that different therapist behaviors result in different changes in different kinds of patients. [10]

Although these phrases become repetitious, the arguments have a compelling logic. Yet the position which they represent has not been consistently held, perhaps because it has failed to be supported by any acceptable system of classification of clients or patients or of their problems or disturbances.

UNITARY THEORIES OF EMOTIONAL DISTURBANCE

Though subject to the charge of oversimplification and of anachronism (see the quote from Ford and Urban), unitary theories of emotional disturbance have persisted. In fact, as Ford and Urban note, every major theory of or approach to psychotherapy, in its acceptance of a single method of treatment, has implicitly if not explicitly assumed that emotional disturbance is unitary in nature. The only exception is behavior therapy, whose development has been the stimulus for the recurrence of interest in diagnosis.

The failure to develop an acceptable diagnostic classification system after decades of effort may be an indication that emotional disturbances cannot be differentiated into meaningful categories. There seems to be no logical—or psychological—system of classification that is satisfying or generally acceptable, that leads to nonoverlapping, discrete categories on the same level of abstraction, and that are related to differential methods of treatment. The failure to find such discrete categories may be due to the fact that they do not exist. Perhaps we are attempting to break up something that is homogeneous. Perhaps the apparent differences, such as symptoms, are all accidental or irrelevant differences in terms of etiology and the essential nature of emotional disturbance. There may be no essential or fundamental differences among so-called functional emotional disorders that will allow us to distinguish classes of disorder.

Menninger and his associates began to write of a unitary concept of mental illness in 1958.[11] The concept later was incorporated in a book, in which they noted that many psychiatrists were coming to the conclusion that there is but one type of mental disturbance.[12] Menninger reported that he began to question diagnosis at the beginning of his career, but remarked: "I am somewhat ashamed to admit that it has taken me a quarter of a century to realize that this formula [treating the patient according to his diagnosis] rarely works out this way in actual practice."[13]

Menninger and his associates did not drop the use of the word *diagnosis,* however. They used it to distinguish differing degrees of severity of disturbance. It is this difference in severity of disturbance that seems to be the basis for recommendations for differential treatment. It is the basis of the difference between disturbances that are labeled neurotic and those that are labeled psychotic, a differentiation that is not always easy to make.

Bergin, in his work on the studies on which Eysenck based his claim that psychotherapy is not effective, notes that the rate of success varies among different diagnostic categories. He suggests that diagnosis or the distinguishing of differences among clients or patients is necessary in evaluating the effects of psychotherapy.[14] However, it appears that the differences can be accounted for in terms of the degree of severity of the condition. A ranking of the diagnostic categories in terms of degree of disturbance, I suggest, would correlate perfectly with the success rates.

The extensive research upon the relation of client variables to continuance in psychotherapy or to outcome has not resulted in the discovery of any classification of clients in terms of diagnosis or personality.[15] Fulkerson and Barry, following their review on predicting outcome by the use of tests, concluded that "the variables which appear to have the strongest relationship to outcome have been non-test variables: severity and duration of illness, acuteness of onset, degree of precipitating stress, etc."[16]

The only client variables consistently related to continuation and/or outcome are client motivation, socioeconomic variables, and severity of the disturbance.[17] Motivation is probably related to severity of disturbance; the most severely disturbed clients often do not recognize the nature or severity of their condition or their need for help. There is research evidence that the less severely disturbed clients persist in therapy and improve, which has led to the statement that those who need psychotherapy least are the ones who receive it. Motivation is essentially the recognition of the need for help and a desire to get help by seeking and persisting in psychotherapy. The relevant variable in the socioeconomic factors is probably what may be called psychological-mindedness. This is a psychological sophistication about emotional disturbance, contrasted with the unsophisticated attitude or belief that disturbance is physical or physiological in nature. This attitude is related to or a part of motivation. Socioeconomic factors also relate to intelligence and ability to verbalize, particularly introspectively, both of which are facilitative for therapy. In addition, the problems of clients at the lower socioeconomic levels often involve situations not suitable for psychotherapy. That is, many people come to or are referred to counselors or psychotherapists with problems that are not essentially psychological, and it should not be expected that counseling or psychotherapy would be helpful.

To summarize, the extensive research on client variables in psychotherapy has turned up little or no evidence upon which relevant classifications of clients could be constructed as a basis for differential treatment. The so-called myth of client homogeneity may not be a myth after all. To be sure, there are differences among clients, but these are essentially irrelevant and, where relevant, are differences not in quality but in quantity, essentially in the degree of disturbance. The notion of a common basic etiology for all functional emotional disturbance is not a new idea. It is implicit at least in all major methods of psychotherapy. Perhaps instead of continuing to act upon the assumption that there are different kinds of emotional disorder and persisting in attempts to discover what they are, we should operate upon the assumption that there is no basic essential difference and attempt to discover and understand the common etiology. The theory presented in this book is such an attempt.

A UNITARY THEORY OF PSYCHOTHERAPY

If there is a single basic cause for emotional disturbance, *then* it follows that there should be a single method of treatment. This is the implicit premise of all major approaches to psychotherapy. As Urban and Ford note:

> It is more parsimonious to presume that all changes in behavior occur as a consequence of learning, and that all learning proceeds in essentially the same fashion, that is, that the same principles govern the

modification of all behavior regardless of its type or the characteristics of the person in whom they are taking place. If all behaviors . . . follow essentially the same sets of laws, then the procedures effective with one category of behavior will be effective for all.[18]

But, it may be asked, if this is so, why are there so many obviously different theories and methods of psychotherapy, all of which are apparently equally successful? The answer is simple. While there may be obvious differences among the various approaches, there are basic common elements, or a common basic element. Parallel to the concept of the unitary nature of emotional disturbance, there has developed the concept of the unitary nature of psychotherapy.

It is the common elements, rather than the obvious but superficial differences, that are responsible for the (equal) effectiveness of all approaches. The basic common element in all psychotherapies is the interpersonal relationship. The nature of this relationship, and its aspects, are now beginning to be understood.

In their 1967 book, Truax and Carkhuff presented the results of their survey of some of the major approaches to counseling or psychotherapy.[19] They indicated that all theories either implicitly or explicitly recognize these basic ingredients or conditions: (1) empathic understanding, (2) nonpossessive warmth or respect, and (3) genuineness. There is now extensive evidence of the effectiveness of these conditions, enough so that it is not too soon to conclude that these conditions, perhaps with the addition of some others (see Chapter 5), are the effective elements in all methods of counseling or psychotherapy. The myth of the uniformity of conditions is, it appears, not entirely a myth.

The significant fact about these conditions is that they are effective with all kinds of clients with all kinds of problems—with children and adults, the poor and disadvantaged as well as the rich and the advantaged, and with educational, vocational, marital, and other so-called personal problems. (See Chapter 13 for a discussion of the research evidence.) The essential variable in which the effectiveness of therapists varies is the quality of the interpersonal relationship they provide. The low level of effectiveness of psychotherapy in general can be attributed to the fact that professionals have not been selected on the basis of their potential to provide a good interpersonal relationship. Their training has not focused upon fostering and developing this capacity. In fact, with the emphasis upon evaluation and diagnostic skills and upon cognitive or intellectual performance in academic subjects and research, those individuals who are high in interpersonal skills to begin with may leave or be dropped from training programs or, if they remain, may even show a drop in the level of their interpersonal relationship skills.

When the levels of the conditions offered by the therapist are high, other variables, including client variables, are less important. Truax and Mitchell concluded that the therapist, rather than the client, is the most important determiner of the conditions.[20] However, client psychological-mindedness, verbal expressive productivity, severity of the condition, and socioeducational level were found to be related to therapist conditions in the Wisconsin study of Rogers and his associates.[21] Clients who are not psychological-minded, who are less verbal, less introspective, and who are concerned about reality problems, are not responded to with as much interest, concern, liking, respect, acceptance, and so on by the therapist and are more difficult for the therapist to understand.

If there is a myth regarding the homogeneity of psychotherapists, it has been that all therapists of all theoretical orientations or using all techniques are equally good. There are, however, as we now know, good therapists and bad therapists. It was fashionable a short time ago to ridicule those who, like me, insisted that there were some counselors, some methods, or some theories that were better than others. We were, it was said, playing the game of setting the people in the black hats against those in the white hats. But in therapy, as in all of life, there *are* black hats and white hats.

THE PLACE FOR DIAGNOSIS

It should not be concluded that there is no place for diagnosis in psychotherapy and, more broadly, in helping relationships. There is a place, in the model developed in this book.

It may be that the development of so-called behavior therapy, with its emphasis upon specific treatments for specific conditions, is related to the resurgence in interest in diagnosis. But it is also the extension of the terms *psychotherapy* and *counseling* (which is in part related to the rise of behavior therapy) that has led to an increased interest in specific treatments for specific conditions. For it is true, as Kiesler notes, that psychotherapy is not homogeneous. Psychotherapy has come to encompass many things, or many kinds of helping relationships, including most if not all of the continuum described in Chapter 1. A major source of the confusion regarding diagnosis, as well as of the disagreements and contradictions in much of the research, is the inclusion of so many different things under the term *psychotherapy*. Urban and Ford recognize this problem:

> One can legitimately ask at this point whether there is a definable realm of psychotherapy any longer, and what the justification is in continuing to speak of it as a field. It has become increasingly clear

that these procedures which operate under the label of psychotherapy no longer represent an homogeneous grouping. Psychotherapy as currently practiced is not a unitary process, applied to unitary problems, by a set of professionals with a definable common background and training and a common set of criteria by which the fruits of their labor can be evaluated.[22]

If this is the case, then it would appear to be desirable to agree upon some definitions of terms to apply to the heterogeneous things that now go by the name of psychotherapy. Yet one encounters great resistance in attempting to do so. No one appears to want to limit the term, even though it is recognized that failure to do so is the source of much confusion. My attempts to delimit counseling or psychotherapy as I have done in this book have led to strong objections. Students often ask: What difference does it make what we call it? But the problem is that "it" is not an "it" but a number of quite different things.

The realm of behavior with which psychotherapists are now concerned has widened, and involves the whole continuum of helping relationships rather than just the treatment of neurotics or psychotics, the "mentally ill," or the emotionally disturbed. Psychotherapists are now being faced with a large number and variety of persons seeking a wide variety of specific behavior changes. *Behavior modification* is a term used to refer to the treatment of many of these specific problems. For some (or many, apparently) *psychotherapy* and *behavior modification* are interchangeable terms. Kiesler, for example, without any justification and apparently without recognizing the implications, states that psychotherapy "has been defined as the science of behavior modification."[23] While it should be apparent that the latter is a much more inclusive term and that the two cannot be equated, their juxtaposition does provide a suggestion for the resolution of the problem of diagnosis.

With the increasing variety and heterogeneity of methods of behavior modification and the increasing variety of persons who are called clients, the matter of distinguishing them and matching one to the other becomes more relevant. The diagnostic question is not: What kind of emotional disturbance does this client have? It is (1) Does this client have an emotional disturbance of psychological origin, or does the disturbance originate from an organic or physiological condition? and (2) If the client has a psychological problem, is it one for which counseling or psychotherapy (defined as a relationship consisting of the conditions dealt with in this book) is appropriate (necessary and sufficient), or is it one that requires another kind of helping relationship (the facilitative conditions plus other methods of helping)? The latter question involves placing the client on the continuum of helping relationships that is described in Chapter 1. Of course, it may be the case, as indicated there, that some if not many clients need or could benefit from more than one kind of helping relationship.

In light of the research indicating that the conditions alone are sufficient for a wide variety of outcomes, it becomes difficult to determine when other kinds of help should be provided. It would be easy to conclude, on the basis of the effectiveness of behavior modification techniques with certain disturbances, that the relationship itself is not sufficient for solving many of the specific problems to which behavior modification techniques have been successfully applied. But there is evidence that the relationship is also effective, at least for some clients with such specific problems. For example, Paul found that systematic desensitization was more effective than "insight therapy" or "attention placebo" (probably a weak relationship therapy) in the treatment of fear of public speaking in college students. But both the insight and the attention placebo groups also improved (or, perhaps more accurately, though Paul did not ascertain this, some of the members improved).[24]

It might be expected that children with reading problems would benefit more from remedial instruction than from relationship therapy or, if it be conceded that there are emotional factors involved, more from instruction and therapy than from either alone. But Bills, in an early study, found that retarded readers who participated in play therapy improved their reading significantly during the therapy period compared to control periods preceding and following the experimental period.[25] In another study, Lawrence found, contrary to his expectation, that poor readers who were provided with both counseling and remedial instruction did not gain as much as those who were provided with counseling alone.[26] Truax's statement, that the effectiveness of behavior modification may be essentially due to the relationship, may be relevant in this study.

It is not clear to what extent the conditions of relationship therapy are necessary and sufficient. When the conditions are successful in leading to a greater level of self-actualization, the self-actualizing client may then, on his or her own and as a by-product of the therapy, change many specific behaviors and/or seek specific kinds of help and assistance to achieve specific goals. But since not all clients do this, it is important to know how they differ from those who do, or how their therapists and/or their therapy differ in the implementation of the action conditions, particularly.

Relationship counseling or psychotherapy is the specific treatment for clients whose self-actualization is hindered by the lack or inadequacy of facilitative interpersonal relationships. This may appear to be an extremely narrow definition, limiting counseling or psychotherapy to only a small proportion of those who need or desire help. However, the evidence that the therapeutic relationship alone is effective with so many clients with so many apparently different problems suggests that the lack of good interpersonal relationships is widespread in our society and is the source of the major part of what we call emotional disturbance, or the failure of so many to become self-actualizing persons, capable of achieving—by themselves in many cases, providing the opportunities are present, or through the help of others—the many specific goals with which psychotherapy has been concerned.

SUMMARY

In this chapter we dealt with the problem of diagnosis in counseling or psychotherapy. Emphasis on diagnosis has increased with the development of the techniques of behavior modification. Writers are calling for studies that will determine what specific techniques used by what kinds of therapists are effective with what kinds of clients with what kinds of problems.

While this may appear to be an eminently logical and desirable approach, the necessary systems for classifying techniques, therapists, clients, and problems are not available. Research to date has not succeeded in identifying relevant variables that would form the basis for such classifications. The results of studies of clients to date indicate that client motivation, socioeconomic level, and degree of disturbance are the only variables significantly and consistently related to continuation in therapy and to successful outcomes.

In the area of therapies and therapist variables, research has supported consistently only the importance of a facilitative interpersonal relationship characterized by high levels of empathic understanding, warmth or respect, genuineness, and concreteness. Therapy that provides high levels of these conditions is successful with a wide variety of clients presenting a wide variety of problems. Changes in many kinds of specific behaviors occur without the use of direct or specific modifying techniques such as are advocated by the behaviorists and the others quoted at the beginning of the chapter.

Thus, it appears that, despite the apparent logic of specific treatments for specific conditions, there is evidence for the unitary nature of emotional disturbance and for a single method of treatment. The human interpersonal relationship is the effective factor in all counseling or psychotherapy. There is no compelling evidence to support the doctrine of specific treatments for specific conditions. In fact, the evidence we have is against this.

Diagnosis does have a place in the practice of counseling or psychotherapy, however. In the first place, it is necessary to determine whether the client's emotional disturbance is of psychological origin or not. Psychotherapy is appropriate only for psychological problems. Second, it may be necessary or desirable to ascertain if the client's problem is one that can be helped by psychotherapy (defined as a facilitative interpersonal relationship) or whether he or she needs, or also needs, other kinds of help, involving a different kind of helping relationship.

NOTES

1. F. C. Thorne. *Principles of psychological examining.* Brandon, VT: Clinical Psychology, 1955, pp. 96–106; F. C. Thorne. Diagnostic classification and nomenclature for psychological states. Monograph Supplement No. 17. *Journal of Clinical Psychology*, 1964. (Also in F. C. Thorne. *Integrative psychology.* Brandon, VT: Clinical Psychology, 1967, pp. 86–157.)
2. D. H. Ford and H. B. Urban. Psychotherapy. *Annual Review of Psychology.* Palo Alto, CA: Annual Reviews, 1967, p. 336.
3. Ford and Urban, Psychotherapy, p. 340. Italics added.
4. H. B. Urban and D. H. Ford. Some historical and conceptual perspectives on psychotherapy and behavior change. In A. E. Bergin and S. L. Garfield (Eds.), *Handbook of psychotherapy and behavior change: An empirical analysis.* New York: Wiley, 1971, p. 20.
5. G. L. Paul. Strategy of outcome research in psychotherapy. *Journal of Consulting Psychology*, 1967, *31*, 111.
6. D. Blocher. What can counseling offer clients? In J. M. Whiteley (Ed.), *Research in counseling.* Columbus, OH: Merrill, 1968, p. 16.
7. H. H. Strupp and A. E. Bergin. Some empirical and conceptual bases for coordinated research in psychotherapy. *International Journal of Psychiatry*, 1969, *7*, 68, 19–20.
8. A. E. Bergin. Preface. In Bergin and Garfield, *Handbook*, pp. ix–xii.
9. A. E. Bergin. The evaluation of therapeutic outcomes. In Bergin and Garfield, *Handbook*, p. 257.
10. D. J. Kiesler. Experimental designs in psychotherapy research. In Bergin and Garfield, *Handbook*, pp. 36–74. For the earlier discussion of myths, see D. J. Kiesler. Some myths of psychotherapy research and the search for a paradigm. *Psychological Bulletin*, 1966, *65*, 110–136.
11. K. Menninger, H. Ellenberger, P. Pruyser, and M. Mayman. The unitary concept of mental illness. *Bulletin of the Menninger Clinic*, 1958, *22*, 4–12.
12. K. Menninger, M. Mayman, and P. Pruyser. *The vital balance.* New York: Viking, 1963.
13. B. Hall (Ed.). *A psychiatrist's world: The selected papers of Karl Menninger.* New York: Viking, 1959, p. 671.
14. Bergin, Evaluation of therapeutic outcomes.
15. S. L. Garfield. Research on client variables in psychotherapy. In S. L. Garfield and A. E. Bergin (Eds.), *Handbook of psychotherapy and behavior change: An empirical analysis* (2nd ed.). New York: Wiley, 1978. S. L. Garfield. *Psychotherapy: An eclectic approach.* New York: Wiley Interscience, 1981.

16. S. C. Fulkerson and J. R. Barry. Methodology of research on the prognostic use of psychological tests. *Psychological Bulletin*, 1961, *58*, 199.
17. Garfield, Research on client variables; *Psychotherapy: An eclectic approach.*
18. Urban and Ford, Some historical and conceptual perspectives, p. 17. They go on to say, however, that the evidence does not support this view.
19. C. B. Truax and R. R. Carkhuff. *Toward effective counseling and psychotherapy.* Chicago: Aldine, 1967, Chap. 2.
20. C. B. Truax and K. M. Mitchell. Research in certain therapist skills in relation to process and outcome. In Bergin and Garfield, *Handbook*, pp. 310, 330.
21. C. R. Rogers, E. T. Gendlin, D. J. Kiesler, and C. B. Truax. *The therapeutic relationship and its impact: A study of psychotherapy with schizophrenics.* Madison: University of Wisconsin Press, 1967.
22. Urban and Ford, Some historical and conceptual perspectives, p. 5.
23. Kiesler, Experimental designs in psychotherapy research, p. 37.
24. G. L. Paul. *Insight vs. desensitization in psychotherapy: An experiment in anxiety reduction.* Stanford, CA: Stanford University Press, 1966.
25. R. E. Bills. Nondirective play therapy with retarded readers. *Journal of Consulting Psychology*, 1950, *14*, 140–149.
26. D. Lawrence. The effects of counseling on retarded readers. *Educational Research*, 1971, *13*, 119–124; see also D. Lawrence. The counseling of retarded readers by non-professionals. *Educational Research*, 1972, *15*, 48–52.

CHAPTER 9

The Relationship
in Group Counseling
or Psychotherapy

We are in the era of the small group. To be sure, humans have always lived in groups. This is a biological necessity, and society has developed its institutions, including the basic group—family—to meet this need. But society has increased in size and complexity, with a resulting increase in impersonality. The increase of formal groups that involve only limited aspects of the person or individual, coupled with the decline of groups that involve the total person—the primary or face-to-face groups—have created problems in human relationships. Society has not been meeting the human need for the close interpersonal relationships of small groups. But a new social institution is arising to fill this gap; this is the group movement, represented by such diverse methodologies as those of the T-group or sensitivity group, the encounter group, and the personal growth group.

In view of the basic need for close interpersonal relationships and the fact that many if not most of the problems bringing people to counselors or therapists involve interpersonal relationships, group therapy is probably the preferred mode of treatment. It makes possible the practice of the principles of good interpersonal relationships as they are learned. It provides an opportunity for experiential learning. We explore in this chapter the role of the group in relationship psychotherapy.

KINDS OF GROUPS

For many years, group guidance has been a part of the counseling and guidance service in secondary schools. The term *group guidance* has been used to refer to such activities as homeroom programs, field trips, clubs, assemblies, college and career days, and the imparting of educational and occupational information and sometimes test scores to students in groups. Less frequently, group guidance has included discussions of social skills and social development, human relations, and adjustment or mental health.

Group guidance is not group counseling but group teaching or instruction, and is differentiated from the usual classroom instruction in that it deals with content that is not considered part of the standard curriculum. The focus is upon content; the process is highly structured, with guided discussion; and the groups are of classroom size.

In the 60s there was a proliferation of groups with varying designations—*T-group, sensitivity group,* and *encounter group* being most common. It has become difficult if not impossible to distinguish among these groups, since there is as much variability among groups having the same designation as among those with different designations. The T (for training) group was originally concerned with the teaching of skills in human relations, through a group experience that was analyzed in terms of what was happening in the group—group dynamics. There was no concern about personal development. However, T-groups have merged into sensitivity groups and become concerned with increasing an individual's sensitivity to his or her own and others' actions and reactions. Encounter groups are concerned with the personal growth and development of their members but do not include analysis and didactic discussion of the process, as do T-groups. There is thus a continuum on the dimension of cognition-affect. Indeed, some groups prohibit any cognitive discussion, and some groups permit only nonverbal behavior. There is also a continuum of structuring that cuts across the group designations. T-groups can be quite unstructured, though they tend to be task-oriented, at least to some extent. Encounter groups are generally unstructured; however, there are encounter group leaders or facilitators who use a highly or completely structured approach, going through an ordered series of exercises or games.

Group psychotherapy is not a new or recent concept. Its origin is generally attributed to a physician named Joseph H. Pratt, who in 1905 introduced group meetings for tuberculosis patients. However, this was not group therapy as it is recognized or practiced today. The meetings were lectures and discussion groups. In the 1920s, group methods were employed with psychiatric patients. These groups also were cognitively oriented or instructional in nature. In the 1930s, psychoanalytically oriented group therapy developed. Client-centered principles were used in groups in the 1950s.

Group counseling as a term has been in use for about three decades. However, just as there is no essential difference between individual counseling and individual psychotherapy, there is no essential difference between group counseling and group psychotherapy. Attempts to differentiate between them have been unsatisfactory, leading to artificial distinctions. Group therapy is what is practiced by psychiatrists, psychologists, and social workers in a medical setting. Group counseling is what is practiced by counselors (and to some extent social workers, clergymen, and others) in a nonmedical setting. The difference, as in the case of individual counseling, is in the degree of disturbance of the clients, not in the process or the goal.

All groups, whether sensitivity groups, encounter groups, personal growth groups, counseling groups, or therapy groups, involve interpersonal relationships. Insofar as there are common ways of relating and general principles of interpersonal relationships, all groups are similar. This probably is strictly true only in free or unstructured groups. Groups that are controlled by the leader, facilitator, or counselor or therapist will differ according to the structure imposed upon them. As Yalom states: "The psychotherapy group, provided its development is unhampered by severe structural restrictions, evolves into a social microcosm" of interpersonal relationships.[1]

THE GROUP RELATIONSHIP

It is often, if not usually, assumed that when one moves from the dyadic relationship to group relationships, one enters an entirely new realm involving new principles and new concepts. But groups are composed of individuals—they do not exist apart from their members. Thus, the group itself is not the focus of the therapist; the focus is the individuals in the group. Group therapy is not therapy of the group but of individuals *in* a group setting. It is necessary to point out here that I do not consider as group therapy the kind of treatment of individuals *in the presence* of a group that is practiced by many Gestalt therapists as well as by those practicing transactional analysis. In group therapy as defined by me and most others there is interaction among the group members.

Groups consist of interrelationships among the individuals who compose them. Members can interact with only one other individual at a time, even though it is in the context of previous interactions with other members of the group and with awareness of the presence of others. The interrelationships among members of groups are not qualitatively different from the interrelationship between two individuals. They are, of course, more complex. The group counselor is not relating to or responding to a group, but to individuals in a group. It is, of course, much more difficult to relate to a number of individuals in a group context, or in the context of the interrelationships among these individuals, than to one person at a time.

It may thus be questioned whether there is such a thing as "group dynamics," at least as something qualitatively different from or involving entirely new principles from interpersonal relationships on a dyadic basis. The acceptance of the concept of group dynamics tends to lead to a reification of the group and the group process as something apart from, above, or in addition to the individuals composing the group and their interrelationships. But there is no such thing as a "group mind." There is no group goal or group task in group therapy as there is in task-oriented groups. Yalom says the task of the group is "to achieve a group culture of intimacy, acceptance, introspection, understanding, and interpersonal honesty."[2] But this is not a group task—it is the task of the individual members, or, as Yalom goes on to note, an interpersonal, and thus a personal, task. The concept of group dynamics grew out of the T-group movement. Its principles or concepts represent the description and terms developed by a particular group of social psychologists. It is possible that other principles or concepts could be used to describe the same process. Perhaps the terms used in the field of group dynamics refer to the same things as other terms used by other psychologists in describing the group process, or the interrelationships of individuals in groups.

As an example, we can take the term *group cohesion,* a basic and perhaps the most important concept of group dynamics. Its importance is emphasized because there is evidence that group cohesiveness is related to successful outcomes in group counseling or psychotherapy.[3] Definitions of this concept and instruments used to measure it include feelings of personal involvement in the group, including feelings of mutual warmth, respect, acceptance, concern, trust, empathy, and genuineness. These are terms we have met before. They are the characteristics of good human relationships as described in earlier chapters. Yalom equates cohesiveness in group therapy to the relationship in individual therapy.[4] Perhaps the basis for the concept of cohesiveness is the sense of "we-ness" or group attractiveness that develops in successful groups. But this is an outcome of the presence of good interpersonal relationships and occurs in dyadic relationships, including individual therapy or a good marriage. Perhaps it is important to note here that most of the research on groups is not relevant to group therapy, since it has usually involved task-oriented, structured, controlled, or artificial groups composed of "normal" individuals meeting in a nontherapy setting over a short period of time.

Relationship therapy, based upon the principles of good human relationships, extends naturally to group therapy. *The conditions for effective individual therapy are the conditions for effective group therapy.*

THE GROUP PROCESS

Most writers see the group as going through a number of stages. Yalom distinguishes three stages in the formation of the group.[5] The first is the initial stage—the stage of orientation, hesitant participation, and search for meaning. There is a search for acceptance and approval, both from other members and the therapist. Members are puzzled, dependent, and are looking for structure. Behavior is socially stereotyped, with impersonal discussion of general topics, and rational discussion of external problems and solutions. Members search for commonalities. Mahler[6] refers to this first phase as the involvement stage. It includes getting acquainted, beginning accepting relationships, and beginning to discuss personal behaviors and feelings. Bonney and Foley call it the establishment stage.[7] This stage is of no specific duration. It may last for one or two or several sessions. Group members have many doubts, anxieties, even fears, about disclosing or exposing themselves to the group. Most ordinary social interaction is at a formal and superficial level, and it takes time to get down to basic feelings and genuine expression of them to others. Mintz refers to "the social masks which participants wear, which they gradually doff with apprehension and relief and finally delight. . . ."[8] The development of trust cannot be forced or accelerated by the therapist but must come at its own pace.

Yalom's second stage is the stage of conflict, dominance, and rebellion. Negative feelings are expressed to other group members and to the therapist, perhaps because of disappointment in the therapist's leadership or his or her lack of special interest in members, or jealousy of the therapist's position. There is preoccupation with dominance, power, and control. Many negative comments and criticisms are offered, and moralistic advice-giving occurs. Scapegoating may appear. Mahler's second stage is called the transition stage, in which the group moves from a social orientation to a therapeutic orientation in which the members recognize that for progress to occur the content must become highly personal in nature. Bonney and Foley describe this state succinctly:

> Early in this stage, they [the group members] realize that the purpose for their existence as a group is to develop a situation that will allow for therapeutic experiences. . . . There ensues a period characterized

by lack of involvement on the part of group members for fear of violating the perceived social norms inhibiting the discussion of personal problems in groups. The incongruency is resolved through the acceptance of a new norm that demands the discussion of personal concerns.[9]

There is resistance and anxiety, which may be reduced by the therapist's structuring the therapy group as different from the social group, as a place where the discussion of personal problems is not only permissible but necessary. The transition stage ends when the group members accept the need for self-disclosure.

Yalom's third stage involves the development of cohesiveness—group members develop trust, mutual acceptance, intimacy, and closeness. An in-group feeling develops—a sense of we-ness. Members engage in self-disclosure. Expressions of negative affect are suppressed. Mahler terms this the working stage in which the members of the group engage in the process of self-exploration and assist each other in the process.

Yalom's fourth stage is the longest stage by far, continuing from the three preliminary stages for the life of the group. In this stage, his working stage, the group is a fully developed, mature working group, engaging in the working-through process. Mahler adds as a fourth stage the ending of the group. This is the process of divorce or disengagement from the close relationships that have been formed, and the movement toward independence from group members and the substitution of close relationships with persons outside the group.

These stages are, of course, not discrete or clear-cut. There are overlappings. Moreover, the group may move back and forth or in cycles as new material emerges. Also, the stages and their nature are influenced by the therapist, both by his or her personality and his or her style or technique. A therapist who directs and gives clear-cut structure will find the group responding differently in its beginning or first stage than the therapist who provides little or no structure. The composition of the group will also influence its functioning and thus the nature of its development.

The description of the process in basic encounter groups by Carl Rogers is particularly relevant because the philosophical and theoretical bases of his approach are essentially those of relationship therapy as developed in this book. The following is in part an adaptation from Rogers.[10]

1. *Milling around.* When the group is initially given freedom, with little structure except that of a place where individuals can relate to each other and get to know each other, there is a period of confusion, silence, frustration, small-talk, lack of continuity. There

is often a demand for the leader to "do something." In one group (conducted by me), after two sessions of this, one member addressed me: "Why haven't you done something, why don't you do something?" Before I could respond, she said: "Well, I'm going to do something," and then she launched into a very personal expression of her problems.

2. *Resistance to personal expression or exploration.* Although one member may reveal something personal, there may be a hesitancy, reluctance, or refusal by the others to respond on a personal level. There may be an embarrassment in the others, who gloss over the personal statement. People don't disclose themselves in ordinary social situations, and it takes time for them to feel comfortable in doing so even when they have been, in effect, given permission to do so. A trust in the group must develop first.

3. *Description of past feelings.* Expressions of feelings begin with telling about past feelings. They are experienced in the past, not in the present. They do not involve members of the group.

4. *Expression of negative feelings.* The first current feelings to be expressed, about other members in the group, are negative. The feelings are often first directed at the counselor. Negative feelings are apt to be expressed first because of feelings of threat, anxiety, defensiveness, because we are not used to expressing positive feelings, and also because of a need to test the freedom and safety of the group.

5. *Expression and exploration of personally meaningful material.* The voicing of negative feelings is followed by someone revealing himself or herself to the group. Rogers says that "the reason for this no doubt is that the individual member has come to realize that this is in part his group. He can help to make of it what he wishes." This is beautifully illustrated by the woman in my group who took responsibility for her contribution to getting the group started. A climate of trust begins to develop. Members are willing to take the risk of disclosing themselves.

6. *Expression of immediate interpersonal feelings in the group.* Members become able to express their feelings and attitudes about each other, both positive and negative. The negative feelings are not critical, bitter attacks but simple statements of feelings and reactions. The result is not conflict but exploration in an atmosphere of trust.

7. *Development of a healing capacity in the group.* Members of the group begin to help each other. They begin to care for each other, to understand each other, to try to help, each in his or her own way.

8. *Self-acceptance and the beginning of change.* This is an awareness of what one is, an admission, even, of what one really is behind the facade. This recognition of what one is, is necessary before one can begin to change. One can then explore what one is. A growing

sense of realness, genuineness, or authenticity develops. Members feel they can be themselves, both their strong and weak selves.

9. *Cracking of facades.* The growing recognition of oneself leads to the throwing off of defenses, the taking off of masks and facades. Each group member, apparently realizing the possibility of a deep relationship where everyone is real and open and honest, demands or requires that other members be themselves.

10. *Giving and receiving of feedback.* As the group members become open and honest with each other, the members learn how they seem to others, how they affect others. Again, this can involve both positive and negative feelings, but the negative expressions take place in a concerned and caring environment. Feedback can lead to greater self-understanding. Feedback lets us see ourselves as others see us.

11. *Confrontation.* When one member reacts to another very strongly, usually in a negative manner, *confrontation* seems to be a better term to use than *feedback*. Sometimes people do feel strongly against others, and these feelings have to come out. But it is only when people have come to know each other well that these feelings can be meaningfully expressed with the possibility of constructive results.

12. *Extension of the helping relationship outside the group sessions.* Group members relate to each other outside the group in a more human way and often are very helpful to another member of the group who is going through the painful process of self-awareness and change.

13. *Development of the basic encounter relationship.* Group members feel close to each other and highly empathic with each other. An extremely close personal relationship develops, a basic human encounter, an I-thou relationship.

14. *Expression of positive feelings and closeness.* The group becomes warm, trusting, with a sense of human togetherness and closeness. This and the preceding stage appear to constitute "cohesiveness."

15. *Change of behavior in the group.* Group members change and become different right before each other's eyes. They become more empathic and understanding, they become more accepting, respecting and warm, they become more honest, real, and genuine—they act like self-actualizing persons! Interpersonal relationships change, personal problems are resolved. A member in one of my groups, who had presented himself as needing to be strong and independent, to have people lean on him (at the age of 6, he had taken his younger brother on a train halfway across the country), began openly to ask for and accept help from others. A man who could not bear to be touched by a woman was unaware later when a woman

touched him and when he touched her. There is considerable evidence that people are different following even a brief but intensive group experience. Too often, though, in the reality of the world outside the group, changes fade away. It is difficult to be really human in a world where there are so few really human beings—or where so few human beings are able to express their humanness.

THE THERAPIST IN THE PROCESS

The major function of the therapist is to create, set up, or "permit" a situation where group members can express themselves, can start out on and continue along the pattern described above. The therapist is not a controller, with a hand on the throttle, pushing and pulling to speed up or slow down the process by manipulating the behavior of group members, as if trying to reach a preconceived destination on a time schedule. The group is a real-life situation and should be allowed to develop naturally. The purpose of the therapist should be to help provide an atmosphere in which the members can interact more naturally, more realistically, more honestly, and more humanly than is possible in the so-called real, but actually artificial, social environment in which we live.

How does the therapist do this? The therapist is not a leader in the usual sense of the word. There is no specific goal for the group. The goal, as in individual therapy, is the development of self-actualizing persons. The purpose of the therapist is to create, or facilitate, the development of the conditions under which members of the group can become more self-actualizing persons. As in individual relationship therapy, the therapist in a group tries to establish the core conditions.

1. *Structuring.* The amount of structuring necessary or desirable depends on the group and the situation. If the group has no idea of what is expected of them, some structuring is necessary. If the group, or some of its members, have some misconceptions about the group and how they are to function, then structuring is necessary. In general, structuring should be kept to a minimum. Because in therapy groups people are expected to function differently than in "real life," some structuring seems to be necessary. Rogers, in meeting for the first time the encounter group depicted in the Academy Award winning film *Journey into Self,* began as follows:

> I'm glad we all had a chance to have dinner together because it gives a little chance to get acquainted, at least a few of us; but I feel as though really, we really are strangers to each other in spite of that—with lots of geographical distance and occupational distance, and everything.

And, I feel like saying just one or two things to start with, from my point of view. One is that this is our group. We really can make of it anything we want to make of it, and, for myself, I don't have any prediction, except that by the time we end Sunday afternoon, we'll probably know each other a lot better than we do right now; but how we may want to go about it, or what we want to do, that's really up to us. And I think that it is an opportunity to *be* in the group as fully as we can; maybe in some respects to try ways of being or ways of relating to each other that we never quite have had nerve enough to try before, where in ordinary life situations it seems like it's too impossible. In a sense, it's an opportunity to try out new ways of behaving with other people; there's that in it too: things that we have sort of wished we might be or do with others and never have quite had the nerve—maybe we will have the nerve here. I don't know, but at any rate from here on in, as far as I'm concerned, it's up to us. . . . Oh, yes, one thing I did want to say: I feel a lot of anticipation about this group; I really look forward to getting to know you. And at the same time, I'm apprehensive; and I don't think it has much to do with the lights and the cameras. I think I'm always a little apprehensive in not knowing what a given group is going to be like. I don't know who we are, how we're going to get along, whether anything is going to come of this. Ah, so I feel a very double feeling; I feel excited and full of anticipation; I feel a little on the scared side too.[11]

A similar approach is appropriate for therapy groups. Structuring is designed to give participants some idea of what to expect and what is expected of them, thus reducing initial anxiety and threat.

2. *Listening.* The therapist listens carefully to *everything* everyone says, focusing upon the feelings being expressed. This is an intense personal listening, to whatever the member of the group is expressing.

3. *Acceptance and respect.* Each member is accepted and respected as he or she is, as a person. There is no pressure for change, no attempt to make the group "jell," "get down to business," begin expressing feelings, or to "speed up" the group process. There is no attempt to get each member involved, to force participation, to "psych out" a silent member, or to delve beneath what persons say. Each person's contribution is taken at face value.

4. *Empathic understanding.* The therapist attempts to understand what each member is thinking, feeling, and trying to express. The therapist attempts to place himself or herself in the place of each person, to understand the personal meaning of what each is saying and feeling.

5. *Responding.* The therapist attempts to convey understanding of what is said by his or her responses. It is not necessary, or desirable, or even possible, that the therapist respond to every statement by a member of the group, for to do so would tend to lead to the development of a two-way interaction. Group members respond to

each other, and the therapist must allow for this. But, as a trained and experienced person, the therapist can often better understand what a member may be trying to say and can often, in communicating his or her understanding, put it in a clearer form, reducing the incoherence or lengthy attempts at expression. By responding to feelings rather than intellectualizing, the therapist can focus the group upon feelings. The therapist can sharpen differences among participants by bringing them out clearly, thus helping participants see their differences more clearly and engage in a more meaningful interaction.

The reader will recognize these methods of facilitating a group. They are the basic conditions of the individual therapy relationship. The group is no exception when it comes to them. As a model for good, open, honest interpersonal relationships, these conditions must be present in the group. While some groups might be able to function without the presence of a therapist, since these characteristics are present to a greater or lesser extent in most individuals, their presence to a sufficient degree cannot be counted on. Groups without a therapist would at best be less efficient—that is, move more slowly. The therapist—as a trained person, an expert, and a constant model—provides a stability to the group as its members flounder and struggle in their relationships with each other. The therapist is thus necessary. He or she is the model for the conditions for a good interpersonal relationship.

The presence of the conditions provided by, and fostered by, the therapist leads to a nonthreatening, safe atmosphere in which people can become less defensive, less inhibited, less constricted, and more open, free, and honest. They can become more real, more human, and thus more the kind of person they are capable of being. And in doing and being so, they make it more possible for others to be so. They become *therapists* for each other. In fact, Yalom goes so far as to say that

> the curative factors in group therapy are primarily mediated not by the therapist but by the other members who provide the acceptance and support, the hope, the experience of universality, the opportunities for altruistic behavior, and the interpersonal feedback, testing and learning.[12]

The fact that group members become, to some extent at least, therapists for each other is an important element in group therapy, making it potentially more powerful and effective than individual therapy. This mutual therapeutic effect has, of course, two elements —one is the experiencing of the therapeutic elements in the behaviors of others, and the second is the experience of being therapeutic for others.

Both these elements of group therapy have been reported by members of groups as being important factors in their experience in successful groups. Dickoff and Lakin found that "more than half of the former patients indicated the primary mode of help in group therapy is through mutual support."[13] Clark and Culbert found that outcomes (as measured by the Walker, Rablen, and Rogers Process Scale) in a T-group were not related to the members' perceived personal relationships with the therapist (as measured by the Barrett-Lennard Relationship Inventory), but were related to the number of two-person mutually therapeutic relationships.[14] Berzon et al. found that among incidents considered most important by group members were feelings of positive regard; acceptance and sympathy for others; witnessing honesty, courage, openness, or expressions of emotionality in others; and feeling responded to by others—incidents involving relationships with the therapist did not rank high.[15]

If the therapist is a model, it may be questioned why he or she doesn't model self-disclosure and self-exploration at the beginning of the group process. One reason, mentioned in the discussion of the therapist as a model in individual therapy (Chapter 7), is that therapy is for clients, not the therapist. The therapist does, of course, engage in some self-disclosure as the group progresses. While it might help for the therapist to model self-disclosure at the beginning, it is not necessary. Its importance can be emphasized through structuring with the group members prior to the beginning of the group. And as one member begins self-disclosure, he or she becomes an example or model for others. As suggested in the discussion of individual therapy, the use of tape recordings or films prior to the start of the group process can be helpful in facilitating the progress of the group.[16] Yalom reports that "successfully treated patients, when interviewed at the conclusion of therapy, have usually expressed a wish that the therapist had been less aloof, more involved in the group. Yet none of the patients wanted the therapists to have contributed more of their personal lives or problems to the group."[17]

The research on the effects of leader or therapist self-disclosure in groups is contradictory. Therapists and leaders who are self-disclosing are perceived as likable, friendly, trustworthy, and helpful.[18] However, self-disclosing therapists were perceived as less mentally healthy in all but one of the studies cited. In the exception (the May and Thompson study), the groups were encounter groups, not therapy groups. Although a study of T-groups by Culbert found leader self-disclosure to be facilitative, Bolman reports that "unexpectedly, trainer openness showed little relationship to participant learning" in a study of 20 trainers and 118 participants in T-groups at Bethel.[19]

The nature of the group appears to be an important factor. Therapist self-disclosure would appear to be less relevant (or appropriate) in counseling or therapy groups than in encounter groups. There are also a number of other variables that influence the effects of leader or therapist self-disclosure. Among these are the timing of self-disclosure in terms of the life of the group (whether at the beginning or early, or later after the group members have become close and have become comfortable with the leader or therapist). While it would appear that to be effective as modeling, therapist self-disclosure should come early, there is some evidence that group members (particularly in therapy groups) disapprove of early self-disclosure.[20] It is apparent that many factors must be taken into account in evaluating the influence of leader or therapist self-disclosure. There also seems to be some confusion between therapist self-disclosure and therapist genuineness, with evidence for the value of the latter sometimes presented as evidence for the value of the former.

There is a further function or responsibility of the therapist that it is necessary to consider because of certain practices of some leaders of encounter groups. This is a function that trained and experienced therapists automatically assume. Beginning therapists and students, however, perhaps under the influence of reports of practices of some encounter group leaders, may not recognize or assume this function. It is the responsibility of the therapist to protect members of the group from being hurt by other members of the group. This is, of course, implicit in the requirement that the group be a therapeutic experience for each member.

Some encounter group leaders apparently believe that the group is not successful unless members express strong negative or aggressive feelings toward each other very early in the process, and they therefore encourage, stimulate, or even provoke such reactions. This misconception is probably based on the fact that usually the first feelings expressed by group members are negative. They are usually directed toward the therapist or facilitator, however. But not all group members necessarily have repressed aggressive feelings toward other members of the group, though no doubt all of us will respond aggressively if provoked enough.

There are two reasons why early expression of uninhibited and indiscriminate aggression or negative reactions toward other group members is undesirable. The first has been alluded to earlier—they can be harmful to the persons to whom such reactions are directed, who may be unable to understand or cope with them, and may be provoked to respond with negative reactions or attacks on others without adequate reason, resulting in later guilt and remorse.

Such negative or hostile reactions are often justified as being desirable because it is claimed they represent feedback to the person to whom they are directed, on the basis that they are responses to that person or his or her behavior. However, it must be recognized that before the members of the group get to know each other their responses or reactions to each other may be inaccurate or mistaken, based on misinterpretations or misperceptions. They are apt to involve projections. They are thus not true feedback. They include much that is based upon transference. Mintz notes that "transference, in the sense of distorted perception of others, is clearly visible in groups, as members misperceive other members initially, often on the basis of subtle resemblances to childhood figures."[21] Members respond to each other in terms of associations with significant persons in their lives or in terms of stereotypes. Mintz, in discussing the technique of having each person, fairly early in the group, select three people whom he or she likes and three of whom he or she feels critical, and to give reasons for these feelings, writes:

> Participants are encouraged to explore the extent to which their feelings are determined by distorted perceptions coming from past experiences, accidental resemblances, or prejudice. On the following day [of the marathon], when group members know one another better and when their behavior has become more open, they are asked to share any changes in their initial reactions. Typically, although a sense of liking is further enhanced by further acquaintance, initial critical feelings become milder and turn into approval.[22]

Thus it is unreasonable to expect the recipients of such early negative reactions to cope with them as accurate feedback and to learn about themselves from them. They are shocked, hurt, or at least puzzled.

After the group members know and accept and understand each other, such feedback can be helpful. Again, Mintz notes that "after an atmosphere of mutual warmth and concern is established, confrontation can occur which might be painful or even injurious under other circumstances."[23]

Early hostile or aggressive feedback or confrontation, while undesirable even in encounter groups with so-called "normal" individuals, is particularly dangerous in therapy groups. While normal individuals may be able to take it (up to a point, at least), clients are more vulnerable because they are especially low in or lacking in self-esteem and are easily threatened. Yalom points out that such individuals are not likely to give accurate feedback, either. Thus, "the therapist . . . must constantly modulate the amount of confrontation, self-disclosure, and tension the group can tolerate."[24]

There is another potential danger in groups that has not been adequately recognized. This is the power of group pressure toward conformity. Individuals are susceptible to the expectations and demands of others, and the majority members of a group can exert tremendous pressure on a minority or on a single individual. This is the reason some people do things in groups that they would not otherwise do. Under group pressure individuals may do things they do not want to do, which cause them pain and discomfort, and which may be damaging to them as persons, because they are led to believe these things are "good for them," because they do not want to be different—"everyone else is doing it"—and it would be an admission of weakness or lack of courage not to do so. And sometimes, members who do conform experience considerable regret or guilt afterwards. Encounter groups often exhibit this phenomenon, and some leaders foster it, in the name of group esprit de corps or as evidence of group cohesiveness. Such extreme cohesiveness is undesirable and can have harmful effects on members who are coerced to conform to so-called group norms. In group therapy the therapist must be careful not to allow any member to be forced into doing something for which he or she is not prepared and which can perhaps be harmful rather than helpful. No member should be expected or required to do anything that he or she does not want to do. This applies particularly to self-disclosure. Group members must be permitted to remain silent and not to disclose themselves if they don't feel ready to do so.

GROUP SIZE AND COMPOSITION

Group size and composition are important variables that the therapist must consider. We look at these variables in this section.

Group Size

There is general agreement that counseling or therapy groups should be small, though the exact number recommended varies from four to ten. Four is perhaps too few, and ten perhaps too many. The larger the number, the less time there is, on the average, for each member to participate or to talk, and the less interaction each member has with each of the other members. In a large group there is a tendency for members to direct communication to a few others (leading to the development of subgroups or cliques) or to the therapist. Another important reason for keeping the group small is the demands upon the therapist made by a large group. Interactions among members increase in geometric proportion to their number.

It becomes very difficult for the therapist to be aware of all the inter-actions, including nonverbal interactions, and to be responsive to each member at the appropriate time.

Selection of Members

Much has been written about selection of clients for group ther-apy; most of it is based on clinical opinion rather than research. Whatever the problem, or kind of client, someone has reported suc-cess in group therapy. Differences in therapists, in the type of ther-apy, in outcome or success criteria, as well as in the composition of the group, are certainly significant factors in the differences reported. In spite of the lack of agreement and of research, most writers feel that selection is necessary and important.

Research on dropouts, who are for all intents and purposes fail-ures and thus poor risks and to be excluded, indicates that they feel less disturbed psychologically (and thus probably not highly moti-vated) but more hostile than continuers, that they complain more frequently of somatic or physical symptoms, are less responsive to others, are subject to external stress or problems, and are isolates in the group. Dropouts appear to be low in psychological-mindedness and introspectiveness. They are lacking in openness, are self-defensive, insensitive to others, and unable to engage in self-disclosure or in interpersonal intimacy.[25] Yet it could be argued that these are just the kind of clients who need group therapy. In most groups, how-ever, it appears that they are not sufficiently accepted by—or accept-able to—the other members to remain in the group.

The converse of the dropout's characteristics would appear to be desirable for continuation or success in group therapy—openness, sensitivity to others, ability to engage in self-disclosure and intimate personal relations. Ohlsen advocates a rigorous selection procedure, using a personal interview, to select such clients—clients who are ready for and committed to disclosing and exploring themselves and to listening to and helping others. He states that "the prospective client must convince not only the counselor but also himself that he is ready for counseling."[26] But while rigorous selection increases the likelihood of success in group counseling and may be justified if only a limited number from many applicants can be accepted, the de-sirability of a highly restrictive admission policy can be questioned. As in the case of highly selective procedures for individual counsel-ing, the result is that the cards are stacked toward successful results, and those accepted are those who are less in need of help. In the case of group counseling, the factors used in selection, such as ability to disclose oneself and to verbalize problems, to listen to and accept others, are actually the characteristics that group counseling is expected to develop and should not be used too restrictively to reject applicants.

It would appear that selection should best focus on rejecting the few applicants who clearly are not ready to function in or to benefit from a group or who give evidence that they might prevent others from functioning in or benefitting from group counseling. This is, in fact, what many writers suggest. Bach, for example, recommends that persons with insufficient reality contact, with culturally deviant symptomatology, who are chronic monopolists or highly impulsive, should be excluded from therapy groups.[27] Yalom, on the basis of a survey of the literature, lists as poor candidates those who are brain-damaged, paranoid, narcissistic, hypochondriacal, suicidal, addicted to alcohol or drugs, acutely psychotic, or sociopathic.[28]

It would appear that concern with selection should best be limited to excluding those individuals who because of extreme characteristics (muteness, withdrawal, isolation, lack of any ability to relate to others coupled with fear of social contacts) are not likely to be helped but might even become worse in a group, and those whose extreme behaviors (impulsivity, aggressiveness, verbal dominance) are likely to interfere with the progress of other members of the group.

Group Composition

The issue of whether groups should be homogeneous or heterogeneous has not been settled; the situation appears to be similar to the one that existed when Furst summarized it over thirty years ago.[29] Yalom agreed with Furst: "There appears to be a general clinical sentiment that heterogeneous groups have advantages over homogeneous groups for intensive interactional group therapy."[30]

The question, of course, is: On what characteristics is homogeneity or heterogeneity to be based? Such variables as problem or diagnosis, age, sex, intelligence, education, socioeconomic level, and cultural and social origin could be bases for group composition. The problem of communication might suggest the desirability of some homogeneity. Persons widely different in age, intelligence, education, socioeconomic level, and culture may have difficulty in accepting, understanding, and communicating with one another. Yalom appears to favor somewhat homogeneous groups (though he doesn't specify in what variables) on the grounds that they foster cohesiveness, which leads to better outcomes. For some groups, relative homogeneity in age, and homogeneity in sex, may be desirable. Children in group therapy probably should be similar in age or developmental level, although if one purpose of the group is to develop mutual understanding between children and teachers, parents, or adults, then this would not be the case. Adolescents, particularly, might benefit from groups with older members. In some instances, however, single-sex groups of adolescents may be desirable or useful.

But it could be argued that it is enough that all group members share the basic characteristics of human beings living in a common society, or segment of society, with its common problems. If the purpose, or one of the purposes, of group therapy is to develop facility in interpersonal relationships, then a wide variety of group members would appear to be desirable.

Extreme heterogeneity can perhaps create problems, but these need not be insurmountable. However, there is one caution that deserves attention. In the discussion of selection, it was suggested that extreme deviants should not be included in a group. Except for the very extremes, this might not apply to a group composed entirely of such persons—such as severely disturbed psychotics. The point to be made is that there should be no individual in the group who is extremely different from all the other members of the group in one or more characteristics that could interfere with communication with or acceptance by other members of the group. Bach's suggestion is appropriate here: "In general, we limit excessive heterogeneity by trying to place a patient in a group where he can find at least one other patient in circumstances which are similar with respect to some other central phase of his own life."[31]

Probably there is too much concern with the heterogeneity-homogeneity issue. Even when we achieve some homogeneity on some variables, sufficient heterogeneity remains on many other variables because of individual differences to keep the group from becoming dull, stale, uninteresting, unproductive, and unsuccessful.

There is one other point about group composition, which is related to the fact that group members become therapists for each other. It would appear to be desirable, if not necessary, that the group have at least one member who is able to listen to others, to accept and respect others, and to understand others, at least to a minimal degree, to supplement the modeling of the therapist.

It is not possible here to go into considerations of the place and duration of group therapy sessions, frequency of meetings, the life span of the group, and whether groups should be closed (fixed membership) or open (members leaving and new members admitted during the life span of the group). These matters are not specifically related to the nature of relationship group therapy.

SUMMARY

Relationship counseling or psychotherapy, with its focus on the interpersonal relationship between the counselor and the client, extends naturally into group counseling or psychotherapy. The conditions for therapeutic progress in individual counseling are also the conditions for progress in group counseling.

While group counseling is more complex than individual counseling, it is not qualitatively different. The vocabulary by which interpersonal relationships in groups are often discussed, such as the vocabulary of group dynamics, differs, but the concepts and principles appear to be the same as those involved in relationship therapy. The concept of group cohesiveness was used as an illustration.

Group counseling offers certain experiences to the client that are not available in individual counseling or psychotherapy. In the group, the client interacts with a variety of other persons, receiving feedback on his or her impact on them. He or she thus has the opportunity to learn how to interact with others in an actual situation. The client also may be helped by others in the group whose behavior is therapeutic—that is, who demonstrate respect and warmth, understanding and empathy, and honesty and genuineness. Finally, the client has the experience of being therapeutic or helpful to others as he or she learns and practices these conditions of facilitative interpersonal relationships.

If, as appears to be the case, many if not most of the problems that individuals bring to counselors or therapists are problems of, or related to, interpersonal relationships, it would appear that the treatment of choice for many if not most clients would be group therapy. However, there are some clients who may not be ready for the group relationship or who may have characteristics that do not allow them to benefit from a group situation or that impede or block the progress of others in groups. Therefore, some attention must be given to the selection of clients and the composition of counseling or therapy groups.

NOTES

1. I. D. Yalom. *The theory and practice of group psychotherapy.* New York: Basic Books, 1970, p. 30.
2. *Ibid.*, p. 176.
3. R. L. Bednar and G. F. Lawlis. Empirical research in group psychotherapy. In A. E. Bergin and S. L. Garfield (Eds.), *Handbook of psychotherapy and behavior change: An empirical analysis.* New York: Wiley, 1971, pp. 812–838; Yalom, *Theory and practice of group psychotherapy*, pp. 40–43.
4. Yalom, *Theory and practice of group psychotherapy*, pp. 36–37.
5. *Ibid.*, pp. 231–241.

6. C. A. Mahler. *Group counseling in the schools.* Boston: Houghton Mifflin, 1969, p. 65.
7. W. C. Bonney and W. J. Foley. The transition stage in group counseling in terms of congruence theory. *Journal of Counseling Psychology,* 1963, *10,* 136–138.
8. E. E. Mintz. *Marathon groups: Symbol and reality.* New York: Appleton-Century-Crofts, 1971, p. 26.
9. W. C. Bonney and W. J. Foley. A developmental model for counseling groups. *Personnel and Guidance Journal,* 1966, *44,* 577.
10. C. R. Rogers. *Carl Rogers on encounter groups.* New York: Harper & Row, 1970, pp. 15–37.
11. In William Coulson. Inside a basic encounter group. *The Counseling Psychologist,* 1970, *2*(2), 1–2.
12. Yalom, *Theory and practice of group psychotherapy,* p. 83.
13. H. Dickoff and M. Lakin. Patients' views of group psychotherapy: Retrospections and interpretations. *International Journal of Group Psychotherapy,* 1963, *13,* 64.
14. J. B. Clark and S. A. Culbert. Mutually therapeutic perception and self-awareness in a T-group. *Journal of Applied Behavioral Science,* 1965, *1,* 180–194.
15. B. Berzon, C. Pious, and R. Parsons. The therapeutic event in group psychotherapy: A study of subjective reports by group members. *Journal of Individual Psychology,* 1963, *19,* 204–212.
16. C. B. Truax and R. R. Carkhuff. Personality change in hospitalized mental patients during group psychotherapy as a function of the use of alternate therapy sessions and vicarious therapy pretraining. *Journal of Clinical Psychology,* 1965, *21,* 225–228; C. B. Truax, D. G. Wargo, R. R. Carkhuff, F. Kodman, and E. A. Moles. Changes in self-concepts during group psychotherapy as a function of alternate sessions and vicarious therapy pretraining on institutionalized mental patients and juvenile delinquents. *Journal of Consulting Psychology,* 1966, *30,* 309–314; C. B. Truax and R. R. Carkhuff. *Toward effective counseling and psychotherapy.* Chicago: Aldine, 1967, pp. 153, 362–363; I. D. Yalom, P. S. Houts, G. Newell, and K. H. Rand. Preparation of patients for group therapy: A controlled study. *Archives of General Psychiatry,* 1967, *17,* 416–427; C. Whalen. Effects of a model and verbal instructions on group verbal behaviors. *Journal of Consulting and Clinical Psychology,* 1969, *33,* 509–521; K. Heller. Effects of modeling procedures in helping relationships. *Journal of Consulting and Clinical Psychology,* 1969, *33,* 522–531.
17. Yalom, *Theory and practice of group psychotherapy,* p. 103.
18. R. R. Dies. Group therapist self-disclosure: An evaluation by clients. *Journal of Counseling Psychology,* 1973, *20,* 344–348; O. P. May and C. L. Thompson. Perceived levels of self-disclosure, mental health and helpfulness of group leaders. *Journal of Counseling Psychology,* 1973, *20,* 349–352; R. G. Weigel, N. Dinges, R. Dyer, and A. A. Straumfjord. Perceived self-disclosure, mental health and who is liked in group treatment. *Journal of Counseling Psychology,* 1972, *19,* 47–52; R. G. Weigel and C. F. Warnath. The effects of group therapy on reported self-disclosure. *International Journal of Group Psychotherapy,* 1968, *18,* 31–41.
19. S. A. Culbert. Trainer self-disclosure and member growth in two T-groups. *Journal of Applied Behavioral Science,* 1968, *4,* 47–73; L. Bolman. Some effects of trainers on their T-groups. *Journal of Applied Behavioral Science,* 1971, *7,* 322–323.

20. R. R. Dies, unpublished study. It should be noted that the leader or therapist self-disclosures that were strongly disapproved of were expressions of negative feelings toward the group and its functioning. Disclosures relating to feelings and experiences external to the group were rated as potentially helpful by the psychology students who were the subjects in this study. Thus, the content of the disclosures and, when they relate to feelings about the group, whether they are positive or negative, are important variables.

21. Mintz, *Marathon groups*, p. 26.

22. *Ibid.*, p. 51.

23. *Ibid.*, p. 133.

24. Yalom, *Theory and practice in group psychotherapy*, p. 369.

25. *Ibid.*, pp. 159–170.

26. M. M. Ohlsen. *Group counseling.* New York: Holt, Rinehart & Winston, 1970, pp. 103–104.

27. G. R. Bach. *Intensive group psychotherapy.* New York: Ronald, 1954.

28. Yalom, *Theory and practice in group psychotherapy*, pp. 157–158.

29. W. Furst. Homogeneous versus heterogeneous groups. *International Journal of Group Psychotherapy*, 1951, *1*, 120–123.

30. Yalom, *Theory and practice in group psychotherapy*, p. 193.

31. Bach, *Intensive group psychotherapy*, p. 26.

CHAPTER 10

Cross-Cultural
Counseling
or Psychotherapy

$\mathbf{W}$arren Weaver, a biological scientist, wrote that "as man's con-trol of his environment has proceeded . . . he has progressively un-covered more and more unifying principles which accept the ever increasing variety, but recognize an underlying unity. He has, in short, discovered the many and the one. . . . The diversity . . . is a surface phenomenon. When one looks underneath and within, the universal unity becomes apparent."[1] This observation applies not only to the physical and biological realms, but also to the human sciences, including psychology. One might substitute the phrase "as man's understanding of man has proceeded" for the first phrase of Weaver's statement, and the remainder would still be relevant.

Harry Stack Sullivan, the American psychiatrist who developed the interpersonal theory of psychotherapy, stated it concisely: "We are all much more simply human than otherwise."[2] This chapter will develop this thesis as the basis for a universal approach to counseling or psychotherapy. This approach is neither time-bound nor culture-bound; it transcends time and cultures, since it is based upon the universal unity of human nature.

We are moving, though very slowly, toward a world culture, which will have room for much diversity but which will nevertheless have a unity derived from the universals of human nature and the human experience. In such a world, while members of different cul-

This chapter was originally published in the *International Journal for the Advancement of Counseling*, 1978, *1*, 231–247. It also appeared in *Hacettepe University Bulletin of Social Sciences* (Turkey), 1978, *1*, 119–134.

tures will vary in opinions, customs, preferences, tastes, and styles, they will share some basic universal values related to the nature, development, and evolution of humankind as a species. These values will be the foundation for the common goal and methods of counselors or psychotherapists in all cultures.

PROBLEMS RELATING TO CULTURAL DIFFERENCES

The last two decades have seen the development of increasing interest in cross-cultural counseling or psychotherapy, as manifested by publications in this area, such as the book *Counseling Across Cultures.*[3] The tenor of the writing appears to be in general negative, focusing upon the numerous problems and difficulties associated with cultural differences. There is little of a positive or constructive nature offered. Furthermore, many of the criticisms of the applicability of counseling methods to clients of other cultures are not related to cultural factors but involve questions of counselor or psychotherapist competence. There is much emphasis, for example, on the ability of the therapist to establish a relationship, to be accepting of the client, to understand the client as a (unique) person, and on the avoidance of stereotyping clients. The problem of excessive positive reactions (sympathy, identification) or negative feelings toward clients is also frequently discussed. Again, considerable attention is given to the necessity of the counselor understanding himself or herself and being aware of his or her attitudes and values, and avoiding their imposition upon clients. The bias of rational or logical explanations of causation and analysis of problems has also been noted.

These are not problems that are peculiar to cross-cultural counseling or psychotherapy. They are problems in therapy with clients from the same culture as the therapist, where there are social and class differences, sectional differences, neighborhood differences, sex differences, and age differences, as well as wide individual differences in speech and mannerisms and in attitudes and values. In the consideration of the special problems posed by cultural differences one must start with the assumption of a competent therapist, even though it may be that there are few such therapists.

Another problem in many discussions involves confusion or disagreement about the essential nature of counseling or psychotherapy. Some criticisms (often by writers who are not counselors) of so-called Western approaches to counseling are criticisms of directive and controlling methods, involving the definition of the problem by the counselor and the imposing of solutions with little if any consideration of individual clients and their perceptions of their situation and problems. Some writers appear to differentiate between counseling and psychotherapy, with the former consisting of rational problem solving directed by the counselor. The problem then inheres in the assumption that the counselor's (or therapist's) function is to diagnose, evaluate, and define the problem, intervene to alleviate the problem or to advise, recommend, suggest, or impose a solution to the problem. To do so without a thorough understanding of the client's culture would of course lead to all sorts of complications beyond those occurring in a situation where the counselor and the client are from the same culture. Certainly this approach would be inapplicable to clients from other cultures, whose problems are influenced by the culture, and whose solutions would also involve cultural considerations. But such an approach to counseling would not be acceptable with clients from the same culture as the therapist. Most counselors and instructors would disagree with such an approach.

More relevant are the discussions of problems actually related to cultural differences. Of particular interest is the comparison of Western culture with other cultures, particularly Eastern cultures, as well as with subcultures, or minority cultures, such as the American Indian culture. Here the concern has been with differing values and personal characteristics. These differences are relevant on the one hand to objectives and goals, and on the other hand to methods and techniques, of the counseling or therapy relationship.

There are two aspects of values that are not recognized or dealt with. (These are also relevant to the consideration of differences within a culture—for example, to social class differences in values.) First, there are many differences that are not basic. There are differences in opinions, preferences, habits, customs, norms, and practices or ways of doing things, differences in dress, attire, and manners, or in style of living. These are essentially choices or preferences that do not involve basic values or goals. They represent acceptable alternatives. But too often these are overemphasized as if they represented important value differences. Counselors become involved in these differences because of their biases and the inability to accept alternatives to their own practices. However, these are not essentially value differences.

But there appear to be some basic differences in significant areas among cultures. Western culture values highly such things as economic productivity and efficiency (including a competitive element), and an obligation to work to support one's family and contribute to society. But there is also a high value placed on the individual, on personal health and happiness, upon individual potentialities. Loyalty is to one's family of procreation (nuclear family) rather than to one's family of origin (the extended family). Love, rather than family choice, is the basis of marriage and the family. Personal satisfaction rather than obligation is its continuing justification. Youth rather than age is respected.

In other cultures, particularly Eastern cultures, there is less concern with material productivity and efficiency. Cooperation rather than competition is emphasized. Marriage is a concern of, and arranged by, families. The individual continues to identify closely with his or her family of origin even after marriage. The individual is expected to sacrifice personal ambitions and development, even career choice and aspirations, to the needs and demands of the family. In return, the family supports its members in crises and times of need. The individual is subordinated to the family group. Age rather than youth is revered.

These differing patterns of cultural organization and values clearly have implications for the definition of normality or abnormality in behavior, and for the acceptable or desirable outcomes or goals of counseling or psychotherapy. Recognition of and emphasis upon these implications pervades the literature of cross-cultural counseling or psychotherapy. But there is little concerning the solution of the problems that they pose. The general position seems to be that one must accept these basic differences, as one should the less basic preferences and attitudes, as equally tenable or desirable without question or discrimination.

These cultural differences are associated with differences in modal personality characteristics that are relevant for counseling or psychotherapy. Individuals in Western cultures are more independent of their families of origin than individuals in some other cultures. They do not feel the same pressures to submerge or sacrifice themselves to the family. Westerners are more independent. They are also more extroverted or more verbal compared to many other cultures. They are more used to introspection, more ready and able to engage in the self-disclosure and self-exploration that is necessary for progress in psychotherapy. Persons from the Oriental and some other cultures, on the other hand, are more reticent, more modest in talking about themselves or personal relationships with others, including their families. They are more respectful to and dependent upon authority.

The problem posed by passive, dependent, nonverbal, non-self-disclosing clients is clear. The solution, however, is not clear. The generally accepted opinion seems to be that psychotherapy as developed and practiced in Western societies is not applicable to other societies. All of the major systems or theories of counseling or psychotherapy, it is pointed out, have developed in Western Europe and America. It is assumed that the theories (if not the nature) of human behavior and its psychopathologies are culture-bound. Thus, it is concluded that new approaches, as yet undefined, are necessary.

It is interesting that some of those who recognize that counseling or psychotherapy requires that clients assume responsibility for self-disclosure and self-exploration and that they take responsibility for developing their own solutions to problems and making their own decisions, suggest that if the client is passive, dependent, and non-verbal then the counselor should change his or her approach. The therapist should direct and control the process, giving clients suggestions and advice and proposing solutions to their problems. Pedersen, for example, referring to American Indian clients, writes: "A counselor who expects counselees to verbalize their feelings is not likely to have much success with Native American clients. The Native American is more likely to withdraw and, using the advice he has received, work out the problem by himself." He concludes that "each cultural group requires a different set of skills, unique areas of emphasis, and specific insights for effective counseling to occur."[4] This statement represents the implicit, if not explicit, conclusion of many writers that the methods of Western counseling and psychotherapy are not appropriate in other cultures, and must be changed or modified by developing methods or techniques to conform with the characteristics of other cultures. No specifications of the necessary skills, methods, or techniques are provided.

This view presumes to avoid a narrow, parochial, culture-bound view of humans and their nature. Yet in a very real sense, it may represent the most parochial, culture-bound view of humanity. It assumes that the accidents of geography, climate, and culture are associated with basic differences in human nature. As the assumption that we must develop a new kind of (simplified, structured) psychotherapy for the poor[5] is a manifestation of extreme bias and prejudice in a subtle disguise, so also may be the assumption that different cultures require different approaches and methods of counseling or psychotherapy.

UNIVERSALITY IN HUMAN NATURE AND VALUES

The belief that all cultural differences should be accepted and respected, and that all differing cultural values are equally good and desirable must be questioned. So must the assumption that there are no universals in human nature, and no universal values, or no universal goals for counseling or psychotherapy. Finally, if there are some universals in human nature and values, one must question the prevailing concept that different approaches, methods, and skills are necessary for counseling individuals from each and every cultural group.

The argument for accepting all cultural differences as being desirable rests upon the doctrine of cultural relativity. This doctrine involves the contention that differences represent basic characteristics of the culture, and that to change them will result in the demise of the culture. This argument overlooks the fact that cultures have changed and do change with changing conditions, and that it is the cultures that do not change that do not survive. Cultural characteristics do develop out of the struggle for existence in a particular physical and social environment, but characteristics that persist when the environment changes result in the demise of the culture.

It is frequently noted that characteristics that are viewed as undesirable in today's Western culture are present, or have been present, and accepted as desirable, in other cultures. Suspiciousness, deception and treachery, and revenge have been present and valued in some societies, and have been necessary for individual survival. But it is likely that these characteristics would not, and no doubt did not, contribute to the survival of such societies. It could be maintained that unless there is a basic minimum of honesty and trustworthiness in a society, no social system can long survive.

Moreover, the survival of a culture is a necessary but not sufficient condition for the survival and, more important, the development of the individual and his or her potentials. Survival is not the highest goal of mankind—life must be worth living, and contribute to the development of the individual as a person. The basic motivation of the human being—a universal motivation—includes but goes beyond survival. As Combs and Snygg phrase it, "From birth to death the maintenance of the phenomenal self is the most pressing, the most crucial, if not the only task of existence. . . . But man seeks not merely the maintenance of the self. . . . Man seeks both to maintain and enhance his perceived self."[6] Or as stated by Rogers: "The organism has one basic tendency and striving—to actualize, maintain and enhance the experiencing organism."[7] The concept of self-actualization incorporates these ideas. It can be stated that the universal and single motivation of every organism, including human beings, is the development and actualization of its potentials. It is this striving that throughout history has been the basis of cultural change, to assure that society recognizes and contributes to the self-actualization of its members. Self-actualization thus represents the basic drive or motivation, and the basic goal or value of the individual and of society or culture.

Here, then, we have a solution to the problem of cultural relativity. We have a criterion for the evaluation of different societies or cultures. As reported by Maslow, Ruth Benedict, the well-known anthropologist, attempted to transcend the doctrine of cultural relativity with which she was erroneously identified.[8] She sought for criteria on the basis of which cultures could be evaluated. On the basis of her study of four pairs of cultures, she identified several characteristics that differentiated "good" from "bad" cultures. The latter were anxious, surly and nasty, hostile and aggressive, and insecure, and the former were not. She coined the term *synergy* to summarize the differences. Societies with high social synergy are "those whose institutions insure mutual advantage from their undertakings," while societies with low social synergy are those "where the advantage of one individual becomes a victory over another, and the majority who are not victorious must shift as they can." In high-synergy societies the good of the individual and of the group or society are not antagonistic; the selfish-unselfish dichotomy is resolved, in that if one gains, others do not have less, but more.

It is interesting that Maslow, at the time he wrote the article, did not tie the concept of synergy in with the concept of self-actualization. Yet later he did propose the development of self-actualizing persons as the criterion by which to judge the adequacy of any society: "I proceed on the assumption that the good society, and therefore the immediate goal of any society which is trying to improve itself, is the self-actualization of all individuals. . . ."[9] The "good," or high-synergy, society or culture is one that fosters the development of self-actualizing persons.

Thus it must be recognized that not all cultures or socie. es are good or desirable, and thus not all cultural institutions, characteristics, or values of all societies are to be respected and maintained. We clearly recognize and accept this when considering our own society,[10] but paradoxically we refuse to do so when considering other cultures. We are concerned about changing social environments in our society that are deleterious to personal development, but seem oblivious to the deleterious effects of social environments in other cultures. A possible exception in our own society is the idealizing by some of the so-called culture of poverty.

Not all cultures should survive; not all the values and forms of every culture should be accepted, respected, and revered. All must be judged or evaluated in terms of their contribution to the self-actualization of the individual. The concept of self-actualization as a value or goal is thus applicable to Eastern cultures that value and require conformity, uniformity, and dependence on the group or the family. Thus, a society that subordinates the individual to the group—even to the family group—to an extreme degree that inhibits or prevents the development of self-actualization, is not acceptable. It must change or eventually not survive because it is inconsistent with, or thwarts, the basic motivation of the individual. The value of self-actualization is an ultimate, universal value, not one that is man-made or culture-bound. It is part of the nature of the human organism. Societies that do not facilitate self-actualization must change. This means not only Eastern cultures, for example, which thwart the independence or autonomy of the individual. Nor should the change necessarily be toward identity with Western culture, with its extreme individualism, selfish aggrandizement, and competitive dog-eat-dog ethics, with the devil taking the hindmost. These characteristics or values do not contribute to self-actualization and must change. The traditional Western concept of individualism is not the only possible kind of individualism. Thus while Eastern cultures must change in the direction of greater concern for individual personal development, Western culture must move in the direction of greater concern for the influence of the individual upon others and upon their development, and of cooperation in fostering personal development in others. While the highly dependent relationship of the individual to the family in Eastern culture must be modified, so must Western culture refrain from going too far toward independence from the family. There needs to be a balance between the individual and the group.

The concept of self-actualization has a number of advantages as an integrating concept for human behavior (see Chapter 3). Of particular importance in a cultural context is that while it recognizes the basic common or universal motivation of human beings, it also allows for individual differences, and cultural differences, in the means for its achievement and the nature of the outcome. These will vary with the various potentialities, aptitudes, and abilities of different persons. Individuality is thus possible and is fostered. But there are limits, related to respecting the need of others for self-actualization. Self-actualization is not to be confused, as it frequently is, with self-centeredness or selfishness (see Chapter 3). The individual needs others to become self-actualizing; he or she must live with others in a society and cannot be self-actualizing without them. However, while there is room for individual and cultural differences, it is not reasonable to expect that the nature of self-actualization is drastically different in different cultures. We are basically similar as human beings, and Maslow's description of the general characteristics of the self-actualizing person is applicable for individuals in any culture.[11]

GOALS AND METHODS IN CROSS-CULTURAL
COUNSELING AND PSYCHOTHERAPY

As noted in Chapter 2, the problem of goals in counseling or psychotherapy has received relatively little attention until the past few years. Every school or method of therapy, indeed every therapist, has developed their own goals, leading to a situation where there has seemed to be great confusion with little agreement. Recently, however, there appears to have developed some consensus, if one looks at what might be considered long-term ultimate or general goals—that is, the kind of persons we want to develop, the nature of so-called "mentally healthy" or psychologically healthy or "adjusted" people. The problem has been one of terminology. The concept that seems to be congealing, and that incorporates many if not all the more specific terms and concepts, is that of self-actualization. The desired outcome of counseling or psychotherapy is a person who might be characterized by Maslow's description of a self-actualizing person. The purpose and goal of counseling or psychotherapy is, as we have emphasized earlier, to help persons who are hampered in their personal development to become more self-actualizing persons.

The major conditions for the development of such persons have been presented in earlier chapters. They are empathic understanding, respect, and therapeutic genuineness. These three conditions appear to be common to all major theories of counseling or psychotherapy, implicitly if not explicitly. They appear to be necessary, if not sufficient, conditions for personality change in the direction of self-actualization. They represent basic principles of human relations that are universal. Wohl contends that

> despite this universality, it is possible, even probable, that the constituents of the "good human relationship" are different in one culture than they are in another. . . . The question needs to be raised as to the extent to which our American conception of the good therapeutic relationship is universally valid.[12]

It is certainly justifiable to raise the question, but neither Wohl nor others who do so have presented any evidence to support differences. The evidence from studies involving a wide variety of clients with a wide variety of problems in various groups in Western society supports their universality, though admittedly studies in quite different cultures have not yet been done. Given the basic similarities of human nature, it is not likely that the conditions would not be necessary in other cultures. As the drive for self-actualization is not limited to a particular culture, so the conditions for its development are not. If counseling or psychotherapy consists of providing these facilitative conditions for self-actualization, then these conditions are universal aspects of counseling or psychotherapy.

Psychotherapy, in some form, has existed and now exists in many if not all non-Western cultures. A study of these other cultures suggests that methods of psychological healing do include these conditions. Frank[13] in his survey refers to them as nonspecific conditions. It is apparent that acceptance, respect, caring, and concern characterize these methods, though they are often (as is also the case in many Western approaches) associated with other aspects of an influencing relationship—prestige, status, suggestion, authority—in short, the ubiquitous placebo. It appears that experience has led to the development of methods that share much in common across time and cultures. Nevertheless, the differences among cultures and some personal characteristics in clients related to cultural differences—characteristics that the authoritative placebo seem designed to deal with—pose some problems. It is to the solution of these problems in the context of maintaining the necessary conditions for therapeutic personality change that we now turn.

SOME SUGGESTED SOLUTIONS TO PROBLEMS RELATING TO CULTURAL FACTORS

We conclude that it is not necessary, nor desirable, that we discover or develop new theories or approaches for counseling clients from or in other cultures. The evidence, from experience and research, as noted earlier, supports the effectiveness of the core conditions as they have been extended to new kinds of clients with different problems and in different situations. The problem is one of implementation of the conditions. There are two major categories of problems. The first consists of those relating to the functioning of the therapist, involving problems in understanding the communications of the client, and communicating this understanding to the client (empathic understanding), and communication of respect, warmth, caring, and concern in a therapeutically genuine manner. The second category of problems consists of those relating to the client, which are essentially problems of preparing or adapting clients to engage in the client behaviors necessary for therapeutic progress.

Cultural differences impose barriers to empathic understanding—to communications of the client about himself or herself to the therapist and to communication of therapist understanding to the client. (So, of course, do other differences, such as sex, age, socioeconomic levels, race, and religion.) The first barrier is of course language. It would no doubt go without saying that the therapist must be fluent in the client's native language. Besides verbal communication, there is the problem of nonverbal communication. This is a difficult area in working with clients from the same culture, since we know so little about nonverbal cues, except for the most obvious. With clients from other cultures the problem is greater, since nonverbal behaviors may have different, even opposite, meanings in different cultures.

An example of cultural differences in nonverbal behavior involves eye contact, an element of attending behavior, which is an aspect of the core conditions. There is currently an emphasis in counselor education on training students in such behaviors, because they are objective and can be measured and thus serve as goals for a competence-based approach to preparing counselors. The use of such behaviors as objectives is questionable even in preparing counselors to work with standard clients in the usual setting in America. It is an apt example of the technologizing of human relations, reducing the qualitative to the quantitative. There is no research to indicate exactly what proportion of time a counselor should maintain eye contact with a client. Certainly it will depend on the client, and on the counselor, and on the quality of the eye contact. Performed by the counselor as a technique it may consist of a nontherapeutic staring at the client. And when used with clients from some other cultures it may also be nontherapeutic. In Japan and some other cultures it is taboo for a female to look males in the eye, and custom and modesty influence eye contact in other cases.

This calls into question the trend toward emphasizing specific techniques in counseling. The attempt to reduce counseling or psychotherapy to such restricted techniques is likely to be detrimental to the counselor or therapist adapting to clients from differing cultures or differing social backgrounds. The greater the emphasis upon techniques, the less the generalizability of an approach to other cultures. Conversely, emphasis upon philosophy and attitudes frees the therapist to discover and to learn culturally appropriate methods of implementation. The core conditions are necessary, but there may be no specific techniques of implementing them that are necessary. If eye contact is necessary, one wonders how Freud and the orthodox psychoanalysts, sitting behind the client, who is on a couch, could ever be successful as therapists. It has been reported that Freud chose this position because he was unable to tolerate prolonged eye contact with clients. No doubt Freud would have failed to graduate from a competence-based counselor education program.

A second barrier involves the content of the client's communications. Here it is clear that the counselor or therapist must have a thorough knowledge of the client's culture if he or she is to understand the content of the client's communications, including the nature of the client's problems. Culture provides the content in which the universals of human experience are clothed. In some instances—great art, literature and drama, and music—the universals of human experience transcend the specific content. The highly sensitive, experienced counselor or therapist may be able to sense this experience in some cases even when it is clothed in unfamiliar content. But the therapist who intends to work in a particular culture clearly must be committed to a time-consuming process of learning to know the culture.

Academic courses may help. But they may also hinder, if they focus, as they often do, upon group characteristics, averages, and the typical or modal personality, leading to stereotypes that interfere with understanding the client as an individual. The literature of the culture is a better source for cultural understanding. But there is no substitute for living in the culture, and the counselor or therapist should be prepared to spend considerable time living in the culture—preferably as a nonprofessional—before engaging in counseling or psychotherapy. To be sure, once the therapist begins to practice, he or she continues to learn from clients.

Stewart, in an interesting discussion of empathy, says that "intercultural counseling, by definition, does not permit a totally accurate interaction, since empathy, defined as understanding others on the basis of shared qualities, cannot occur."[14] He goes on to note, however, that "there are universals of human behavior" that provide similarities in experience that serve as a basis for shared qualities. Perfect understanding, and thus perfect empathy, cannot be achieved with any client, or any other human being, since each has had unique experiences that cannot be completely communicated to, or understood by, another. It is not required for therapeutic success that perfect empathy be achieved. There is always a gap in understanding, but it must not be too wide, and the client must feel that the therapist understands to a minimal degree and that he or she is constantly striving to understand better.

While the problems involving the therapist are difficult, problems involving the client may be greater in certain cultures. The evidence from research indicates that certain conditions or behaviors are necessary in the client if therapy is to be successful. The major requirement in the client is that he or she be willing and able to engage in the process of self-exploration, which begins with self-disclosure. It is possible that to some extent this can occur without overt vocalization on the part of the client. But in general, clients must be able to verbalize about themselves and their experiences, to communicate to the therapist their perceptions of themselves and their problems, and to engage in active exploration of these areas.

It has been suggested that self-disclosure, and its lack, are cultural values. Sue writes that counselors who "value verbal, emotional, and behavioral expressiveness as goals in counseling are transmitting their own cultural values."[15] Thus lack of self-disclosure, it would appear, should be accepted as a cultural value, and counselors should change their methods to adapt to it, abandoning "the belief in the desirability of self-disclosure." But the desirability of client self-disclosure is more than a belief. Experience and the research evidence indicate that it is a necessary condition for progress in counseling or psychotherapy. Certainly there is a problem with those clients who find it difficult to engage in self-disclosure because of their cultural backgrounds. But it is an obstacle to be overcome, not accepted. If it cannot be overcome, then the client is unable to enter a therapeutic relationship, and is unlikely to be able to benefit from counseling or psychotherapy, to achieve the desired outcome of becoming a more responsible, independent, and self-actualizing person. Psychotherapy, by definition, cannot occur without the participation of the client. It is clearly no solution, as some writers have proposed, for the counselor or therapist to take the responsibility for defining and exploring what he or she conceives to be the client's problem. Even if the counselor should perceive the problem correctly, the goals of client responsibility, independence, and problem solving are being abandoned. But if the client cannot verbalize about himself or herself, cannot communicate ideas, thoughts, attitudes, feelings, and perceptions, then the therapist has no basis for empathic understanding. It does not help for the therapist to assume responsibility, to make suggestions, to give advice, and to make decisions for the client. To do so is to abandon the goals of counseling or psychotherapy.

Similarly, there is a problem if the client, as is often the case in other cultures (as well as in segments of Western cultures), expects the therapist to assume an authoritarian, expert, directive role, making suggestions and giving advice. If, as has been noted, such a role is not therapeutic where an objective of therapy is that the client take responsibility for himself or herself, then to accede to these expectations is to abandon the goals of therapy. But what is the counselor or therapist to do?

And what if the client defines his or her problem in such a way that it cannot be solved by a method depending upon a relationship or upon the client's accepting responsibility for the problem? Wohl[16] discusses a situation in which a client attributed his problem to a demonic power that he had offended. This is similar to externalization, where clients attribute their difficulties to forces outside themselves or to other people, taking no responsibility for them. Counseling or psychotherapy is not successful, or applicable, in such situations, even when the counselor or therapist and the client are members of the same cultural group.

Thus it must be recognized that therapy is not effective with, or applicable to, every person who seeks help or every problem presented to the therapist. But where client attitudes and expectations are inconsistent with the conditions necessary for effective psychotherapy an effort can be made to modify these attitudes and expectations before abandoning the conditions and resorting to other methods that, though they may give the client a temporary feeling of being helped, are not psychotherapy. Structuring, in which the counselor or therapist explains the requirements of therapy and the roles and activities of each participant, can be useful in many cases. Another approach is pretherapy education or training to prepare the client for his or her role in the process. Instruction may be given in groups; the instructor should be someone other than the therapist. But if the client is unable to assume the role of a client and engage in the activities necessary for successful psychotherapy, therapy cannot take place, and whatever else the therapist may do is not psychotherapy.

If the culture is not one that is conducive to the development of self-actualizing persons, then a problem arises if therapy is successful, since the client will find himself or herself in a difficult social position. He or she may be more "maladjusted" than before therapy. But while the purpose of therapy is not to make clients better adjusted to their societies, neither is the purpose, as some have suggested,[17] to produce revolutionaries. Clients can decide, without being criticized or pressured by the therapist, to forego any change in directions that will bring them into conflict with their society—clients do not have to choose to be more self-actualizing persons if they feel the price is too great. But if, knowing the price, clients do make the choice, they will become sources of change within their culture or society, whether as activists or not.[18] Self-actualizing persons facilitate the self-actualization of other persons.

SUMMARY

We have reviewed the problems in counseling or psychotherapy posed by cultural differences, and have noted that few if any solutions to these problems have been proposed. It has been the general conclusion that theories and methods of psychotherapy developed in Western culture are not applicable in other cultures.

This view was rejected on the basis that there are universals of human nature, a basic one being the common motive of self-actualization. The goal of counseling or psychotherapy is to facilitate the development of self-actualization in clients. Cultures can be evaluated in terms of their contribution to the self-actualization of their members. The major conditions for the development of self-actualizing persons are known, and must be present in counseling or psychotherapy as practiced with any client, regardless of his or her culture. These conditions are not time-bound nor culture-bound. The problems of practicing counseling or psychotherapy in other cultures can be viewed as problems of implementing these conditions.

Certain characteristics of clients that present obstacles to the implementation of the conditions are associated with certain cultures. Until cultural changes lead to changes in these characteristics, counseling or psychotherapy will be difficult and in some cases impossible with certain clients from certain cultures. Structuring and client education and training may change client expectations and make therapy possible. In any case, however, to accede to client expectations, abandoning methods that have been demonstrated to be related to self-actualization as an outcome of counseling or psychotherapy, is to abandon self-actualization as the goal, and to accept goals that are often inconsistent with self-actualization.

NOTES

1. W. Weaver. Confessions of a scientist-humanist. *Saturday Review*, May 28, 1966, p. 13.
2. H. S. Sullivan. *Conceptions of modern psychiatry*. Washington, DC: William Alanson White Psychiatric Foundation, 1947, p. 16.
3. P. Pedersen, W. J. Lonner, and J. G. Draguns (Eds.). *Counseling across cultures*. Honolulu: University Press of Hawaii, 1976; P. Pedersen, J. G. Draguns, W. J. Lonner, and J. E. Trimble (Eds.). *Counseling across cultures* (2nd ed.). Honolulu: University Press of Hawaii, 1981. See also A. J. Marsella and P. Pedersen (Eds.). *Cross-cultural counseling and psychotherapy*. New York: Pergamon Press, 1981; A. J. Marsella, R. Tharp, and T. Cibbrowski (Eds.). *Perspectives on cross-cultural psychotherapy*. New York: Academic Press, 1980; G. R. Walz and L. Benjamin (Eds.). *Transcultural counseling: Needs, programs, and techniques*. New York: Human Sciences Press, 1978.
4. P. Pedersen. The field of intercultural counseling. In Pedersen, Lonner, and Draguns, *Counseling across cultures*, pp. 26, 30.
5. A. P. Goldstein. *Structured learning therapy: Toward a psychotherapy for the poor*. New York: Wiley, 1973.
6. A. W. Combs and D. Snygg. *Individual behavior* (2nd ed.). New York: Harper & Row, 1959, p. 45.
7. C. R. Rogers. *Client-centered therapy*. Boston: Houghton Mifflin, 1951, p. 487.

8. A. H. Maslow. Synergy in society and the individual. *Journal of Individual Psychology*, 1964, *20*, 153–164. Also in A. H. Maslow. *The farther reaches of human nature*. New York: Viking, 1971, pp. 199–211. I am indebted to Dr. Feriha Baymur of Hacettepe University, Ankara, Turkey, for calling my attention to these papers.

9. A. H. Maslow. Questions for the normative psychologist. In Maslow, *The farther reaches*, p. 213.

10. S. Halleck. *The politics of therapy*. New York: Science House, 1971.

11. A. H. Maslow. Self-actualizing people: A study of psychological growth. In C. E. Moustakas (Ed.), *The self: Explorations in personal growth*. New York: Harper & Row, 1956.

12. J. Wohl. Intercultural psychotherapy: Issues, questions, and reflections. In Pedersen, Lonner, and Draguns, *Counseling across cultures*, pp. 192–193.

13. J. D. Frank. *Persuasion and healing: A comparative study of psychotherapy* (2nd ed.). Baltimore: Johns Hopkins Press, 1973.

14. E. C. Stewart. Cultural sensitivity in counseling. In Pedersen, Lonner, and Draguns, *Counseling across cultures*, p. 101.

15. D. W. Sue. *Counseling the culturally different: Theory and practice*. New York: Wiley, 1981, p. 38. Also in D. W. Sue and D. Sue. Barriers to effective cross-cultural counseling. *Journal of Counseling Psychology*, 1977, *24*, 420–429.

16. Wohl, Intercultural psychotherapy.

17. Halleck, *The politics of therapy*.

18. Two recent publications should be noted here: D. W. Sue et al. Position paper: Cross-cultural counseling competencies. *The Counseling Psychologist*, 1982, *10*(2), 45–52; E. J. Smith. Counseling Psychology in the marketplace: The status of ethnic minorities. *The Counseling Psychologist*, 1982, *10*(2), 61–68.

PART THREE

Implications

CHAPTER 11

The Therapeutic Relationship: Essence or Placebo?

Nearly 25 years ago I titled a chapter in *Counseling and Psychotherapy: Theory and Practice*[1] "Common Elements in Psychotherapy: Essence or Placebo?" At that time I suggested a division of the common elements in all psychotherapies into those that were essentially specific treatment variables and those that were essentially placebos. In the first edition of this book the suggestion was repeated. The suggestion has been ignored in the literature on psychotherapy and the placebo effect. In this chapter I shall develop this suggestion further, in the light of more recent discussions of the psychotherapy relationship, particularly the attention to social psychological variables.

THE PLACEBO EFFECT

The most extensive discussion of the placebo effect is that by Shapiro and Morris[2] (28 pages and 523 references). A placebo is defined as

any therapy or component of therapy that is deliberately used for its nonspecific, psychological, or psychophysiological effect, or that is used for its presumed specific effect, but is without specific activity for the condition being treated. A *placebo*, when used as a control in experimental studies, is defined as a substance or procedure that is without specific activity for the condition being evaluated. The *placebo effect* is defined as the psychological or psychophysiological effect produced by placebos.[3]

These authors consider placebo effects in both medical treatment and psychotherapy. They note that

> the placebo effect may have greater implications for psychotherapy than any other form of treatment because both psychotherapy and the placebo effect function primarily through psychological mechanisms. . . . The placebo effect is an important component and perhaps the entire basis for the existence, popularity, and effectiveness of numerous methods of psychotherapy.[4]

It perhaps should be noted here that the placebo as an inert substance does not exist in psychotherapy.[5] All the variables in the psychotherapy relationship are psychological and all are active, having some direct or specific effects on the client or patient. By the placebo in psychotherapy is meant nonspecific effects—that is, though the placebo may have some specific effects, these effects are not the objectives the therapist is attempting to achieve. Placebo elements may promote such effects, but they presumably are not used deliberately to achieve such effects. The word *deliberately* is used here because, as will be noted later, there are those who, viewing psychotherapy as nothing but the placebo, propose deliberately using the placebo.

In his earlier chapter in the first edition of the *Handbook of Psychotherapy and Behavior Change,* Shapiro stated that the chapter would be "an examination of psychotherapy as a placebo effect,"[6] thus suggesting that psychotherapy is nothing more than a placebo. Shapiro and Morris don't go quite so far. However, they view the total psychotherapy *relationship* as a placebo. They refer to a review by Luborsky, Singer, and Luborsky[7] that found, after a comparison of the effectiveness of several types of psychotherapy, that all were about equally effective, and that concluded that this improvement was related to the presence of the therapist-patient relationship in all forms of psychotherapy. Shapiro and Morris refer to this as a demonstration of the placebo effect.

Rosenthal and Frank much earlier came to a similar conclusion. Referring to the placebo effect as a nonspecific form of psychotherapy, they continue: "The similarity of the forces operating in psychotherapy and the placebo effect may account for the high consistency of improvement rates found with various therapies, from that conducted by physicians to intensive psychoanalysis."[8] Most recently Pentony, in his extensive analysis of the placebo as a model of psychotherapy, suggests that "the placebo effect constitutes the most parsimonious explanation that would account for the apparently equal success achieved by each of the diverse collection of therapies practiced."[9]

There are many writers of diverse origin who view the total psychotherapeutic relationship as nonspecific, and therefore, at least by implication, a placebo. Frank[10] has long maintained this position. Bergin[11] and Strupp[12] also have emphasized the nonspecific nature of the relationship. They repeatedly emphasize that specific techniques are necessary in addition to the nonspecific relationship, without being clear just what these techniques are. (See Chapter 13 for further discussion.) Bergin, however, perhaps unintentionally, implies that techniques themselves are placebos: "Technique is crucial to the extent that it produces a believable rationale and congenial modus operandi for the change agent and the client."[13]

Behaviorists also view the therapeutic relationship as nonspecific, and the techniques of behavior therapy as specific. Wolpe, for example, claims that his method of reciprocal inhibition, as well as other behavioristic techniques, increase the improvement rate over that of the relationship alone, stating that "the procedures of behavior therapy have effects additional to those relational effects that are common to all forms of psychotherapy."[14] Such claims have been disputed and do not seem to be supported; indeed, it appears that many, if not most, of the specific techniques in the various approaches to psychotherapy, including behavior therapy, operate through the placebo effect—that is, they are themselves placebos. It has been noted, for example, that systematic desensitization, which specifies certain conditions for its effectiveness, is effective when none of the conditions are present. This suggests that it is the placebo element in the persuasive ritual that gives the method its effectiveness.

Paraphrasing Pentony, we would say that the therapy relationship is the most parsimonious explanation of the relatively equal success of the diverse approaches to psychotherapy, since all approaches share the relationship. If the relationship is entirely a placebo, this statement and Pentony's are equivalent. But it is the thesis of this chapter that the complex therapy relationship may be separated into two major components, or classes of variables: the nonspecific and the specific. Moreover, in speaking of the relatively equal success of various therapies, we must be concerned about the definition of success—that is, the goal or goals of the treatment process. The success, or outcomes, of those therapies that are mainly placebo may differ from the outcomes of therapy focusing on the specific variables in the therapy relationship.

While recognizing the client's important contributions to the placebo effect, in the discussion to follow we will concentrate on the therapist's contribution, in effect hypothetically considering the client's contributions equivalent or constant across therapists and therapies.

SOCIAL PSYCHOLOGY AND PSYCHOTHERAPY

> *To be persuasive, we must be*
> *believable;*
> *To be believable, we must be*
> *credible;*
> *To be credible, we must be*
> *truthful.*
>
> EDWARD R. MURROW

In 1961 Jerome Frank suggested that psychotherapy is a process of persuasion.[15] In 1966 Goldstein proposed that research in psychotherapy should be directed toward study of variables derived from research in social psychology, particularly the psychology of interpersonal attraction, and he, with Heller and Sechrest, provided an analysis of relevant research in social psychology.[16] There was a considerable literature on the process of persuasion in social psychology[17] that was drawn upon.

In 1968 Strong proposed applying the social psychological concept of cognitive dissonance to the interpersonal influence process in counseling or psychotherapy.[18] He suggested that the greater the extent to which counselors are perceived as expert, attractive, and trustworthy, the greater would be their credibility, and thus their power to influence clients.

There are three main therapist variables in the concept of psychotherapy as a social influence process. The first is actually a loose cluster of variables designated as perceived expertness, or credibility. It also appears to include respect and perceived competence. Contributing to this perception by the client of expertness are indications of status (degrees, diplomas, office decor, and furnishings); prestige (reputation); power and authority. While trustworthiness is often considered a separate variable, it is also included with expertness in the concept of credibility.

The second variable is perceived attractiveness. Included in this are therapist-client similarities in opinions, attitudes, beliefs, values, and background; therapist liking for the client; therapist likability, friendliness, and warmth; and therapist self-disclosure.

The third variable is therapist expectancy. Therapist confidence in himself or herself, and/or in the methods and techniques used, leads to expectation of change or improvement in the client. This expectancy is communicated to the client through various subtle, unintentional ways as well as through direct expressions of optimism, suggestions, and reassurance.

Strong's article stimulated a series of research studies. This research has been reviewed by Beutler,[19] Strong,[20] and Corrigan, Dell, Lewis, and Schmidt.[21] Almost all of the studies (68 out of the 70 reviewed by Corrigan et al.) were analogue studies, involving the presentation of audiotapes or videotapes, or a single contrived interview with nonclients, usually college students, as subjects. Most of the studies were concerned with correlates of or cues for expertness and attractiveness. The measures or criteria used in outcome studies included subject reports or self-ratings of changes in attitudes or opinions, of improvement or satisfaction, or of likelihood of self-referral. The results of these studies have been varied, inconsistent within and between studies, and even directly contradictory. Beutler concludes that "it is not clear from these findings that credibility consistently produces attendant attitude change in psychotherapy. . . . These persuader variables serve only as a basis for facilitating a therapeutic relationship and are not necessarily a direct contributor to therapeutic change."[22] In other words, they are nonspecific variables.

Strong, in spite of the mixed results and the fact that the studies reviewed were analogue studies and did not include outcome studies, states that "as a whole, these studies show that therapist credibility is an important variable in psychotherapy."[23] This would seem to be an unjustifiable conclusion. In regard to perceived therapist attractiveness he concludes that "studies of the effect of client attraction to the therapist on the ability of the therapist to influence the client have obtained mixed and generally pessimistic results."

Corrigan et al. conclude that "the effects of expertness and attractiveness on counselors' ability to influence clients are, at best, unclear. . . . Those studies that successfully manipulated attractiveness failed to find differential effects on client change."[24] Yet these authors recommend further research on these social influence variables in counseling as "interesting and reasonable," though they admit that "the question of the utility of considering counseling as a social influence process remains."

These conclusions, as negative as they are, would appear to be too optimistic. It is difficult to understand the continued enthusiasm for this line of research. The reviewers have all been among the major researchers in the field, however, and this commitment and identification with the area probably influences their conclusions. A study published after these reviews were written should be noted. This study, by LaCrosse,[25] was not an analogue study, but involved 36 clients in a drug counseling program whose counseling ranged from 4 to 31 sessions. Clients rated their counselors at the beginning and end of counseling on an instrument devised to measure client perceptions of expertness, attractiveness, and trustworthiness. They also rated themselves on change following counseling. There was a highly significant relationship between the clients' ratings of their counselors and their self-ratings of outcome. However, not only is there questionable validity of the self-ratings of outcome, but there is a distinct possibility of a spurious element in the correlations, since both variables were ratings by clients. In addition, only two of the clients came to counseling voluntarily, so there is a real question about the relevance of the research for the usual situation in counseling or psychotherapy, where clients come voluntarily for help.

These mixed and inconsistent results are exactly what would be expected if the variables operating were placebos. Placebo effects are highly varied and unreliable—not all subjects respond to the placebo—and are usually temporary in nature. It is interesting that Shapiro and Morris discuss these variables, including expectancy, among others, as methods by which the placebo operates.

Related to or an element in therapists' expectations of positive results are their belief and faith in themselves and in their methods or techniques, factors that Shapiro emphasizes as important elements in the placebo effect. These factors appear to be the same factors that Orne[26] has called the "demand characteristics" in psychological experiments. Rosenthal,[27] among others, has demonstrated the influence of the experimenter's beliefs, expectations, and desires on the outcome of psychological experiments both in and outside the laboratory. In psychological research these are unwanted, or placebo, effects. It would seem that they should be regarded as such in psychotherapy, as indeed they are by Shapiro and Morris.

These variables appear to constitute the "good guy" factor in psychotherapy.[28] LaCrosse and Barak suggest that the common factor in expertness, attractiveness, and trustworthiness is the "influence" of Strong, the "persuasiveness" of Frank and of LaCrosse, or the "power" of Strong and Matross and of Dell. They then note that "these terms are also related to what might be described as 'charisma' or 'impressiveness.' "[29] All of this suggests an image of the counselor or therapist as a person exuding or projecting self-confidence, self-assurance, competence, power, and persuasiveness—a charismatic snake-oil salesperson.

If psychotherapy is nothing but a placebo, then it would appear to be desirable to maximize the effect. As Krasner and Ullmann note:

> Whereas the problem had previously been conceptualized in terms of eliminating "placebo effects," it would seem desirable to maximize placebo effects in the treatment situation to increase the likelihood

of client change. The evidence is growing that "placebo effect" is a euphemism for examiner influence variables.[30]

This is exactly what Fish attempts to do in his systematic development of what he calls placebo therapy.[31]

PLACEBO THERAPY

In placebo therapy, the therapist does everything possible to establish himself or herself as an expert and an authority in the eyes of the client. Then this is used as a power base to influence the client. Recognizing that "the social influence process has been considered the active ingredient in the placebo," Fish states that placebo therapy "denotes a broad frame of reference for considering all forms of human interaction, especially psychotherapy, in terms of social influence process."[32] It also refers to "a method of conducting psychotherapy based on social influence principles."[33]

The therapist fosters the client's belief in the potency of the therapeutic intervention by an impressive and detailed interrogation and exploration of the client's history and current behaviors. This process itself sets the therapist up as an authority, using a thorough "scientific" approach. It also assesses the client's susceptibility to influence and persuasion. The process implies to the patient that "once I know what is wrong with you I can cure you." A treatment strategy is formulated and communicated to the client in a plausible manner, tailored to the individual client's belief system. The major techniques used are those of behavior modification, together with suggestion and hypnosis. "Placebo therapy is a strategy for getting the maximum impact from such techniques regardless of their validity."[34] The placebo formulation and communication

> is designed to activate one powerful set of the patient's beliefs (his faith) to change another set of beliefs (*his problems*). Placebo therapy can thus be seen as a form of spiritual judo in which the therapist uses the power of the patient's own faith to force him to have a therapeutic conversion experience. . . . The patient must be persuaded that it is what *he* does, not what the therapist does, which results in his being cured. . . . Thus a therapist must encourage his patient to believe that he is curing himself, whether or not the therapist believes it.[35]

Placebo communications are used not because they are true but because of their effect. It is the patient's faith or belief in psychotherapy and in whatever methods or techniques the therapist uses that is the source of cure. Thus, the validity of the techniques, or the therapeutic ritual, to use Fish's term, is important only as it enhances the patient's faith—that is, only as it is persuasive, believable, intriguing, or impressive to the patient. "The therapist's role in placebo therapy involves acting in ways which inspire faith because he believes that the patient's faith cures him."[36] The therapist

> says things for the effect they will have rather than for his belief that they are true. Thus, instead of speaking empathically because he believes that empathy cures, he does so because he sees that such statements add to his credibility in the patient's eyes.[37]

The patient's expectations of help tend to result in some improvement, producing increasing pressure in him or her for further change. The knowledge—or belief—that he or she is receiving expert treatment is likely to increase this improvement. The patient has faith in the truth of "high status sources, such as the therapist. . . . One of the strong points in the therapist's role as a socially sanctioned healer is his status as an agent in psychotherapy."[38]

Whether or not this presentation is a tour de force is a question that might be raised. Someone has suggested that the author may have been writing with tongue in cheek. Yet the presentation seems to be sincere, though doubts may be raised by some statements such as that placebo therapy is "a nonschool of persuasion whose therapeutic title is intended ironically."[39] It may be viewed as carrying the social influence approach to an absurd extreme. For example, "lying to a patient is desirable if the lie furthers the therapeutic goals, is unlikely to be discovered (and hence backfire), and is likely to be more effective than any other strategy."[40]

A number of questions or objections may be raised about placebo therapy. First, of course, is the fact that there is little if any research support for it. Fish, who claims that it works, urges that the reasons need to be researched. The unreliability of the placebo effect—not all subjects respond to the placebo—also is a limiting factor. Fish notes that many are called but few are chosen. It is not possible to predict who will respond—who are placebo reactors. Fish refers to the problem client who expects and desires a (different) relationship with the therapist. Pentony writes that "it seems questionable whether a treatment procedure based on suggestion [or persuasion] alone will be universally applicable," given the existence of strong resistance to change.

> The placebo model would seem to be most appropriate for clients who are disposed to accept the therapist's message. Such clients typically have relatively specific problems, often involving low self-esteem, lack of self-confidence, and anxiety. Their disabilities range from physical symptoms to inability to assert themselves in social contexts. Their life goals are relatively realistic and attainable once they gain confidence in themselves. But not all cases which come to the attention of therapists fall into such a category.[41]

Nor is it necessarily true that placebo therapy is the most appropriate therapy even for them.

And there are other objections that must be raised against placebo therapy. The placebo effect is often, if not usually, temporary. No studies of the social influence process in psychotherapy have gone beyond the evaluation of immediate or short-term effects.

Pentony raises three other questions about placebo therapy:

> 1. Is it ethical to mislead the client in regard to the therapeutic strategy? 2. Will the therapist be convincing when he is not a true believer in the ritual he is carrying through? 3. If placebo therapy becomes general and clients become aware of its nature, will they lose faith in the healing ritual and hence render these ineffective?[42]

Fish's attempts to handle these questions are less than convincing.

Placebo therapy—and the social influence model of psychotherapy—assumes not only that psychotherapy is an influencing process, which few would deny, but that it is a process of influencing through persuasion. The therapist is concerned only with those actions or techniques that enhance his or her persuasiveness. Having achieved a power base from which to operate, the therapist then uses whatever methods or techniques are necessary to influence the client toward goals chosen by the client and the therapist. It becomes a situation where the ends justify the means. Moreover, there is no consideration of unintended outcomes or side effects, such as increase in client dependency. Reading the procedures considered by Fish, one has a *deja vu* experience of being regressed to the practices of counselors and psychotherapists in the 1930s and 1940s, before the influence of Rogers began to be felt.

THE THERAPEUTIC RELATIONSHIP

If perceived expertness, attractiveness, and trustworthiness are essentially placebos, that does not mean that the entire therapy relationship is a placebo. There is more to the therapeutic relationship than these three variables. Three other variables have been extensively studied: empathic understanding, warmth or respect, and genuineness, all in terms of client perceptions. These variables, or core conditions as they have become known, are defined and described in many places, including the preceding chapters of this book. The evidence for the specific effects of these conditions has been accumulating for over 25 years. This research is evaluated in Chapter 13.

On the basis of this research, it is proposed that these variables are the specific conditions for certain client behaviors in the counseling or therapy process and for certain outcomes of the process. In the process, the client responds to these conditions with self-disclosure, self-exploration, and self-understanding. The client assumes responsibility for himself or herself in the process, engages in problem solving, and makes choices and decisions. The client becomes more understanding, respecting, and accepting of others, more honest and genuine in relationships with others. These behaviors continue outside and after the therapy process ends, and are thus also outcomes of the process. They constitute aspects of a self-actualizing person, which is the ultimate goal of counseling or psychotherapy.

These conditions and the social influence variables are probably not entirely independent. LaCrosse[43] found significant correlations between the Counselor Rating Form, measuring client perceptions of counselor expertness, attractiveness, and trustworthiness, and the Barret-Lennard Relationship Inventory, measuring client perceptions of counselor empathic understanding, congruence, level of regard, and unconditional positive regard. Observer ratings were also highly correlated, though ratings by the counselors themselves were not, raising some question about the presence of an artifact, such as the halo effect, in the client and observer ratings.

The presence of relationships between these two groups of relationship variables poses the question of which is primary, or which causes or leads to the others. That the core conditions are primary is suggested by the fact that they have been shown to be related to various therapy outcomes in numerous studies, while this has not been done for the social influence variables. Krumboltz and his associates have indicated the direction of the relationship when they suggest, after their review of the research, that *"counselors who want to be seen as attractive should be empathic, warm and active."*[44] It also would appear, from LaCrosse's research, that counselors who want to appear to be experts should also be empathic, show respect and warmth, and be congruent or genuine. Similarly, it might be suggested that counselors who want to be perceived as trustworthy should show respect and warmth and be genuine or congruent. And if the therapist really respects clients, he or she will expect the best from them, and will probably find that clients respond in expected ways—that is, by assuming responsibility for the conduct of therapy, making choices and decisions, and solving problems.

It thus appears that the complex therapeutic relationship cannot be prevented from being "contaminated" by placebo elements. Clients perceive the therapist, to some extent at least, as an authority and an expert. They attribute status and prestige to the therapist. They put trust in the therapist. The therapist's belief in his or her methods or approach is inextricable from the methods or techniques used. If the therapist did not have confidence in them, he or she would use other methods or techniques. Similarly, if the therapist did not have confidence in himself or herself as a therapist, he or she would not continue to practice.

But if the placebo elements cannot be eliminated from psychotherapy, they can be either minimized or maximized. If they are maximized, then the therapist is engaging in placebo therapy, with the possibility that results may be limited, superficial, or temporary. When the placebo elements are minimized, as in client-centered or relationship therapy, the therapist is focusing on those conditions that appear to be specific for the outcomes that are the goals of this approach to psychotherapy.

SUMMARY

This chapter has considered the question: What is the placebo in psychotherapy? Since in psychotherapy there is no inert substance comparable to the placebo in medicine, the discussion has concerned the specific versus the nonspecific elements in psychotherapy. Many, if not most, of the writers on psychotherapy, including the behaviorists, view the entire therapy relationship as nonspecific, and thus as essentially a placebo. The behaviorists have been almost the only ones who have been clear in proposing specific factors, claiming that the various techniques of behavior therapy are specific. However, this claim has been increasingly disputed. Not only does behavior therapy depend on the relationship between the therapist and the client, but the specific methods and techniques of behavior therapy may be essentially placebos.

During the last 15 years, increasing attention has been given to what has become known as the social influence model of psychotherapy, derived from the social psychological research on the nature of the persuasive process. The three variables that have been emphasized are perceived expertness, attractiveness, and trustworthiness. The research on these variables, almost entirely analogue research, is inconsistent and contradictory in its results. It was suggested that this is consistent with the hypothesis that these variables are essentially placebos. Fish has systematically developed an approach that he calls placebo therapy that includes these variables, particularly perceived expertness, as its central focus.

There are other variables in the psychotherapy relationship that have received considerable support from extensive research not involving analogue situations. Three of these variables are empathic understanding, respect or warmth, and therapeutic genuineness. It was proposed that these are specific conditions for certain desirable outcomes in counseling or psychotherapy.

It appears to be impossible to separate out or to eliminate placebo elements from psychotherapy, since the client attributes a certain degree of expertness, authority, and attractiveness to the therapist, and the therapist's belief or confidence in himself or herself and in his or her methods lead to certain expectations for favorable response in the client, which is communicated to the client in various ways. The therapist, however, has the choice of maximizing or minimizing the placebo elements. It was suggested that maximizing the placebo elements, which is essentially placebo therapy, has the disadvantages of the placebo effect. That is, it is not reliable or consistent in that not all clients are strong placebo reactors, and its effects can be limited and temporary in nature.

NOTES

1. C. H. Patterson. *Counseling and psychotherapy: Theory and practice.* New York: Harper & Row, 1959.
2. A. K. Shapiro and L. A. Morris. The placebo effect in medical and psychological therapies. In S. L. Garfield and A. E. Bergin (Eds.), *Handbook of psychotherapy and behavior change: An empirical analysis* (2nd ed.). New York: Wiley, 1978, pp. 369–410.
3. *Ibid.,* p. 371.
4. *Ibid.,* p. 369.
5. Paradoxically, it appears that the "inert" placebo may be an active and specific treatment for pain by triggering the release of endorphins in the brain. See R. C. Bolles and M. S. Franselow. Endorphins and behavior. *Annual Review of Psychology*, 1982, *33*, 87–102.
6. A. K. Shapiro. Placebo effects in medicine, psychotherapy, and psychoanalysis. In A. E. Bergin and S. L. Garfield (Eds.), *Handbook of psychotherapy and behavior change: An empirical analysis.* New York: Wiley, 1971, p. 443.
7. L. Luborsky, B. Singer, and L. Luborsky. Comparative studies of psychotherapy. *Archives of General Psychiatry*, 1975, *32*, 995–1008. See also M. L. Smith and G. V. Glass. Meta-analysis of psychotherapy outcome studies. *American Psychologist*, 1977, *32*, 752–760; and M. L. Smith, G. V. Glass, and T. I. Miller. *The benefits of psychotherapy.* Baltimore: Johns Hopkins Press, 1980.
8. D. Rosenthal and J. D. Frank. Psychotherapy and the placebo effect. *Psychological Bulletin*, 1956, *53*, p. 297.
9. P. Pentony. *Models of influence in psychotherapy.* New York: The Free Press, 1981, p. 56.
10. J. D. Frank. *Persuasion and healing.* Baltimore: Johns Hopkins Press, 1961, 1973.
11. See, for example, A. E. Bergin and M. J. Lambert. The evaluation of therapeutic outcomes. In Garfield and Bergin, *Handbook*, pp. 139–190.
12. See, for example, H. H. Strupp. Psychotherapy research and practice: An overview. In Garfield and Bergin, *Handbook*, pp. 3–22.

13. Bergin and Lambert, Evaluation of therapeutic outcomes, p. 180.
14. J. Wolpe. *The practice of behavior therapy* (2nd ed.). New York: Pergamon Press, 1973, p. 9.
15. Frank, *Persuasion and healing.*
16. A. P. Goldstein. Psychotherapy research by extrapolation from social psychology. *Journal of Counseling Psychology*, 1966, *13*, 38–45; A. P. Goldstein, K. Heller, and L. B. Sechrest. *Psychotherapy and the psychology of behavior change.* New York: Wiley, 1966.
17. An early report of such studies was that of C. L. Hovland, I. L. Janis, and H. H. Kelley. *Communication and persuasion: Psychological studies of opinion change.* New Haven: Yale University Press, 1953.
18. S. R. Strong. Counseling: An interpersonal process. *Journal of Counseling Psychology*, 1968, *15*, 215–224; S. R. Strong and R. Matross. Change processes in psychotherapy. *Journal of Counseling Psychology*, 1973, *20*, 25–37.
19. L. E. Beutler. Psychotherapy and persuasion. In L. E. Beutler and R. Greene (Eds.), *Special problems in child and adolescent behavior.* Westport, CT: Technomic, 1978, pp. 119–159.
20. S. R. Strong. Social psychological approach to psychotherapy research. In Garfield and Bergin, *Handbook*, pp. 101–135.
21. J. D. Corrigan, D. M. Dell, K. N. Lewis, and L. D. Schmidt. Counseling as a social influence process. *Journal of Counseling Psychology Monograph*, 1980, *27*, 395–441.
22. Beutler, Psychotherapy and persuasion, pp. 125, 129.
23. Strong, Social psychological approach, p. 108.
24. Corrigan et al., Counseling as a social influence process, pp. 425, 437.
25. M. B. LaCrosse. Perceived counselor social influence and counseling outcomes: Validity of the Counselor Rating Form. *Journal of Counseling Psychology*, 1980, *27*, 320–327.
26. M. E. Orne. On the social psychology of the psychological experiment: With particular reference to demand characteristics and their implications. *American Psychologist*, 1962, *17*, 776–783.
27. R. Rosenthal. *Experimenter effects in behavioral research.* Englewood Cliffs, NJ: Prentice-Hall, 1966.
28. N. Muehlberg, R. Pierce, and J. Drasgow. A factor analysis of therapeutically facilitative conditions. *Journal of Clinical Psychology*, 1969, *25*, 93–95.
29. M. B. LaCrosse and A. Barak. Differential perception of counselor behavior. *Journal of Counseling Psychology*, 1976, *23*, 170–172.
30. L. Krasner and L. P. Ullmann (Eds.). *Research in behavior modification.* New York: Holt, Rinehart & Winston, 1965, p. 230.
31. J. M. Fish. *Placebo therapy.* San Francisco: Jossey-Bass, 1973. See also J. S. Gillis. *Social influence in psychotherapy: A description of the process and some tactical implications.* Jonesboro, TN: Pilgrimage Press, 1979.
32. Fish, *Placebo therapy*, p. vi.
33. *Ibid.*, pp. vi–vii.
34. *Ibid.*, p. vii.
35. *Ibid.*, pp. 16, 17.
36. *Ibid.*, p. 30.
37. *Ibid.*, p. 32.
38. *Ibid.*, pp. 45, 46.
39. *Ibid.*, p. vii.

40. *Ibid.*, p. 39.
41. Pentony, *Models of influence*, p. 8.
42. *Ibid.*, pp. 63–64.
43. M. B. LaCrosse. Comparative perceptions of counselor behavior: A replication and an extension. *Journal of Counseling Psychology*, 1977, *24*, 464–471.
44. J. D. Krumboltz, J. F. Becker-Haven, and K. F. Burnett. Counseling psychology. *Annual Review of Psychology*, 1979, *30*, 574.

CHAPTER 12

Other Issues
and Questions

In this chapter we consider some of the issues and implications developing from the relationship-client-centered position. First, it is necessary to clear up some of the misconceptions that have persisted over a long period of time.

SOME MISCONCEPTIONS

One of the oldest misconceptions about client-centered or relationship therapy is that the therapist is a purely passive participant in the process. Perhaps the use of the term *nondirective* with reference to the therapist has encouraged this view. The still continuing use of the term keeps this misconception alive.

It was about 1948 that an apocryphal story began circulating that parodied the idea of passivity. Carl Rogers, it was said, was counseling a client in an office high up in an office building. The client: "I feel terrible." Rogers: "You feel terrible." The client: "I really feel terrible." Rogers: "You really feel terrible." The client: "For two cents I'd jump out of that window." Rogers: "For two cents you'd jump out of that window." Client, getting up and going to the window: "Here I go." He jumps out of the window. Rogers, getting up and going to the window: "There you go." Another line was apparently added later. The client hits the ground with a plop sound. Rogers: "Plop."

It should be apparent from earlier chapters that the counselor or therapist is far from being a passive participant. The therapist is a highly sensitive, active, empathic listener, constantly struggling to understand the client, from the client's frame of reference, and to communicate this understanding in a way that facilitates the client's further self-exploration. The therapist is active in responding to the client, rather than in initiating or leading.

This story also illustrates two other misconceptions. First, that client-centered or relationship therapy is simple, even simplistic. It has been referred to as the grunt and groan method, or the uh-uh system. Again, it should be clear from earlier chapters, and from the writings of Carl Rogers and others, that it is far from a simple parrot-ing back of the words of the client. The other misconception that appears in the story is that the method is purely a matter of tech-nique—indeed, of one technique, that of reflecting the statements of the client, or paraphrasing them. But it should be clear at this point that relationship therapy is far from a simple technique or a bag of techniques. It involves the whole therapist as a person—his or her attitudes, values, and philosophy. No array of techniques, no matter how skillfully practiced, can lead to a real therapeutic relationship.

Another persisting misconception is that relationship therapy is useful, but only with a limited group of clients and problems. That is, it is appropriate only with clients of above average intelligence, such as college students, with simple adjustment problems, but not with seriously disturbed clients or those labeled or diagnosed as psychotic. Yet it has been successful with such clients. Gendlin,[1] among others, has reported on his work with schizophrenic patients. The extensive research by Rogers and his associates at the University of Wisconsin[2] should have dispelled the myth that client-centered therapy was not effective with psychotics. Critics have apparently misunderstood or misrepresented this study and have dismissed it, or have complained that not every patient improved. No method, of course, claims or should be expected to achieve 100 percent success.

A final misconception about relationship or client-centered therapy is that it is purely or essentially affective in nature, dealing only with feelings, and ignoring or rejecting cognitive or intellective aspects of clients and their problems. While it is true that client-centered therapy in its beginnings focused on affect, in contrast to the focus of other counseling approaches on cognitive factors, and while the emphasis is still upon affective elements, it is not possible to exclude cognitive factors, either in the client or the therapist, from the therapy relationship. The therapist relates to the client as a whole and total person, including thoughts, intentions, and actions as well as feelings and emotions. Contributors to the volume edited by Wexler and Rice[3] consider the cognitive, information processing, and language factors in the therapy process.

SHORT-TERM AND LONG-TERM PSYCHOTHERAPY

What might also be considered a misconception is that relationship therapy is long-term therapy. A method that leaves the initiative and responsibility with the client must be slow, and to allow the client to decide when to terminate therapy must prolong it. But this is not necessarily true.

Currently there is a strong emphasis on short-term or brief psychotherapy. It is interesting that it is in America, with its focus upon efficiency, where this emphasis is greatest. The psychoanalysts have been criticized because their methods result in therapy that lasts for several years. Some have developed methods to shorten the orthodox approach, calling these briefer approaches psychoanalytic psychotherapy to distinguish them from orthodox psychoanalysis.[4]

A common characteristic of the brief psychotherapies is their active, directing, and controlling nature. These therapies go beyond the responsive conditions, employing a wide variety of directive techniques. Where time is limited, either by pressures upon therapist time, as in mental health centers, or by client factors such as limited financial resources and mobility, it is felt to be necessary or desirable to resort to methods to speed up the process. It is assumed that the client-centered or relationship approach is too lengthy.

Two comments are in order here. First it should be noted that the objectives of brief therapy are different from those of extended therapy. The accepted or recognized objective is to provide immediate, if temporary, relief for the client's distress, and to resolve current specific problems. But this has some unintended outcomes. The use of directive methods means the abandonment of the objective of client responsibility for choices, for solving problems, even for his or her own life. Dependency can be fostered, so that whenever the client encounters another problem or difficult situation, he or she returns for help. Or, if the client feels that he or she was not helped, or was pushed out of therapy too soon, a new source of help is sought. The result can be a revolving door phenomenon. It is possible that this short-term, sometimes limited time policy of community mental health centers is creating a large group of dependent persons who will continue to need help for long periods of time. A student of mine in a practicum at a community mental health center was assigned such a returning client. The client wanted to know whether she would be limited to six interviews this time before she would enter a relationship.

The second comment is simply that relationship or client-centered therapy is not usually long-term therapy. Giving the decision of when to terminate to the client does not lead to interminable therapy. Yet it must be recognized that clients need therapy of varying duration. Some need only a few interviews, but some need lifelong therapy if they are to remain out of an institution. It is much more cost-effective to provide an hour a week of therapy than to commit a person to an institution, perhaps for the rest of his or her life.

The basic principle of the approach represented in this book is that the best way to help any client, whether only for an hour or for a hundred hours or more, is to provide the highest level of a therapeutic relationship of which the therapist is capable.

THE RELATIONSHIP: SPECIFIC OR NONSPECIFIC?

There is currently general agreement among theorists and therapists that the relationship factors of empathic understanding, respect or warmth, and therapeutic genuineness are present in all systems or methods of psychotherapy. Therapy, by almost any definition, involves a personal contact between the therapist and the client. This universal presence of a psychological relationship constitutes an obstacle to research attempting to study the influence or effect of other factors, such as specific techniques, apart from the relationship; the relationship cannot be eliminated and is difficult to control. No study to date has been successful in this respect. One study purporting to do so was not in fact free from relationship factors.[5] This study involved a laboratory study of fear modification using an automated desensitization procedure. Instructions to the subjects were taped; the subjects listened to the tapes instead of being involved with the therapist. But the tapes were of a human voice, and the experimental situation involved relationship elements—the subjects were introduced to the experiment by persons. The possibility that the subjects anthropomorphized the machine was present. In fact, the experimenters themselves may have done, and encouraged, this —the machine was designated as DAD (device for automated desensitization).

Thus, that there are relationship factors in all counseling or psychotherapy is seldom denied. But most of those who recognize the presence, and importance, of the relationship view it as a nonspecific factor, as noted in Chapter 11. It is not considered as directly related to the client's problems or to their solution. It is considered as the general environment in which, or the base from which, the therapist operates, using specific methods or techniques. It may be viewed as rapport, or the method of inducing the client to develop trust in the therapist. This is essentially the view of behavior therapists.

There are two arguments against this view, and in favor of the position taken in this book that the relationship is the specific treatment element in psychotherapy:

1. If it is assumed, as is done here—and there is evidence for this as noted earlier (see Chapter 1)—that the source of much if not most of the problems of clients involves interpersonal relationships, mainly the lack of or inadequacy of good human relationships—then a therapy that provides, and models, a good human relationship is a relevant and specific treatment method.

2. There is evidence that the relationship, without the addition of any techniques, is effective with many clients with many kinds of problems. This point will be considered later, and the evidence is presented in Chapter 13.

THE RELATIONSHIP: NECESSARY *AND* SUFFICIENT?

In addition to recognition of the relationship as a common element in all counseling or psychotherapy, there is widespread acceptance of its importance and even necessity. Goldstein, after reviewing the literature on therapist-patient expectancies in psychotherapy, concluded: "There can no longer be any doubt as to the primary status which must be accorded the therapeutic transaction."[6]

Menninger and Holzman, in *Theory of Psychoanalytic Techniques,* view the process of psychoanalysis as a two-person contractual relationship.[7] Goodstein, reviewing a collection of papers published under the title *What Makes Behavior Change Possible?* states that among virtually all the contributors there is an awareness of and attention to the therapeutic relationship as an essential ingredient of behavior change.[8] The fourteen contributors included Frank, Strupp, Burton, Ellis, Raimy, Polster, Bandura, and Wolpe.

Behaviorists recognize the presence of the relationship, though sometimes minimizing its importance. Observers of Wolpe and of Lazarus (when he was associated with Wolpe) noted that relationship variables were present. Lazarus acknowledged this in commenting on the report: "Both Wolpe and I have explicitly stated that relationship variables are often extremely important in behavior therapy. Factors such as warmth, empathy and authenticity are considered necessary but often insufficient."[9] Subsequently Wolpe insisted that "no basis exists for the idea that others have more compassion than behavior therapists."[10] More recently he wrote that "the more the patient feels a responsive warmth towards the therapist, the more likely to be inhibited are those of his anxieties that are evident during the interview."[11]

The question of the presence and importance of the relationship in counseling or psychotherapy is thus not an issue nor, it would appear, is the question of its necessity. But there are few who would agree that the relationship is not only necessary but also sufficient.

A major implication of the model presented in Chapter 1 is that the relationship is not only necessary but sufficient for therapeutic behavior change. Note the adjective *therapeutic*. No one would deny that there are other ways to change behavior—force or threat of force, drugs, psychosurgery, brainwashing, and, to a very limited extent with human beings, conditioning. But for positive changes in voluntary clients, the conditions of a therapeutic relationship are sufficient for a wide variety of changes with a wide variety of problems. There may be limits, but if so it is not yet clear what these limits are. As the conditions are tested in more and more situations, without the addition of other specific methods or techniques such as interpretation or behavior modification techniques, they demonstrate their effectiveness. They work with all kinds of problems and all kinds of people—the poor and disadvantaged as well as the rich and middle-class. The problem with certain kinds of clients is not the ineffectiveness of the conditions but of implementing or communicating them. The conditions themselves are not time- nor culture-bound, as noted in Chapter 10.

The question of sufficiency involves the question: Sufficient for what? Rogers,[12] in his initial statement of the hypothesis of the necessary and sufficient conditions, used the term *therapeutic personality change*. This needs definition. In this book it has been argued that a relationship characterized by empathic understanding, respect, and therapeutic genuineness leads, in the client who perceives these conditions, to progress in self-actualization. It leads, in part, to the development of these characteristics themselves, which constitute elements of self-actualization.

But what about other outcomes? People often come to counselors or therapists with problems involving lack of information or knowledge, lack of skills of various kinds—deficiencies of a cognitive or motor nature. Surely where these are lacking or inadequate, the providing of a relationship is not sufficient. But it may be, and is here, argued that dealing with such problems would appear to be education (or reeducation) or teaching, rather than therapy. While it may be difficult to draw a line between therapy and (remedial) teaching, there would seem to be some value in doing so. One difference is that therapy is concerned with persons who are not lacking in knowledge or skills but are unable for some reason to use their knowledge or skills. Their problem, in the distinction made by many learning theorists, is not one of learning but of performance. Therapy as a relationship is sufficient for enabling them to do those things that they are capable of doing. On the other hand, the relationship may not be sufficient where there is a lack or deficit. It is here that cognitive methods and techniques would be relevant and appropriate. To include these methods in counseling or psychotherapy simply because clients want or need such approaches is to unduly extend therapy to cover educational methods and practices.

However, even here, two comments are in order. First, it is becoming increasingly recognized that learning is not simply a cognitive process, as Rogers and other writers on humanistic education have emphasized.[13] Cognitive therapists often appear to ignore or be unaware of this. Second, the teacher-student interaction involves a personal relationship, and evidence is accumulating that the same factors that lead to therapeutic personality change also facilitate cognitive learning.[14] In fact, in some teaching—perhaps the best teaching—creating a suitable relationship may be sufficient for some kinds of learning by some learners.

In addition, evidence is accumulating that a therapy relationship characterized by empathic understanding, respect, and therapeutic genuineness, *without the addition of other methods or techniques* such as direct instruction or remedial teaching or cognitive techniques, can lead to client changes in behavior beyond those represented by the conditions themselves. As noted in the model presented in Chapter 1, clients may engage in seeking information and skill training and other learning experiences on their own, perhaps as a by-product of becoming more self-actualizing persons.

In the light of research indicating that the conditions alone are sufficient for a wide variety of outcomes, it becomes difficult to determine when other methods or techniques or other kinds of help should be included. It would appear that a client who lacks information should be given the information, or that a client who possesses incorrect or false information should be provided with accurate information. On the other hand, client responsibility might be increased if clients were simply told where to obtain lacking or accurate information. Similarly, where skills are lacking, clients could be informed where they could obtain instruction. Certainly therapists do not, and could not, provide instruction in all the kinds of skills that might be lacking in their clients—or provide all the kinds of information that they could lack.

Not every client will improve in a relationship that includes the core conditions. There is, of course, the possibility that the therapist conditions are not present at high enough levels in some cases. Even the best therapists encounter clients with whom they cannot fully empathize, or whom they cannot respect, like, feel warm toward, or be highly genuine with. Then there is always the possibility that in spite of the therapist's offering of high levels of the conditions, as rated by an outside observer, the client does not perceive these conditions. It is difficult, and sometimes impossible, to break through to some clients. The nature of the disturbance in some clients—for example, paranoia—may prevent it. Some clients may be so defensive that they cannot perceive anyone as genuinely interested in them. Other clients may be too threatened to trust anyone or to enter a relationship even with the best therapist. In addition, it is possible that even though the conditions may be present, they may be nullified or rendered ineffective by other, inconsistent and negative, elements introduced in the relationship by the therapist. Some therapists, after establishing a relationship, may attempt to use it to manipulate, persuade, or guide the client, leading to client confusion or resistance.

An apparent reason for the wide variety of changes in clients who are provided a therapeutic relationship without direct instruction or specific training is found in one of the effects of the relationship conditions in the therapy process. The presence of the conditions leads the client to engage in the process of self-exploration. Clients learn to take responsibility for themselves when they are expected to and allowed to do so. They make necessary choices and decisions. They seek and obtain necessary information when it is lacking. They look for and obtain training in necessary or desirable skills.

Since therapy is effective without specific methods or techniques beyond the relationship itself with a wide variety of clients with a wide variety of problems, a number of questions arise. When is the relationship not sufficient? Since results are obtained without the use of information-giving, advice, suggestions, interpretations, persuasion, and so on, then it is clear that none of these is necessary. The question then is: Do these other techniques help when added to the relationship, without undesirable side effects? When do they help? And a final question, which has not been investigated: If the relationship is not only necessary but sufficient for so many outcomes, is it efficient?[15] Again, are there other methods or techniques that would increase the efficiency of therapy, when added to the relationship, in achieving the same outcomes, and again without other undesirable side effects?

RESISTANCE TO ACCEPTANCE OF THE MODEL

There is considerable resistance to acceptance of a model that says that a good interpersonal relationship is not only necessary but sufficient for therapeutic personality change. Such a model poses a threat to many counselors and psychotherapists. Strupp's statement is a clear example of this threat: "The trained psychotherapist, whether he be a psychoanalyst or a behavior therapist, will reject as naive the suggestion that a large segment of the therapeutic influence —that is, the motive power for therapeutic change—might be encompassed by 'nonspecific' interpersonal factors. . . . On the basis of his clinical experience, he is deeply convinced that a good human relationship, which he might liken to the laying on of hands, sentimentality, moral treatment, or gross ignorance of the realities of therapeutic work, is severely limited in its therapeutic effects."[16] This resistance is also evident among reviewers of the research supporting this model (see Chapter 13), research that does not support Strupp's statement.

There are a number of reasons why this model is threatening.

1. The idea that the essence of psychotherapy is the relationship between the therapist and the client appears to be too simple. It is difficult to accept the fact that the relationship can have such profound effects on so many different problems and so many different kinds of clients. The idea that there must be different techniques for different problems and for different clients—indeed, for different therapists—appears to be more logical. The preoccupation with this thinking has led to reluctance or inability to recognize or accept the evidence for the power of the therapeutic relationship.

This idea and the model that includes it is simple, but it is not simplistic. It has the elegant simplicity of all the basic concepts or principles in science.

2. The concept that the relationship is the essence of psychotherapy is threatening because it places responsibility squarely on the person of the therapist. He or she has no place to hide. He or she cannot excuse himself or herself by disclaiming responsibility for lack of effectiveness, blaming it on lack of suitable techniques, and arguing that more research is needed to discover specific effective techniques. There are frequent statements to the effect that the most important element in psychotherapy is the personality of the psychotherapist. As long as the nature of the personality characteristics are not stated or identified, or it is implied that there are many different kinds of therapeutic personalities, this statement is innocuous or even meaningless. The research on the therapy relationship identifies and specifies those personality characteristics that are therapeutic, and provides evidence that high levels of these characteristics lead to therapeutic personality changes, while low levels do not.

3. Perhaps the most threatening implication of the relationship as the core of psychotherapy is that psychotherapy is not a

profession. The threat to professionalism is clearly reflected by Strupp: "If the contribution of a good human relationship to a specific therapeutic outcome is subtracted, what is left over? The development of psychotherapy as a set of theories and as a prestigious profession in the twentieth century is predicated on the assumption that the residue is substantial."[17] But the assumption is not supported by research. The emperor is without any clothes. Albee writes that

> a *profession* must jealously guard its secrets! Historically, one of the hallmarks of a profession has been the *privacy* of its knowledge. If the knowledge of the professional, his techniques, and his skills are available to anyone, and could be performed by anyone, a profession would disintegrate. Secrecy and mystery are essential.[18]

If psychotherapy consists of the providing of a good human relationship, it cannot be the monopoly of a professional group. It can and should be disseminated throughout society. It does not require a degree, neither the B.A., M.A., Ph.D., or M.D., many of the requirements of which are unnecessary or irrelevant—if not detrimental—to the providing of a therapeutic relationship. If, to paraphrase Miller,[19] psychotherapy is to be given away to the people, it cannot remain a profession.

To be sure, for a long time to come there will be a need for those who are gifted or expert in providing a therapeutic relationship, and whose time and commitment will be worth payments. Psychotherapy may be likened to the purchase of friendship as Schofield noted,[20] but it is something more—viewing it simply as bought friendship places the psychotherapist in the same category as taxi dancers, gigolos, and call girls. While it may not be a profession, psychotherapy is on a somewhat different level.

There is another element in client-centered or relationship therapy that creates resistance, and that is its revolutionary nature. This has become increasingly evident, especially with the recent proliferation of so-called innovative methods and techniques or strategies of intervention, all of which seem to have in common an active, directive, and controlling view of psychotherapy.

THE REAL REVOLUTION IN
COUNSELING AND PSYCHOTHERAPY

In 1966 John Krumboltz, in the title of a book that he edited, proclaimed a "Revolution in Counseling."[21] It was a behavioristic revolution. That revolution, if it ever amounted to a real revolution, petered out. In 1942, and again in 1951, when Carl Rogers[22] presented client-centered therapy he did not claim it to be revolutionary. He actually was cautious and tentative in proposing it. Yet it has become increasingly evident, particularly as newer methods and techniques have been proliferating, that client-centered or relationship therapy is revolutionary, and that its revolutionary implications go beyond psychotherapy. In a recent book, Carl Rogers[23] deals with some of the broad implications of what he terms the person-centered view of psychotherapy, and I shall draw upon this in some of my comments. The broad question that he poses concerns "the political effects (in the new sense of political) of all that I, and my many colleagues throughout the world, have done and are doing."[24] He is aware of the resistance noted above when he writes that "the very effectiveness of this unified person-centered approach constitutes a threat to professionals, administrators and others, and steps are taken—consciously and unconsciously—to destroy it."[25] Why should there be such a reaction to an approach to psychotherapy that is so effective? Haven't we been seeking such an approach, and haven't we—or some of us—hailed behavior therapy because it appeared to be so effective? Let us look at the implications of this approach for a clue as to its threatening nature.

Relationship or client-centered therapy turns upside down the traditional concept of the therapist-client relationship. Rogers states it as follows: "The person-centered view drastically alters the therapist-patient relationship as previously conceived."[26] He tells of an experience, some years ago, when he was asked a question about the politics of client-centered therapy. He replied that there was no politics in client-centered therapy. He was met by laughter from the audience. He asked his questioner to explain his question. The response is reported as follows: "I spent three years of graduate school learning to be an expert in clinical psychology. I learned to make accurate diagnostic judgments. I learned the various techniques of altering the subject's attitudes and behavior. I learned subtle modes of manipulation, under the labels of interpretation and guidance. Then I began to read your material, which upset everything I had learned. You were saying that the power rests not in my mind but in his organism. You completely reversed the relationship of power and control which had been built up in me over three years. And then you say there is no politics in client-centered therapy!"[27]

In client-centered therapy the therapist is not the expert on the client—the client is the expert on himself or herself, and the therapist learns from him or her. To the extent that the therapy relationship is a one-way street in the sense that the client (we hope) gains or benefits more than the therapist, it is a one-way street on the *level*. The relationship is a *horizontal* rather than a *vertical* one as it is in most other approaches to psychotherapy. This concept of equality between the therapist and the client is difficult to elucidate. The therapist does know more about some if not many things than the client does. But the therapist doesn't know more about the most essential subject of therapy, the patient, though the therapist often thinks he or she does. As Rogers says: "The more this person-centered approach is implemented and put into practice, the more it is found to challenge the hierarchical models of 'treatment' and hierarchical models of organization."[28] "The politics of the client-centered approach is a conscious renunciation and avoidance by the therapist of all control over, or decision-making for, the client."[29] And again, in noting the many apparent disagreements of this approach with common sense, he writes: "It is nonsensical to think that therapy can be democratic. *But*—when the therapy relationship is equalitarian, when each takes responsibility for himself in the relationship, independent (and mutual) growth is much more rapid."[30] And again, he notes, common sense says "it is unreasonable to think that a troubled person can make progress without the guidance and direction of a wise psychotherapist. *But*—there is ample evidence that in a relationship marked by the facilitative conditions, the troubled person can engage in self-exploration, and become self-directing in profoundly wise ways."[31]

The concept of equality between the therapist and the client is threatening to many. The desire to be an expert, to feel knowledgeable and influential—if not omniscient and omnipotent—to be an authority, to be looked up to, is widespread and strong. There are those who have a need to control others, or who gain satisfaction from feeling superior, or who need even to be in control of the therapy relationship. Many, besides George Burns, would like to play God. Rogers writes: "It has taken me years to recognize that the violent opposition to a client-centered therapy sprang not only from its newness, and the fact that it came from a psychologist rather than a psychiatrist, but primarily because it struck such an outrageous blow to the therapist's power. It was the politics that was threatening."[32] The attraction of many of the so-called innovative methods lies, I believe, in the fact that they emphasize the therapist as an expert, even if, as in behavior therapy, he or she is only a technician.

The basic attitude of the person-centered therapist toward his or her client thus differs from that represented in most traditional approaches. I will not go so far as to label these approaches object-centered, though many therapists of these schools seem to view their clients as interesting species to be studied to see "what makes them tick." The very origin of clients' difficulties involves their having been, or being, treated as an object, as inadequate, inferior, unworthy, rather than respected as a person with potential.

The person-centered therapist not only views the client as a person, but as potentially capable of being *his or her own person.* The therapist has confidence in the client's ability to solve his or her own problems—that is, to engage in self-discovery learning—when provided the conditions for doing so, and in the client's ability to make his or her own decisions and choices. The therapist trusts clients, or the growth forces within them. Again, Rogers notes that it is regarded as "hopelessly idealistic to think that the human organism is basically trustworthy. *But*—the research and actions based upon this hypothesis tend to confirm the view, even strongly confirm it."[33]

The person-centered therapist thus operates in the best traditions of medicine, as Hippocrates phrased them: first, to do no harm and, second, to depend on and collaborate with the natural drive toward health of the organism. I have called it the principle of minimal intervention; it is sometimes referred to in medicine as the principle of conservative management. Every intervention poses a risk—the greater the intervention the greater the risk—and this is true psychologically as well as physiologically. The therapist's function is to remove blocks to natural healing and growth. Client-centered therapy is almost the only therapy—orthodox psychoanalysis is one of the few others—that does not actively intervene, control, guide, direct, teach, advise, interpret, suggest, recommend, persuade, and so on.

It appears that many therapists with various orientations and kinds of training tend with experience to focus more and more upon the providing of a facilitative relationship. As Rogers notes: "A sensitive person, trying to be of help, becomes more person-centered, no matter what orientation s(he) starts from, because s(he) finds that approach more effective." Moreover, "it is found that those who can create an effective person-centered relationship do not necessarily come from the professionally trained group."[34] And again, "the modes of 'helping' most popular in our culture—the diagnostic, evaluative, interpretive, prescriptive, and punitive approaches" are being put aside by the nonprofessionals for human acceptance and caring.[35]

SUMMARY

In this chapter, after noting some of the misconceptions about relationship therapy, we considered a number of questions and issues raised by the model presented in this book, which places primary importance in therapy on the conditions of empathic understanding, respect, and therapeutic genuineness. Few, if any, would dispute that these conditions are important, even necessary, for therapy to be effective. Many view them as nonspecific elements, however, contending that there are, or must be, more specific factors or techniques involved. These techniques have never been specified or identified, however. We argued that a good relationship provided by the therapist is the specific remedy for the lack of or inadequacy of such relationships in the client's life. That these conditions are not only necessary but sufficient would be admitted by few theorists or therapists. Arguments for this position were presented.

There appears to be increasing resistance to client-centered or relationship therapy. Some of the reasons for this were noted. A major reason is the revolutionary nature of this approach, which has been recognized only recently, perhaps as its almost diametric opposition to new methods and techniques has become apparent. There are basic differences between relationship or client-centered therapy and most other theories and methods. While it may be oversimplifying to some extent, these differences appear to amount to the difference between a democratic, egalitarian philosophy that views the client as able, responsible, trustworthy, and capable of resolving his or her own problems and a more authoritarian philosophy that views the client as inadequate, helpless, and dependent on the therapist for the solutions to his or her problems.

NOTES

1. E. T. Gendlin. Client-centered developments in work with schizophrenics. *Journal of Consulting Psychology*, 1962, *9*, 205-212.
2. C. R. Rogers, E. Gendlin, D. J. Kiesler, and C. B. Truax (Eds.). *The therapeutic relationship and its impact: A study of psychotherapy with schizophrenics*. Madison: University of Wisconsin, 1967.
3. D. A. Wexler and L. N. Rice (Eds.). *Innovations in client-centered therapy*. New York: Wiley, 1974.
4. For example, F. Alexander and T. French. *Psychoanalytic therapy*. New York: Ronald Press, 1946.
5. P. J. Lang, B. G. Melamed, and J. Hart. A psychophysical analysis of fear modification using an automated desensitization procedure. *Journal of Abnormal Psychology*, 1970, *76*, 220-234.
6. A. P. Goldstein. *Therapist-patient expectancies in psychotherapy*. New York: Macmillan, 1962, p. 105.
7. K. A. Menninger and P. S. Holzman. *Theory of psychoanalytic techniques* (2nd ed.). New York: Basic Books, 1973. In describing psychoanalysis as a two-person contract, they note that in a business contract the relationship between the two parties is not important but that "in psychotherapy these relations are by no means incidental; they are the basic elements in the transaction" (p. 22).

8. L. D. Goodstein. Detente in psychotherapy. Review of A. Burton (Ed.), *What makes behavior change possible?* in *Contemporary Psychology*, 1977, *22*, 578-579.

9. M. Klein, A. J. Dittman, M. B. Parloff, and M. M. Gill. Behavior therapy: Observations and reflections. (With comment by A. Lazarus.) *Journal of Consulting and Clinical Psychology*, 1969, *33*, p. 262.

10. J. Wolpe. *The practice of behavior therapy* (2nd ed.). New York: Pergamon Press, 1973, p. 9.

11. In A. Burton (Ed.), *What makes behavior change possible?* New York: Brunner/Mazel, 1976, p. 66.

12. C. R. Rogers. The necessary and sufficient conditions of therapeutic personality change. *Journal of Consulting Psychology*, 1957, *21*, 95-103.

13. C. R. Rogers. *Freedom to learn.* Columbus, OH: Merrill, 1969; C. H. Patterson. *Humanistic education.* Englewood Cliffs, NJ: Prentice-Hall, 1973; C. H. Patterson. *Foundations for a theory of instruction and educational psychology.* New York: Harper & Row, 1977.

14. D. N. Aspy. *Toward a technology for humanizing education.* Champaign, IL: Research Press, 1972.

15. Albert Ellis has recently addressed this question in A. Ellis, The value of efficiency in psychotherapy. *Psychotherapy: Theory, Research and Practice*, 1980, *17*, 414-419.

16. H. H. Strupp. A reformulation of the dynamics of the therapist's contribution. In A. S. Gurman and A. M. Razin (Eds.), *Effective psychotherapy.* New York: Pergamon Press, 1977, p. 9.

17. *Ibid.*, p. 9.

18. G. W. Albee. The uncertain future of clinical psychology. *American Psychologist*, 1970, *25*, 1075.

19. G. A. Miller. Psychology as a means of promoting human welfare. *American Psychologist*, 1969, *24*, 1063-1075.

20. W. Schofield. *Psychotherapy: The purchase of friendship.* Englewood Cliffs, NJ: Prentice-Hall, 1964.

21. J. D. Krumboltz (Ed.). *Revolution in counseling.* Boston: Houghton Mifflin, 1966.

22. C. R. Rogers. *Counseling and psychotherapy.* Boston: Houghton Mifflin, 1942; C. R. Rogers. *Client-centered therapy.* Boston: Houghton Mifflin, 1951.

23. C. R. Rogers. *Carl Rogers on personal power.* New York: Delacorte, 1977.

24. *Ibid.*, p. 5.

25. *Ibid.*, p. 28.

26. *Ibid.*, p. 15.

27. *Ibid.*, p. 3.

28. *Ibid.*, p. 28.

29. *Ibid.*, p. 14.

30. *Ibid.*, p. 287.

31. *Ibid.*, p. 287.

32. *Ibid.*, p. 16.

33. *Ibid.*, p. 287.

34. *Ibid.*, p. 28.

35. *Ibid.*, p. 270.

PART FOUR

Research
Evidence

CHAPTER 13

Evaluation of
the Research

Research on the core conditions of the counseling and psychotherapy relationship is voluminous. It constitutes a body of research that is among the largest for any topic of similar size in the field of psychology. In the 1967 review of Truax and Carkhuff,[1] 439 references were listed. In the 1971 review of Truax and Mitchell,[2] there were 92 references. It is manifestly impossible within the limits of this chapter to review all these studies. Moreover, it is not necessary to do so, since there are several more recent reviews. The second edition of the *Handbook of Psychotherapy and Behavior Change*[3] includes four chapters that review research related to this topic.

In this chapter we shall present a critical analysis and evaluation of these recent reviews. This is necessary because the conclusions of the reviewers in many cases do not appear to follow from their own summaries of the research studies. Since these conclusions are likely to be accepted as valid by most students, and others, who do not have the time or opportunity to read the original studies, it is important that their deficiencies be revealed.

REVIEWER BIAS

It probably goes without saying that all reviewers are biased. Reviewers do not identify their biases, however, even when they are aware of them. Many of the recent reviewers are biased against recognition or acceptance of the effectiveness of the core conditions in counseling or psychotherapy, perhaps in part at least for some of the

This chapter was originally published in *Psychology*, 1984, *21*, 431–438.

reasons noted earlier (Chapter 12). The evidence for these biases becomes clear when one examines the analysis of the individual research studies. Consider the following points:

1. Reviewers are biased in the selection of the studies that they review. Criteria for selection often seem to vary depending on the conclusions of the studies. Strict criteria are applied to reject inclusion of those studies that disagree with the bias of the reviewer, while lesser criteria are applied to select those studies that support the reviewer's bias. Thus, the conclusions of the review are biased, even though they seem justified by the studies selected for review.

2. Similarly, of those studies admitted to the review, whether bias has entered into the selection or not, standards applied in the critiques of methodology and procedures and analysis of the data vary according to the reviewer's bias. Strict standards are applied to those studies inconsistent with the reviewer's bias, leading to rejection or minimizing of the results, while less strict standards are applied to other studies, leading to acceptance of the results.

3. Sometimes results of a single study or two or three studies that are in accordance with a reviewer's bias are emphasized or given great weight in conclusions. If two of three studies agree with the reviewer's bias, strong statements are made. Yet if, as noted later, 14 out of 21 studies yield results against the reviewer's bias, little emphasis is placed on "only" two-thirds agreement.

4. When results are positive on some outcome measures and negative on others, a reviewer may fail to mention or may deemphasize the positive results or may reject the measures yielding the positive results unacceptable to the reviewer. Yet if in another study such measures yield results acceptable to the reviewer, these measures are accepted.

These kinds of biases became evident in many of the reviews to be considered here. In addition, other evidences of bias were apparent. The language and phrasing frequently indicate bias, as will be seen in some of the statements of reviewers as we evaluate their reviews. Bias leads to misunderstanding, misinterpretation, or even misrepresentation of the findings of the original studies. It also leads to inconsistencies or discrepancies among statements—the stated results of studies reviewed are not consistent with the reviewer's conclusions. The existence of bias is also indicated by the differing evaluations and conclusions by different reviewers of the same studies.

MAJOR REVIEWS

We look here at a number of recent major reviews and point out where they are flawed in their critiques or their conclusions.

Mitchell, Bozarth, and Krauft

The review by Mitchell, Bozarth, and Krauft[4] is particularly interesting since the earlier review by Truax and Mitchell was highly positive. Its conclusion read as follows:

> Therapists or counselors who are accurately empathic, non-possessively warm in attitude and genuine are indeed effective. Also, these findings seem to hold with a wide variety of therapists and counselors, regardless of their training or theoretic orientation, and with a wide variety of clients or patients, including college underachievers, juvenile delinquents, hospitalized schizophrenics, college counselees, mild to severe outpatient neurotics, and a mixed variety of hospitalized patients. Further, the evidence suggests that these findings hold in a variety of therapeutic contexts and in both individual and group psychotherapy or counseling.[5]

Mitchell, Bozarth, and Krauft question, but do not refute, these conclusions, in their negatively toned review. Their evaluation rests heavily upon the Arkansas study by Mitchell, Truax, Bozarth, and Krauft.[6] Mitchell, Bozarth, and Krauft performed various statistical analyses and state that "in no instance was either empathy or warmth found to be related to client change. Genuineness was found to be related to client change in a sufficient number of analyses to allow us to say that minimal levels of genuineness were related modestly to outcome."[7]

There are, however, several flaws in this study. The 75 therapists included represented only 5 percent of those invited to participate in the study. Moreover, in this highly (self-) selected sample of therapists, "the interpersonal interaction levels of the therapists with their clients were relatively superficial. Almost all the therapists in this sample were below minimal levels and as a group, were not facilitative."[8] The low levels and restricted ranges of the facilitative conditions would operate against obtaining any significant relationships with outcome variables. The authors recognize this problem when they note that "a reasonable proportion of therapists in any particular study *must* provide *at least* minimally facilitative levels before the study can be seen as even testing the central hypothesis" that "*high* levels of skills lead to client improvement."[9]

Fifteen studies conducted between 1970 and 1975 are reviewed, even though the authors estimate that none of them actually tested the central hypothesis. They summarize their evaluation as follows: "Perhaps seven [47 percent] offer at least minimal support for the hypothesis of *higher* levels of empathy (whether truly facilitative or not) and positive client outcome. Similarly, perhaps four [27 percent] offer such support for *higher* levels of warmth, and perhaps three studies (20 percent) offer such support for *higher* levels of genuineness."[10] It would seem to be difficult to argue that such high levels of the conditions are not facilitative in the face of positive relationships with outcome. However, the authors state that *"our conclusion must be that the relationship between the interpersonal skills and client outcome has not been investigated adequately and, consequently, nothing definitive can be said about the relative efficacy of high and low levels of empathy, warmth, and genuineness."*[11] (Italics in the original.)

On the basis of these 15 studies and the Arkansas study the authors offer the following equivocal conclusion:

> It seems to us to be increasingly clear that *the mass of data neither supports nor rejects the overriding influence of such variables as empathy, warmth, and genuineness in all cases.* . . . The recent evidence, although equivocal, does seem to suggest that empathy, warmth, and genuineness are related in some way to client change, but that their potency and generalizability are not as great as some thought.[12]

Parloff, Waskow, and Wolfe

Parloff, Waskow, and Wolfe[13] are perhaps the most negative in their evaluation of the research on therapist variables. While noting that "all schools of psychotherapy appear to be in accord that a positive relationship between patient and therapist is a necessary precondition for any form of psychotherapy" they add that "relevant clinical observations have . . . cast doubt on the universal applicability of the principle that the greater the degree of genuineness, empathy, and warmth, the greater the benefit to all patients."[14] The validity of clinical observations is not questioned; moreover, no one claims that *all* patients benefit.

Parloff, Waskow, and Wolfe criticize and reject the favorable conclusion of the Truax and Mitchell review, and quote approvingly from the more negative review of Mitchell, Bozarth, and Krauft. They recognize that there are positive findings, but emphasize the negative, failing to note that there are more positive than negative studies, or to note that the negative studies are not without serious problems or flaws. They make the important point that Rogers's 1957 statement included as a necessary condition the client's perception of the therapist's empathy, warmth, and genuineness, and note that most studies do not involve measures of client perceptions of the conditions, but rather use observer's ratings of the conditions. They fail, however, to recognize that this would lead to attenuation of the relationship between the conditions and outcomes, or to negative results in some cases where client ratings might produce positive results. Thus it is significant that positive results are obtained where the conditions are measured from an observer's rather than from the client's viewpoint.

These reviewers end by stating that "it must be concluded that the unqualified claim that 'high' levels (absolute or relative) of accurate empathy, warmth, and genuineness (independent of the source of rating or the nature of the instrument) represent 'the necessary and sufficient' conditions for effective therapy (independent of the outcome measures or conditions) is not supported."[15] This is an equivocating and essentially meaningless statement. No one makes such an unqualified claim. No one claims that the case has been absolutely proven. Parloff, Waskow, and Wolfe do not, on the other hand, disprove it.

Orlinsky and Howard

Orlinsky and Howard[16] review much of the same research as do Mitchell, Bozarth, and Krauft, and Parloff, Waskow, and Wolfe, but with somewhat different conclusions. They state that "approximately two-thirds of the 23 studies of warmth and a similar percentage of the 35 studies of empathy show a significant positive relationship between the externally rated aspects of therapist interpersonal behavior and therapeutic outcome."[17] Of 20 studies of therapist congruence or genuineness, a similar proportion, two-thirds or 14, show a significantly positive relationship with outcome. They state that

> the studies done thus far suggest that the positive quality of the relational bond, as exemplified in the reciprocal interpersonal relationship behaviors of the participants, is more clearly related to patient improvement than are any of the particular treatment techniques used by therapists.[18]

This is a strong statement, in view of the emphasis on techniques by most therapists and current therapies. They go on to say that

> cumulatively these studies [of congruence] seem to warrant the conclusion that therapist genuineness is at least innocuous, is generally predictive of good outcome, and at most may be a causal element in promoting client improvement. Beyond a reasonable minimum, however, it is probably neither a necessary nor a sufficient condition of therapeutic benefit.[19]

This is a rather innocuous, if not negative, statement and one that cannot be drawn directly from the research they review. It seems to be inconsistent with the statements quoted above.

Orlinsky and Howard also review studies using measures of client perception of the therapist conditions. Fifteen studies of client perception of empathy vary some in results, but "generally these studies support the notion that the sense of being understood by one's therapist is a fairly consistent feature of beneficial therapy as experienced by patients."[20] Again, regarding respect (or warmth):

> The evidence of 13 studies ... is unanimous in indicating that the patient's perception of the therapist's manner as affirming the patient's value is positively and significantly associated with good therapeutic outcome. ... It would seem foolish to discount the patient's sense of affirmation by the therapist as one probable ingredient of productive therapeutic experience.[21]

This is rather a weak conclusion for unanimous evidence.

Orlinsky and Howard reviewed other studies of client perceptions of their therapists and of themselves that support the importance of the relationship established in client-centered or relationship psychotherapy. These studies indicated that patients who saw their therapists as "independence-encouraging" had better outcomes than those who viewed their therapists as "authoritarian." Patients' perception of their therapists as being personally involved was also related to positive outcome. Other variables related to positive outcome were the patients' view of the relationship as warm, close, and intimate, rather than cold, domineering, or confrontative.

Clients who perceived themselves as expressing their thoughts and feelings with greater openness (greater self-disclosure) improved more than those showing lesser openness. Patients who saw themselves as accepting of the therapist improved more than those who did not. Patients who perceived themselves as actively involved and as actively initiating in their therapy (engaging in self-exploration) improved more than those who did not so perceive themselves. Those who felt a greater sense of self-responsibility for solving their own problems and changing their own behavior had better outcomes. Clients who were successful in psychotherapy tended to talk about themselves with feeling, in a concrete way, with increasing self-awareness; viewed their problems as internal rather than external; and showed a willingness to "own" their feelings. A number of studies involved the use of Rogers's process scale and Gendlin's experiencing scales. Nine of ten studies using the process scales found significant positive relationships with outcomes. Fifty percent of the studies using Truax's client self-exploration scale showed positive results. All the client perceptions of their therapists and of themselves are fostered in client-centered or relationship therapy.

Gurman's earlier review of research on client perception of the therapeutic relationship agrees with Orlinsky and Howard, stating the strong conclusion that "there exists substantial, if not overwhelming, evidence in support of the hypothesized relationship between patient-perceived therapeutic conditions and outcome in individual psychotherapy and counseling."[22]

Lambert, DeJulio, and Stein

The work by Lambert, DeJulio, and Stein[23] is not actually a comprehensive review of the research on interpersonal skills. Eighteen studies done up to 1977 were selected as "the best this area has to offer." The authors conclude that

> despite more than 20 years of research and some improvements in methodology, only a modest relationship between the so-called facilitative conditions and therapeutic outcomes has been found. Contrary to frequent claims for the potency of these therapist-offered relationship variables, experimental evidence suggests that neither a clear test nor unequivocal support for the Rogerian hypothesis has appeared.

Of course, if there has not been a clear test, one could not expect to find unequivocal support.

Most of the review is concerned with methodological issues, including the following:

1. Who should rate the conditions—clients, therapists, or outside raters? Relationships among these ratings are low.

2. When audiotapes are used as the basis of ratings, nonverbal behaviors are not observable.

3. Should the raters be experienced therapists or naive observers?

4. Should raters be trained or not?

5. Does the sex of the raters influence the ratings?

6. There are problems of sampling, both of interviews during the course of therapy, and within interviews.

7. Are the facilitative conditions independent, constituting three dimensions, or are they aspects of a single dimension, such as the "good guy" therapist?

These are all sources of "confounding variables that must be taken into account when carrying out research in this area," and the low relationships found are probably a function of these variables. "Improvements in methodology may yet lead to a significant revision of the client-centered hypothesis and an increase in its ability to specify conditions leading to therapeutic change."

These authors also mention some of the problems to be discussed below, including inadequate sampling of therapy excerpts, the low levels of ratings of the conditions, and their restricted range. Referring to the negative results of two major studies, they note that "it would be a shame to see researchers discontinue the examination of the facilitative conditions because of these negative results."

Annual Review of Psychology

The *Annual Review of Psychology* includes reviews of psychotherapy at three-year intervals. These reviews cover much more than the research in which we are interested here, and only the material relevant to our interests will be discussed.

The review by Bergin and Suinn[24] covers the years 1971 through 1973. Bergin, the author of the individual psychotherapy section of the review, puts much emphasis on three studies: the Temple University study (Sloane et al.),[25] the DiLoreto study,[26] and the Mitchell et al. (Arkansas) study mentioned earlier. The first two studies were comparative studies, and they found little or no difference in the effects of a wide variety of techniques. Bergin fails to recognize that this is evidence for the importance of a common element (the relationship). He also is uncritical in his acceptance of the results of the second two studies as not supporting the effectiveness of the core conditions. Lambert, DeJulio, and Stein in their review pointed out several deficiencies in the Temple University study, some similar to those in the Arkansas study: the restricted range of the ratings of the therapist conditions (though the levels were relatively high); the fact that ratings were based on one sample from one interview; and the fact that the ratings of the behaviorists were on samples selected when they "were acting like therapists." In addition, there were only three psychoanalytic and three behavioristic therapists involved in this study. Bergin concludes that "it is clearer now that these variables are not as prepotent as once believed; but their presence and influence is ubiquitous, even showing up strongly in behavior therapies."

Bergin makes the interesting statement that "in recent years, a number of studies have induced skepticism concerning the potency of these variables except in highly specific, client-centered type conditions." It is not clear just what Bergin means or could mean by this statement. But there is an interesting implication. Since the conditions constitute or are the essence of client-centered therapy, then only client-centered therapy is an effective therapy. Though these conditions may be present in other therapies, they can be nullified or counteracted by other conditions or therapist variables. Support for this conclusion is provided by the fact that *there is no good evidence for the effectiveness of any other variables or techniques— or for the effectiveness of other approaches in the absence of these conditions.*

The review by Gomes-Schwartz, Hadley, and Strupp[27] three years later devotes one paragraph to the research on warmth, empathy, and genuineness, citing eight studies. Only one of these studies, that by Sloane et al., related the conditions to outcome; this study was considered in the earlier review by Bergin. The other studies were of interrelationships among the conditions, and problems in their measurement by ratings. Nevertheless, the author (Gomes-Schwartz, who authored this part of the review) perpetuates the negative evaluation: "Earlier assertions of strong empirical support for the relationship between therapist's facilitative 'conditions' and therapy outcome [by Truax and Mitchell] have been challenged by recent findings" [citing Bergin's review]. Yet she also equivocates: "This does not imply that the quality of the therapeutic relationship is not of major importance in determining the effectiveness of psychotherapy."[28]

It is very interesting that in a later section on the therapeutic relationship it is stated that

> in a relationship marked by warmth, closeness, and a sense that the therapist was involved and cared about the patient, patients were more likely to remain in therapy than terminate [four studies cited], to be satisfied with the ongoing therapy process [two studies], and to show greater improvement [three studies]. The therapeutic relationship characterized by relaxed rapport and open communication was likely to promote continuation in therapy [two studies] and better outcome [two studies].[29]

It is curious that these studies are separated from the section on warmth, empathy, and genuineness—they certainly are relevant supporting studies, making the negative conclusion questionable at least.

Hadley, in his section on behavioral interventions, noting that "in the past, relationship variables have often been subsumed under 'nonspecific effects,'" continues:

> Recently there has been increased attention to the importance of a good patient-therapist relationship, in effecting positive change. The thrust of most of these discussions is that the relationship, while not sufficient for *change*, is vital for *substantial improvement*. Furthermore, there is a growing consensus that an empirical, learning-based approach to clinical practice is not antithetical to recognition of the importance of "relationship" factors.[30]

Here, as in most of the previous reviews, one notes the inconsistencies and contradictions among the various statements and conclusions regarding relationship variables.

The 1979 volume of the *Annual Review* includes a chapter on "Counseling Psychology."[31] A brief section on genuineness, warmth, and empathy notes an "apparent substantiation of Rogers's triad of therapist genuineness, warmth, and empathy," but the reference is to the 1971 review of Truax and Mitchell. Further references are to studies of the reliability of ratings of the variables. In 1981 the chapter reviewing psychotherapy[32] makes no mention of studies on empathy, warmth, or genuineness. It is inconceivable that there were no such studies during the period covered (1976-1980). The review simply does not cover research on the therapy process or relationship. The review of counseling psychology in this issue of the *Annual Review of Psychology*[33] concerns itself only with career interventions, research, and theory.

EVALUATION

If one reads these reviews of research—by often biased reviewers—one cannot help being impressed with the direction of the evidence. Yet the conclusions of the reviews do not adequately or accurately reflect the reviewers' own reports of the studies reviewed. The reviewers are more than cautious in their conclusions—they are often inconsistent, ambivalent, and unable to accept the results of their own reviews. Allen Bergin and Hans Strupp, who have produced earlier biased reviews, show the same inconsistency and ambivalence in their overview chapters in Garfield and Bergin. Bergin and Lambert write, presumably after reading the other chapters considered above: "Our hope that the study of specific treatments with specific problems would result in practically useful information has not been realized, with but few exceptions."[34] This is true as regards the case of behavior therapy, to which they are referring in this statement. But they do not go on to note that this is not true regarding the conditions of client-centered or relationship therapy. They continue:

> Interpersonal and nonspecific or nontechnical factors still loom large as stimulators of patient improvement. It should come as no surprise that helping people . . . can be greatly facilitated in an interpersonal relationship that is characterized by trust, warmth, acceptance, and human wisdom. It appears that these personal factors are crucial ingredients even in the more technical [behavioral] therapies. This is not to say that techniques are irrelevant but that their power for change pales when compared to personal influence. Technique is crucial to the extent that it provides a believable rationale and congenial modus operandi for the change agent and the client.[35]

Bergin and Strupp have been writing for years about the "crucial" importance of techniques in addition to the relationship. But neither they nor anyone else have clearly identified or specified these techniques or produced any evidence for the effectiveness of techniques. It is interesting that Gomes-Schwartz, a colleague of Strupp, states that "it remains to be demonstrated that what the therapist does has an impact over and above the effects of a supportive relationship."[36]

If techniques "provide a believable rationale and congenial modus operandi" they are not specific—in fact they are part of the placebo. Bergin and Lambert state that

> although it was once felt that this hypothesis [that a positive relationship exists between therapist interpersonal skills and therapy outcomes] had been confirmed [an apparent reference to the 1971 review of Truax and Mitchell], it now appears that the relationship between these variables and outcome is more ambiguous than was once believed.[37]

Complex, perhaps, but hardly ambiguous—this statement is a misleading evaluation of the reviews that follow. They continue: "We assume that as interpersonal dimensions of therapy interactions are more carefully examined, . . . it will become possible to define more clearly what kinds of persons help which kinds of clients most effectively."[38] This goes back to the research model considered earlier (Chapter 12). Not only is this an impossible model to apply at this time, as noted there, but it is also inconsistent with the research evidence to date, which indicates that the relationship variables are positively related to outcome with a wide variety of clients with a wide variety of problems.

Strupp, in his opening overview chapter to Bergin and Garfield's *Handbook,* takes a similar position—again after presumably having read the other chapters. He says: "Although the hypothesis of nonspecific variables [that is, relationship variables or common elements] may be correct, it is still possible that *some* technical operations may be superior to others with particular patients, particular problems, and under particular circumstances."[39] This is pure speculation—he does not even suggest what these particular techniques, patients, problems, and circumstances might be. It is interesting that in the face of the evidence for the effectiveness of the relationship variables over many kinds of clients with many kinds of problems, Bergin and Strupp, along with all other writers, persist in labeling them as nonspecific variables. This approach classifies them with placebo factors, to be eliminated or controlled for in research on psychotherapy as placebo variables are in medical research. But to do this would be to dismiss or eliminate the very active ingredients we are looking for.

Bergin and Strupp have been particularly persistent in relegating the relationship variables to the nonspecific, or noncausal, class of factors—noncausal in contrast to specific causal techniques, which, as has been noted, they never clearly specify—while at the same time they acknowledge the necessity and importance of the relationship in all therapy. In an otherwise excellent article titled "The Therapist's Theoretical Orientation: An Overrated Variable," Strupp ends by saying: "The best therapists, in my view, are those whose empathic capacity and technical skills have become thoroughly blended in such a way that they interact flexibly with the unique constellation presented by each patient's personality."[40] Nowhere in the article are the technical skills identified. In another article by Strupp titled "Humanism and Psychotherapy: A Personal Statement of the Therapist's Essential Values," there is only one use of the word *technique*. In discussing Freud as representing an extreme position, now considered superseded, he says that Freud

> likens psychotherapy to a set of technical operations, analogous to surgery, in which the therapist, as a person, plays a negligible role. [The other extreme is] the view of psychotherapy as a unique human encounter, exemplified by client-centered, humanistic, existential writers, in which the therapist's personality is of the utmost importance.

He continues:

> In my view, the therapist's personality, including his or her values, is inextricably intertwined with the technical operations brought to bear on the dyadic interaction. Accordingly, it is meaningless to speak of techniques in the abstract, just as it is meaningless to speak of the therapist's personality in the abstract.[41]

Yet this is exactly what he does—no further mention is made of any concrete techniques. In the case of personality he does essentially the same thing, with no reference to specific characteristics of the therapist other than his value commitments.

Strupp opens his paper by saying that "most therapists and students of psychotherapy now seem to agree that the therapist's personality plays an important role in the formation of the patient-therapist relationship which in turn has a critical bearing on therapeutic outcomes." It is curious, however, that those who accept this view, including Strupp, seldom go on to identify the characteristics of the therapeutic personality. They are peculiarly blind to the fact that the relationship variables provide a definition of the therapeutic personality.

There are a number of factors that militate against the obtaining of significant positive relationships between the therapist variables and therapeutic outcomes. These include problems in the design and analysis of research studies. Some of these factors are recognized by reviewers (such as Lambert et al.) in their critiques of the research. However, reviewers use these problems to reject or minimize the results of studies with positive outcomes, failing to recognize that the obtaining of positive results against such handicaps is an indication of the strength of the relationships. The following factors are in addition to the methodological problems enumerated by Lambert, DeJulio, and Stein.

1. Not all therapists are therapeutic. Much of the research involves inexperienced therapists, therapists in training, or interns. The averaging of studies including such therapists with those involving experienced therapists attenuates relationships. As some reviewers have noted, most of the studies have included therapists offering low levels of the therapeutic conditions, often borderline or below— below level 3 on the five-point scale. Furthermore, the ranges of scores on the measures are usually restricted; the resulting reduced variability attenuates relationships between the variables and outcome measures.

2. Critics have pointed to the small numbers of therapists and clients in most studies. Yet they do not recognize that the probability of obtaining significant results is directly related to the size of the sample.

3. Critics have complained about the small amount or percentage of variance in the outcome criteria accounted for by the therapist variables. Correlations between .50 and .65, the highest obtained, account for between 25 and 40 percent of the variance. There are several factors that must be considered, however. No one expects perfect correlations in studies of human behavior. And the correlations are attenuated by (1) the relatively low reliabilities of measures of the therapeutic conditions; (2) similar low reliabilities of the outcome measures; (3) the less-than-perfect validities of the outcome measures; and (4) restricted ranges of scores on the predictor variables. Statistical corrections for unreliability of the therapist and outcome measures would increase the obtained correlations significantly. No one appears to have considered this. Smith, Glass, and Miller[42] did not apply such corrections in their metanalysis of the effectiveness of psychotherapy.

4. Outcome measures used in the various studies vary widely. The various measures show low intercorrelations. It appears that there is no single outcome measure, or group of highly related measures, that is generally accepted. This problem of an appropriate criterion influences all outcome studies.

5. No one seems to have applied, or suggested the use of, probability statistics to estimate the probability of obtaining by chance the proportions of positive results in a series of studies.

All studies, as the critics have pointed out, are flawed, but the critics do not seem to be aware that these flaws, in almost all cases, militate against, not for, the obtaining of significant positive results.

CONCLUSION

Considering the obstacles to research on the relationship between therapist variables and therapy outcomes, the magnitude of the evidence is nothing short of amazing. It might be ventured that there are few things in the field of psychology for which the evidence is so strong. The evidence for the necessity, if not the sufficiency, of the therapist conditions of accurate empathy, respect or warmth, and therapeutic genuineness is incontrovertible.

As Orlinsky and Howard conclude: "If study after flawed study seemed to point in the same general direction, we could not help believing that somewhere in all that variance there must be a reliable effect."[43] And a powerful effect. There is certainly more than meets the eyes of most reviewers.

The effectiveness of all methods of counseling or psychotherapy may be due to the presence of a therapeutic relationship. The crucial study to determine if this is so by eliminating the relationship is difficult if not impossible to conduct. It could be possible to vary the therapeutic level of the relationship; this is, in effect, what is done in comparing studies in which the level of therapeutic conditions vary. The fact that therapeutic change occurs in a therapeutic relationship without the addition of so-called specific techniques, such as interpretation, suggestion, instruction, and so on, is also evidence of the sufficiency of the relationship by itself.

The consistent positive findings regarding the elements of the therapeutic relationship are encouraging. This is particularly so in view of the lack of consistent findings in the area of (developmental) psychopathology in the search for specific causal factors. Thus there is no basis for specific interventions related to specific causal factors of psychopathology. The research on the effectiveness of the relationship over a wide range of client conditions or problems provides a basis for a therapy that does not depend on identifying specific causal pathological factors. This suggests either that the specific content of the client's disturbance is unimportant, or that the cause of much, if not most, psychological disturbance is related to the absence of good human relationships, or deficiencies in such relationships. It is also possible that improvement in the client's relationships springing from the therapeutic relationship leads to improvement in other areas of the client's life.

NOTES

1. C. B. Truax and R. R. Carkhuff. *Toward effective counseling and psychotherapy*. Chicago: Aldine, 1967.
2. C. B. Truax and K. M. Mitchell. Research on certain therapist interpersonal skills in relation to process and outcome. In A. E. Bergin and S. L. Garfield

(Eds.), *Handbook of psychotherapy and behavior change.* New York: Wiley, 1971, pp. 299–344.

3. S. L. Garfield and A. E. Bergin (Eds.). *Handbook of psychotherapy and behavior change* (2nd ed.). New York: Wiley, 1978.

4. K. M. Mitchell, J. D. Bozarth, and C. C. Krauft. A reappraisal of the therapeutic effectiveness of accurate empathy, non-possessive warmth, and genuineness. In A. S. Gurman and A. M. Razin (Eds.), *Effective psychotherapy.* New York: Pergamon Press, 1977, pp. 482–502.

5. Truax and Mitchell, Research on certain therapist interpersonal skills, p. 310.

6. K. M. Mitchell, C. B. Truax, J. D. Bozarth, and C. C. Krauft. *Antecedents to psychotherapeutic outcome.* NIMH Grant Report (12306), Arkansas Rehabilitation Research and Training Center, Arkansas Rehabilitation Services, Hot Springs, AR, March 1973.

7. Mitchell, Bozarth, and Krauft, A reappraisal, p. 485.

8. *Ibid.*

9. *Ibid.*, p. 486.

10. *Ibid.*, p. 488.

11. *Ibid.* (Italics in the original.)

12. *Ibid.*, p. 483. (Italics in the original.)

13. M. B. Parloff, I. E. Waskow, and B. E. Wolfe. Research on therapist variables in relation to process and outcome. In Garfield and Bergin, *Handbook,* pp. 233–282.

14. *Ibid.*, pp. 243, 244.

15. *Ibid.*, p. 249.

16. D. E. Orlinsky and K. I. Howard. The relation of process to outcome in psychotherapy. In Garfield and Bergin, *Handbook,* pp. 283–330.

17. *Ibid.*, p. 293.

18. *Ibid.*, p. 296.

19. *Ibid.*, p. 307.

20. *Ibid.*, p. 299.

21. *Ibid.*, p. 298.

22. A. S. Gurman. The patient's perception of the therapeutic relationship. In Gurman and Razin, *Effective psychotherapy,* pp. 523.

23. M. J. Lambert, S. S. DeJulio, and D. Stein. Therapist interpersonal skills. *Psychological Bulletin,* 1978, *85,* 467–489.

24. A. E. Bergin and R. M. Suinn. Individual psychotherapy and behavior therapy. *Annual Review of Psychology,* 1975, *26,* 509–556.

25. R. B. Sloane, F. R. Staples, A. H. Cristol, N. J. Yorkston, and K. Whipple. *Psychotherapy vs. behavior therapy.* Cambridge, MA: Harvard University Press, 1975.

26. A. O. DiLoreto. *Comparative psychotherapy: An experimental analysis.* Chicago: Aldine-Atherton, 1971.

27. B. Gomes-Schwartz, S. W. Hadley, and H. H. Strupp. Individual psychotherapy and behavior therapy. *Annual Review of Psychology,* 1978, *29,* 435–471.

28. *Ibid.*, p. 440.

29. *Ibid.*, p. 442.

30. *Ibid.*, p. 456. (Italics added.)

31. J. D. Krumboltz, J. F. Becker-Haven, and K. F. Burnett. Counseling psychology. *Annual Review of Psychology,* 1979, *30,* 555–602.

32. J. S. Phillips and K. L. Bierman. Clinical psychology: Individual methods. *Annual Review of Psychology,* 1981, *32,* 405–438.

33. J. L. Holland, T. M. Magoon, and A. R. Spokane. Counseling psychology:

Career interventions, research, and theory. *Annual Review of Psychology,* 1981, *32,* 279–305.

34. A. E. Bergin and M. J. Lambert. The evaluation of therapeutic outcomes. In Garfield and Bergin, *Handbook,* p. 180.
35. *Ibid.*
36. Gomes-Schwartz, Hadley, and Strupp, Individual psychotherapy, p. 445.
37. Bergin and Lambert, Evaluation of therapeutic outcomes, p. 167.
38. *Ibid.,* p. 180.
39. H. H. Strupp. Psychotherapy research and practice. In Garfield and Bergin, *Handbook,* p. 12.
40. H. H. Strupp. The therapist's theoretical orientation: An overrated variable. *Psychotherapy: Theory, Research and Practice,* 1978, *15,* 317.
41. H. H. Strupp. Humanism and psychotherapy: A personal statement of the therapist's essential values. *Psychotherapy: Theory, Research and Practice,* 1980, *17,* 396–397.
42. M. L. Smith, G. V. Glass, and T. I. Miller. *The benefits of psychotherapy.* Baltimore: Johns Hopkins University Press, 1980.
43. Orlinsky and Howard, Relation of process to outcome, pp. 288–289.

Name Index

Adler, A., 17, 33, 35
Ahbex, E., 8
Albee, G. W., 222
Alexander, F., 215
Alland, A., Jr., 33
Allport, G. W., 30
Anderson, S., 77
Angydal, A., 34, 149
Ansbacher, H. L., 33, 35
Ansbacher, R. R., 33, 35
Aristotle, 17, 36
Aspy, D. N., 219
Auden, W. H., 9

Bach, G. R., 176, 177
Ban, T. A., 149
Bandura, A., 26, 134, 140, 141, 217
Barak, A., 204
Barret-Lennard, G. T., 60
Barry, J. R., 151
Battle, O. L., 142
Baumrind, D., 8
Becker-Haven, J. F., 208, 239
Bednar, R. L., 163
Beethoven, L., 38
Bender, L., 33
Benedict, R., 187
Benjamin, L., 182
Berenson, B. G., 52, 57–58, 59–60, 61, 64, 68, 72, 75, 77, 79, 80, 89–90, 102, 112, 113, 115, 116, 117, 118, 125, 126, 131, 141, 142
Bergin, A. E., 65, 66, 101, 149–150, 210, 231, 238, 239, 240, 241
Berne, E., 63
Berzon, B., 171
Beutler, L. E., 203
Bibring, E., 33
Bierman, K. L., 239–240

Biestek, F. P., 59
Bills, R. E., 155
Binswanger, L., 17
Blocher, D., 149
Bolman, L., 171
Bonner, H., 14
Bonney, W. C., 164–165
Bower, G. H., 133
Bozarth, J. D., 87, 233–234, 235
Buhler, C., 33
Burnett, K. F., 208, 239
Burton, A., 8, 13, 91, 119, 217

Carkhuff, R. R., vi, 6, 51, 52, 55–57, 57–58, 59–60, 60–61, 62, 63, 64, 66–67, 68, 69, 69–70, 71, 72, 75, 76, 77, 78–79, 80, 82–83, 84, 85, 86, 87–90, 91, 96, 101, 102, 112, 113, 115, 116, 117, 118, 125, 126, 127–129, 131, 132, 133, 134–135, 136, 137, 139, 141–142, 153, 171, 231
Carr, A. C., 8
Chaiken, A. L., 80
Chance, J. E., 26
Cibbrowski, T., 182
Claiborn, C. D., 80
Clark, J. B., 171
Collins, J. L., 101
Combs, A. W., 16, 34, 35, 37, 38, 39, 40, 133, 186
Corrigan, J. D., 203
Coulson, W., 168–169
Cristol, A. H., 238, 239
Cuchetti, D. V., 115
Cudney, M. R., 85
Culbert, S. A., 171

Day, W. F., 94
DeGrazin, S., 13

Subject Index